Bomber Pilot on the Eastern Front

THE RED AIR FORCE AT WAR

Bomber Pilot on the Eastern Front

307 Missions Behind Enemy Lines

VASILIY RESHETNIKOV

Translators: Vladimir Kroupnik and John Armstrong
Editor: Serguey Anisimov
English text: Sarah Bryce

Publication made possible by www.iremember.ru

Pen & Sword
MILITARY

Published in Great Britain in 2008 by
PEN & SWORD MILITARY
an imprint of
Pen & Sword Books Ltd
47 Church Street
Barnsley
South Yorkshire
S70 2AS

ISBN 978-1-84415-660-3

A CIP catalogue record for this book is
available from the British Library.

Typeset in 10/12 Sabon by Concept, Huddersfield, West Yorkshire
Printed and bound in Great Britain by CPI UK

Pen & Sword Books Ltd incorporates the imprints of
Pen & Sword Aviation, Pen & Sword Maritime, Pen & Sword Military,
Wharncliffe Local History, Pen & Sword Select,
Pen & Sword Military Classics and Leo Cooper.

For a complete list of Pen & Sword titles please contact
PEN & SWORD BOOKS LIMITED
47 Church Street, Barnsley, South Yorkshire, S70 2AS, England.
E-mail: enquiries@pen-and-sword.co.uk
Website: www.pen-and-sword.co.uk

Contents

Introduction: The Elite Squad

The seasoned flyers, aircraft covers tucked around them, had been squeezed together for days now in the semidarkness of the huge fuselage with all its rivets jingling, time passing as slowly as a glacier moves. In their leather, fur-lined coats they were hard to tell apart by rank. Hiding my own tabs under my fur collar I nevertheless felt totally one of them, but I didn't say who I was to those around me or those I talked to, understanding intuitively that these were senior and long-serving commanders.

The heavy, long-outdated, four-engine TB-3 bomber had flown in from far away – from the Pacific, in fact. On the way it had landed at aerodromes to pick up flyers and navigators who had been assigned to a new night-bomber regiment which was still being formed. Our last overnight stop was at an aerodrome near the Volga river. At last, having taken on board two or three newcomers, our plane rumbled across the snow-covered airstrip of our final landing spot in the thick and foul twilight of the early winter of 1941.

The town of Sasovo, Riazan region. The new regiment was based here. While we were tossed from board to board in the back of an old *polutorka* [a 1½-tonne truck – translator's note] on a snow-covered road, the town had time to drown in impermeable darkness. Its blurred outlines were just discernible as the contours of squat roofs and high fences. We couldn't help looking around, but we couldn't tell if anyone was even living in these black houses. There was not a light, no barking dogs. The war had managed to crush this small provincial town thoroughly, just as it had so many others.

The regimental headquarters and the officers' barracks were in a small school building. Educational posters still hung on the walls of classrooms and corridors, and indoor plants were withering away on window-sills. It was nearly night on the same day when they called us together. With difficulty we squeezed ourselves behind the low desks, and then we began. We all introduced ourselves but not as equals, for ranks were so different – senior lieutenants, captains, and even majors were present. All of the rest were regiment and squadron commanders or their deputies. I was only a junior lieutenant, a flight commander.

The flyers and navigators began to get together in crews, apparently spontaneously, decisions based on feelings of mutual sympathy rather than anything else. A young navigator called Volodya Samosudov, a tall, red-haired, intelligent guy, joined me – I was not claimed by anyone else. Everyone was waiting for the commander – Major Tikhonov: he came into the classroom at a slow, soft pace. Having asked us to sit down – we had all jumped to attention – he greeted us quietly and without ceremony. Then he was silent for a bit, looking closely at his 'recruits' and perhaps also intending to give us our first chance to have a good look at him, the new commander. Then he got down to business.

He was an unusually good-looking man – tall and with good proportions, dignified, with a handsome and youthful face. I couldn't take my eyes off him: his broad chest and strong arms, his blouse fitting like a glove and tightly belted, his long strong legs in tight quilted pants tucked into leather working jackboots. A decoration and a Gold Star adorned his chest, and there were two bars on his collar badges. A beautiful sight! This man's whole appearance and bearing were stern and dominating. I knew very well what aura of fame, even the beginnings of a sort of myth, hovered around his name, although all the events shaping this reputation had happened quite recently, not sufficiently long ago for inclusion in the ranks of legend. But it was all true – he'd started his war right from Berlin!

Operating from the Aste aerodrome on the Island of Esel in the Baltic Sea, an aviation group led by Colonel Preobrazhenskiy – commander of the 1st mine-torpedo regiment of the Baltic Fleet's Air Arm – bombed Berlin from 8 August 1941. Tikhonov's squadron was one of two reinforcing Preobrazhenskiy's group. The way to Berlin lay over the Baltic Sea and was extremely difficult and hazardous. More than once the flyers met powerful thunderstorms and thick cloud fronts. There were no reference points to go by, no direction-finders, no guiding radio stations – only compass, watch and airspeed indicator. In the morning, when it was time for the crews to return, the island would be covered by mist. And our flyers had no dispersal airfields. Take-offs were incredibly hard too. On hot evenings when the power of the worn-out engines would drop even more than usual, the planes, overloaded with bombs, would barely get off the ground before they reached the very end of the short earth airstrip.

Berlin defended itself furiously: the skies were pierced by many dozens of searchlights; a dense cloud of large-calibre flak shells kept bursting at the bombers' flight altitude. On the attack heading and at the beginning of the backtrack nearly all aircraft were caught in the intersection of searchlight rays and under the well-aimed fire of anti-aircraft guns. The raids on Berlin continued, but with every new day it was becoming harder and harder to make the aircraft battle-ready: fuel was nearly gone, ammunition was running out. Pouring the last leftovers of petrol from one plane into another, single crews were going on missions alone. The world was agitated and electrified: the very same aircraft the Germans thought they had destroyed long ago was now bombing Berlin, and so far they couldn't do anything to stop it.

At the end of August, having used up all its resources, the group left Aste one plane after another. Tikhonov was the last to take off, escorted by renowned fighter pilots Kokkinaki and Brinko. A group of flyers from the Baltic Fleet kept operating from the island for a while after that, but at the beginning of September 1941 they were completely exhausted and withdrew to the mainland.

A day after landing at an airstrip near Moscow, Major Tikhonov was called up to the Stavka [general headquarters of the armed forces – translator's note] to report on the results of the Berlin raids. He went to Moscow in a great hurry well before the meeting was due to start, and waited for his appointment in Air Force Headquarters, but that evening the city was raided by the Luftwaffe again and the streets were closed to traffic. Tikhonov was advised that the appointment at the Stavka had been cancelled but General Zhigarev – the Air Force Commander – had been assigned to speak to him. Tikhonov had to stay overnight at head-quarters. In the morning Zhigarev announced an order signed by Stalin that Major Tikhonov had been appointed commander of a special long-range bomber regiment assigned to strike at objectives in the enemy's far rear. The time frame for recruitment was set very rigidly and Zhigarev, risking the possibility of frustrating the plan, provided the young major with fairly broad rights to select night-bomber command flyers, regard-less of their rank and position, from any Air Force unit that was not part of front-line formations, as well as from the permanent teaching staff of flying school instructors and reserve units, something that had previously been strictly prohibited. In this way the Air Force Department removed all obstacles in the way of manning the regiment with hand picked flyers and navigators.

Now, in the dimly lit classroom with its tightly curtained windows, the regiment commander looked closely into our faces and unhurriedly conversed with each of us in turn. He'd known many of the flyers and navigators in the past. He'd served with some of them just recently in the

Far East region of Russia, and apparently for this reason he had selected the strongest and most experienced of them into his regiment. Gradually I began to realise the awkwardness of my position. The other flyers were reporting on their many hundreds or even thousands of hours of flying, not just in the daytime, but also at night, in cloud. At the same time they recalled their considerable battle experience and their participation in manoeuvres and exercises. There was nothing like this in my flying record.

Following the rules of rank, I was the last to stand up. My report on my flying record, especially with regard to night flying, amused the whole audience. The commander smiled too: nearly 400 hours' experience meant nothing here. A enquiry about my age followed. The commander smiled again. There were no more questions. A feeling of foreboding seized me. All my cherished aspirations might be dashed instantly! It needed only one word, short as a shot, to be pronounced by this incredibly unapproachable man – 'No!' – and my fate would be left hanging in the air. But the commander said nothing and I kept hoping.

After midnight, crashing the lids of our desks as one, we stood to see him out of the classroom. The commander left us with a reminder that he would expect brave and resolute action from us in the struggle against the enemy. Our noisy crowd spilled out into the corridor, filling it with excited voices and thick tobacco smoke. I felt like an outsider and stood apart, drawing on a cigarette. My 'control wheel brothers' didn't seem to know I was there – pilots are clannish. A phrase thrown by someone reached me – and who else could it be about: 'Well, that guy won't last.' I felt upset and angry. It seemed that to fight in this regiment against the Germans was a special honour not available to everyone.

CHAPTER ONE

The Instructors' Squadron

Some years earlier, after graduating from flying school, I had been assigned to my first unit – the Orel high-speed bomber regiment. The regiment was quite new, not yet really a flying unit, and was doing more sitting on the ground than buzzing through the air. In our squadron, which consisted almost entirely of junior lieutenants, shooting was the most popular exercise, which was not a big organisational burden for the commanders. In the mornings, having armed themselves with Nagans and taken as much ammo as possible, the pilots would head off to the shooting range in a leisurely formation. We would smoke, chat and bang away at the targets as much as we wanted. The time went quickly. Sometimes classes were organised for us and the squadron engineer would expound time and again the intricacies of water-cooling in and lubrication of the M-100 engine. On top of that, the regimental navigator would fill our brains with the fine points of flying guided by radio beacons, which, as it turned out, didn't even exist within the operating range of our planes. I'd say the only thing the squadron commander, Pomortsev, taught me properly was how to make steep-banking classic combat turns in an SB [Skorostnoy Bombardirovshik: high-speed bomber – translator's note]. These turns were unlike the protracted slow ones I'd been taught before which allowed a significant gain in altitude but only at the expense of quite a substantial loss of speed.

At the end of 1939 the regiment was preparing to take part in the Soviet-Finnish War and we patiently kept running our fingers over outline maps, memorising the locations of reference points and learning by heart the names of Finnish towns and railway junctions unfamiliar to our ears. We also had another task – the regiment was to be re-equipped with DB-3 planes [Dalniy Bombardirovshik: long-range bomber – translator's note]. This Ilyushin-designed long-range bomber was famed not only for long-distance flights and lifting loads up to record altitudes but also for the 'death loops' that test pilot Kokkinaki used to make in the heavy twin-engine craft above Tushino aerodrome [near Moscow – translator's note], to the delight and consternation of everyone who saw this incredible sight. To fly such a machine was beyond my dreams and would be fantastic. Several regiments had already been armed with the aircraft; now it was our turn to get it. But the commanders were hesitant and, anticipating the departure to the Finnish front, they didn't take the risk of sending experienced flyers for retraining. They sent us, the most junior.

On the morning of the first day of 1940, having not yet come down from a celebratory evening in a city club, I stood on a platform at Orel railway station. The next day I got off the train in Voronezh. My friends who were burdened with wives rolled up later. The Voronezh reserve brigade was also quite young and still hadn't completely organised itself. Everyone was a novice here and even my new squadron commander, Kazmin, who had flown for many years in the Moscow Academic Aviabrigade, had only just taken over the squadron. He was no ordinary flyer: a very experienced instructor superbly skilled in 'blind' flights by day and night in any weather conditions. By the standards of that time (and later times too) this was an achievement of the highest level, rare for many of his contemporaries and even for senior aviation commanders. As would later become routine, the night flight training of the brigade's commanding officers started with Kazmin testing the instructors himself; only after that, having obtained his approval, would they join the flights.

He was a bit chubby, with heavy, unhurried gait, thick eyebrows, light hair and light-blue unblinking eyes, a slightly podgy face and a large fleshy nose. He didn't say much and he talked slowly, in muffled voice, weighing up every word, knowing its worth. The squadron commander immediately set his newcomers to learning the aircraft's design, its aerodynamics and armaments, and when the time came to examine us he was already casting glances at the sky, looking out for the right kind of flying weather. The March snow still lay thick on the aerodrome, the pale sun barely shining through the low clouds, but the squadron was already making flights.

Deputy squadron commander Lieutenant Tokunov, a man with the kindest soul, an excellent flyer and instructor, was my trainer. I didn't master handling the aircraft straight away – I couldn't land well. This was either the result of a long break in flying or insufficient training (which was most likely), and maybe the unstable weather had an influence. Flights would frequently be cancelled and training interrupted by the expectation of another flying day; we had to wait for days at a time. But Tokunov was wise and patient – he would correct my mistakes during flying and landing, and would meticulously and graphically analyse them on the ground. Alas, one flight followed another with the same depressing lack of success, until suddenly I felt I'd got it. At last I had just the right feel for the ground to enable me to see every centimetre of the plane's altitude before it landed. Things began to work. Now I flew on my own, delving deeper and deeper into other intricacies of piloting techniques and then exploring their combat deployment.

The programme was approaching its end. What would happen to me? Would they send me back to my former regiment? In fact things were to turn out differently: they planned for me to fly in the instructor's seat. It was strange to sit in the closed spherical shell of the navigator's cockpit. It had numerous, dimly gleaming, small windows filled with faded celluloid offering a view of the surrounding space, and the ground could be watched during take-off and landing through a small open vertical slot left by a machine-gun barrel which had been turned aside. A tubular handle on a catch, collapsible pedals made of steel rods, two short power levers on the port side with balls on the ends – all this control gear was very different from the customary cockpit equipment. But strangely enough it was sufficient to make the massive machine absolutely docile – as long as, of course, the levers were shifted at the right time and for the right distance. A pair of instruments – an altimeter and an airspeed indicator – was supposed to provide some idea of the position of the aircraft in the air. Generally speaking, with help from Tokunov (whose limitless patience I admired) I mastered the task of being an instructor too.

Soon the order went out – a small group of flyers, including me, were appointed as instructors. This decision greatly upset me. I was eager to join my combat regiment where flyers flew not in the instructor's cockpit but in the pilot's seat – where there were alarms, drills, long-range flights, unfamiliar aerodromes and bombing ranges. Here everything was so down to earth and routine. The laurels of instructor did not attract me at all. I'd regarded the instructors with reverence, almost worshipped them, since flying school, but I'd always thought that these exceptional flyers and superb commanders had been cheated by life of something essential.

The Orel regiment flew off to fight the Finnish War and this intensified my disappointment. The first flyers who had completed their retraining were going back to their flying units, but nobody wanted me. There was no way out. They gave me a troublesome machine with number 13 on its tail, a flying and a ground crew, and assigned to me a small group of flyers and navigators of varying ranks and abilities. They were to be trained to fly machines new to them. Now, first thing every morning I would seat myself in the front cockpit and day after day, like clockwork, in turn with instructors in other aircraft, make rectangular circles over the aerodrome or leave for the training area to work with my group on all the elements of flying technique peculiar to this machine.

The squadron commander realised that the instructors were over-loaded with the work of taking the flyers out, but nevertheless he didn't deprive us of flying for ourselves. In accordance with his orders, we would make the first flight of every day piloting in a training area or taking the cockpit for a flight to the camp aerodrome. Sometimes of an early morning in quiet and clear weather on my way to the camp I would divert towards the Don, plunge down to its steep banks and racing just above the water, following its smooth curves, I would exultantly enjoy the flight, watching the country people waving to me. Oh, how I loved flying! Achieving the thrilling sensation of huge happiness, almost joy, stirred up by every flight no matter what it was like – simple or very difficult – was the main goal of my life for many years, its highest and best manifestation. Perhaps for this reason, when they pushed me as hard as they could to join the Academy after the war, for many years I would spurn the suit of my well-meaning superiors, fearing to give up flying even for a short while.

Working as an instructor, I obtained priceless experience, learned how to position myself exactly on a map and make navigational calculations. In our young squadron there were quite a few superb airmen who flew with fire in their hearts and prized flying and combat skills above any-thing in the world. We didn't waste our time, but it went by slowly it seemed to me. I felt that I'd been gaining flying experience and the clouds were now calling me. However, my first acquaintances with clouds were scary and promised no good. More than once I dropped out from their underside, either banking and sliding onto one wing or in a steep descent. After catching my breath I climbed back into those turbulent, wet clumps. They seemed to be impregnable, striving to spit out of their menacing realm anyone who would impertinently try to approach them. My machine, so quiet and acquiescent when there was light and sun, would suddenly change character in the clouds, becoming disobedient and showing off its hidden rebelliousness. Nevertheless, between one flight and another I began to notice that my machine was becoming more compliant and soon my troubles with the clouds were over.

As autumn approached, Kazmin found out about my wilfulness and said sternly, 'Stop rushing things. When it comes to the clouds, they'll train you. Now, see how low they are? You'll drop out and won't have time to grunt. The ground is not that soft!'

'Actually, Comrade Captain, I don't drop out anymore.'

' I'll check and then I'll be the judge of what you can really do. But for now, stop it!'

Then one nasty cold day the squadron commander came up to my aircraft and sat in front of the instructor's controls.

'Off to the training area and into the clouds. Altitude 1,500. A steep one to port, a steep one to starboard. On one engine. Do spirals. That's it.' And he fell silent.

I'd never flown like this – I'd mostly undertaken straight flights with smooth turns: now I was going to do steep ones. But there was no way round it. I could do steep turns in clear weather, and I would have to be able to do them blind as well. The training area was nearby; the clouds were dark and turbulent. Storm clouds! I quietly set up the flight regime and bravely swung into a port turn. Everything seemed all right but the machine was shaking, tossing up and down. And suddenly I heard an angry voice in my headphones.

'I thought you could really fly, but you can't even set the machine on the given course. You can't hold altitude and you wobble when you bank. Do to the starboard at forty five.'

I gathered all my courage and went into a steep turn. But the nose kept diving and climbing and the needles on the instruments wouldn't stand still. 'Hell,' I thought, 'he's driven me into the bumpiest spot!'

On the way out I heard, 'Let go the controls!' Kazmin sped the plane up and sharply tilted it, stopping it at exactly 60 degrees, and after that the machine flew very smoothly, just quivering slightly as if it was suffering from a fever. The control wheel was nearly motionless; the pedals were barely moving. We were shaken roughly coming out of the turn which meant we'd been caught by our own airstream – it was a sure sign that the manoeuvre had been executed perfectly. Our course as we came out of the turn was precise down to a single degree. And the turbulence was nothing to him.

'Now you do it.' I was wet all over with sweat, trying my hardest. The left turn went reasonably well but during the right one I began to bank and my rate of roll was not stable. Perspiration was pouring from my eyebrows, obscuring my vision; my hands were slipping on the control wheel.

'All right,' Kazmin concluded. 'Until next time. Did you understand everything? You still have plenty of work to do. You'll train with an instructor. I'll check you later on.' It was a harsh lesson. I now understood how far I was from the real art of flying.

The time for regular flying by instruments wasn't long in coming, but it began with training sessions on the ground. On days when the weather prevented flying, the young instructors, spelling each other, would spend hours sitting in Link cockpits. These were simulators for blind flights. The foreign machine – a humpbacked black box – was simple in design, worked reliably and rendered quite naturally the conditions of flying with no horizon in sight. That was the whole genius of it. The plywood construction was covered by a tall, hard box. The instruments flickered with weak phosphorescent light, providing precise information about the 'flight' regime. A pilot using the steering lever and pedals could turn this compact mechanical installation in all directions, tilt it forward and backward, and could even execute banks of up to 30 degrees. Back then whole rows of these cockpits stood in the classrooms and corridors of many aviation garrisons, regardless of the type of aircraft based there, modestly doing their great work. Of course the training provided in Link cockpits was not sufficient for the experience required of flying by instruments for real and it couldn't replace flying conditions, so I would climb into the clouds at any suitable opportunity or would isolate myself in clear weather by rigging up a tarpaulin shelter on steel cross-pieces. Then we were led in turn into the training area by the flight commanders – or sometimes even by the deputy squadron commander, Tokunov. It would be a long time before Kazmin tested me in clouds again. But this time I worked calmly and didn't sweat. He said nothing during the flight, not letting out a sound. That meant everything was all right. He gave me top marks in my flight log.

A bomber pilot who couldn't fly in cloud, at night and in battle formation was nothing, even by the standards of that time. He wasn't a bomber pilot at all, let alone a long-range one. In some places there were enough of that sort of pilot, but not in our unit. Our squadron's young corps of instructors learned to fly in close wing-to-wing formations earlier than the rest. Kazmin liked to lead the squadron himself. Having placed himself ahead of it, looking back, left and right, he kept a strict watch on the formation's symmetry with his stern gaze and we stuck to our positions as if we were bound there. Of course the purpose of maintaining formation lay not in parade constraints but in that fact that skills were sharpened most finely by just such exact geometrical forms of flying.

When a flying day on our distant training field in Levaya Rossosh was nearing its end, Kazmin would lead us into the air, line the squadron up into V-shaped flights or draw it into one long V, and towards evening he would bring us back to the aerodrome in a close, symmetrically lined formation. We would fly over the residential area and the regimental headquarters, and after dispersing would land one behind another. The brigade and the whole town knew Captain Kazmin had brought his squadron back.

Sometimes they put us in festival parades. During the 1940 October festivities [anniversary of the 1917 October Revolution – translator's note], an aviation parade of two brigades – ours and one from Kursk – was arranged. We took off on the wet, dank day of the festival in an icy wind. Heavy, dark clouds flew swiftly by, swirling over the town; the gusty wind threw the machines from one wing to another, scattering the formation. I turned the control wheel with all my might, sometimes rotating it to the limit in order to stay in my place to the right of the flight commander Pasha Korchagin [Pavel – translator's note], and not to break alignment with the left wingman, Ivan Velichay, or to disgrace myself in front of the spectators. Ivan held out tenaciously, visibly jerking the rudders on his aircraft too.

Meanwhile the weather was getting even worse. The long, nearly shapeless parade column somehow whizzed over the town square and immediately split into regimental groups in order to get back to their respective aerodromes as soon as possible. Ours was nearby and having turned towards it and reshaped our Vs into columns, we landed quickly and safely. But the aircraft from Kursk came across low-level cloud and thick blizzards; they scattered to random airstrips and some crews landed in the open – some on their wheels, some on their bellies.

The flight debriefing called by General Kotov – the Orel Military District Air Force Commander – was a heated one. A long strip of photomontage of the whole air show flowed over his hands, spreading across the stage. The general was discontentedly scrutinising its details, making one commander after another stand up to explain, then sternly reprimanding them and handing out punishments. But his attention was drawn to one of the niners [squadrons consisted of nine planes – editor's note] that had kept its formation, distance and timing. Several times he checked who this niner belonged to and each time it turned out to be Kazmin's. The general made him stand up and then us too, the aircraft commanders. He said some kind words and expressed his gratitude. Class will out!

Although it didn't happen as quickly as we wanted, the squadron eventually switched to night flights. At the time our machines were quite old, still the original versions with numerous exhaust nozzles around star-shaped engines. On dark nights the long orange tongues of flame from these nozzles would be almost completely blinding: it was impossible to see anything – especially in front – and piloting could be conducted only by instruments. Nevertheless we learned to cope with this too. A new flying season was already under way. We confidently travelled the flight paths at night, bombed our ranges, flew in formation and, as instructors in night flying, we proceeded with no hanging about to train the changing group of pilots who kept coming to us.

But 1941 began with some strange changes. In January I returned from leave and immediately heard some overwhelming news: under orders from the new *narcom* [Narodnyi Kommissar Oborony: People's Commissar of Defence – translator's note], Timoshenko, all the young officers had been moved from their apartments into barracks to complete their four years of compulsory service. In addition, so as not to have to repeat such transfers in the future, he had ordered that flyers graduate from aviation schools with the rank of sergeant and not junior lieutenant, as they had done previously.

It was not the first blow the aviation cadres had taken, but it turned out to be the most painful, and it immediately discouraged a significant, and I would say the best, part of the nation's youth from casting their lot with the Air Force. Flying cadets even began to break away from aviation schools under various pretexts, preferring other, more reliable jobs. Voluntary enlistment into aviation schools dropped off. It was replaced by the usual draft via recruiting offices and the resulting intake of low-quality 'human resources' differed sharply from the men taken on through the former special enlistment process. The wound dealt to the self-esteem of the young commanders was deep and painful. But of course no one in authority worried about that.

Having left our quarters (and, for many of the flyers, their families as well), our squadron lieutenants occupied a huge, enlisted men's barracks, noisy as a hangar. They shoved narrow cots with mattresses stuffed with straw into the corners and along the walls, and lounged on them wearing whatever they liked; they were not in a hurry to set up proper military order. That's how I found them. They received me noisily and, vying with one another, they invited me to be their neighbour, sometimes laughing nervously at their fate, sometimes swearing desperately and foully. Cheerful, proud of their mission and full of the feeling that they were the lucky ones chosen by fate, the young officers were deeply humiliated and offended by their relocation and found themselves completely defenceless in the face of official high-handedness.

Quite a few instructor-pilots were among the involuntary prisoners of the barracks because at least some of their experience had been gained in a flying club, not in the army, which meant that under the new order they were second-class citizens. The stinging absurdity of their situation was that all the 'apprentices' previously attached to them – flyers and navigators of various groups who had managed to run up a significant record of service in line units – freely billeted themselves in flats, some in the city, some in the township, because they were army trained. I was lucky in this regard – although I was younger than the rest, I was in my fifth year of army service.

With the arrival of warm days the squadron moved to the camp. Now we were using to the full all the flying time provided by the weather, which left very little time for rest, recreation and aircraft servicing. The possibility of imminent war was hanging over us like a ghost – we felt its presence more than knew it to be there. But during political information sessions we were told simply and clearly that we had a pact with Germany not only of non-aggression but also of friendship. Friendship with the fascists? But it wasn't the custom back then to ask questions, just to keep out of trouble. I remember that a week before the war broke out there was a TASS [Telegraphic Agency of the Soviet Union – translator's note] report stating that 'rumours about Germany's intention to breach the pact and undertake an act of aggression against the USSR were completely unfounded'.

While higher circles were busy with predictions of war and peace, we, having no idea about any of that, were recklessly using up the last remnants of our pre-war life and somehow coping with the discomfort of service existence, not knowing any better. Yet despite our dedication, we still fell prey to worldly passions. On Saturdays, when the roar of plane engines ceased and the aerodrome dust settled, the married contingent was gripped by twitchy excitement, hoping for the commander's grace and a chance to sneak away to Voronezh for the weekend. The lucky ones were few. But on Sundays after the arrival of the morning train a picturesque file of young wives and brides-to-be festooned with bundles and baskets would ceremoniously stretch from the nearest station to the camp. They were flushed and happy, their impatience for a meeting with their beloved, handsome guys shining on their pretty faces. And the 'handsome guys' – baked by sun and wind, with peeling noses and faded eyebrows, quivering with anticipation, but restrained and solemn – primly met them as they were still walking the dusty country road that led to the camp. What an idyll! What a sight! Juicy topics for bachelor jokes ...

As if to confirm the strength and reliability of our unbreakable friendship with the Germans, on the first Saturday after the TASS report – the Saturday which would be the last in peacetime – even the unmarried folk were granted city leave in an act of unheard of generosity. Only a handful of headquarters servicemen stayed in the camp, as well as the regular roster orderlies and part of the technical staff who always had some urgent work to do on the planes, even on Sundays. And that was the situation not only in our brigade. A surge of unprecedented freedom engulfed many garrisons on that fateful pre-war night. The military threw itself into irrepressible merrymaking, filling clubs, parks and music halls. Parties went on in apartments and lights shone in windows until the small hours.

That night the girlfriend of a young instructor-pilot and my buddy, Vasya Skaldin – a very cute girl called Galochka – threw a party for her girlfriends and for his squadron mates. We all went round to her place with flowers and gifts. The gramophone played foxtrots, laughter erupted, the happy, dancing girls squealed in the pilots' tight paws. The long table was crowded with closely packed guests and Vasya, who had long ago served his term in the role of official suitor, self-confidently sat down at its narrow end, near Galochka. The festivities were gathering momentum. We barely managed to tumble into an empty carriage on the last tram rolling towards the outskirts and our township. Vasya was not with us.

A deep and untroubled sleep immediately gripped me when I got home. It was a rare joy for there to be no threat of an early wake up and the next day promised freedom. Heavy rain drummed outside the wide-open window; bursts of thunder could be heard. Then I sensed silence and sank into a blissful condition of even deeper calm. But my most impenetrable sleep of the not-so-early morning was suddenly invaded by the anxious voice of my neighbour, Nikolay Telkov. 'Get up, get up, Vasiliy.' He was pulling at my shoulder. 'We're at war!'

'What do you mean? How do you know?'

'The Germans have crossed our border. They're bombing our cities.'

'How can that be – bombing?' I was taken aback. But the next minute, doing up buttons on the way, I was heading towards the train station with other guys who were darting out of doorways. A freight train was the first to come through. It would do. It didn't stop at our substation near Kolodeznaya but that wasn't a problem because I was like a tram passenger who pays no attention to stops – a throwback to my student days.

The aerodrome was halfway to headquarters and I went to my plane first. The fuel tanks were full; the bombs were being attached. There was no operational information at headquarters – and there wasn't any later either. A ready-to-bomb roster was drawn up and heaps of maps were issued – the navigators were montaging them nearly up to Berlin.

The new times did not bring changes to our lives, however. The Germans were alleged to fly as far as Voronezh, but we didn't see them. Anyway, there were no fighter planes nearby. Were we going to pursue the German bombers in our DB-3s? Yes, I would have given chase with my ShKAS machine guns [7.62mm rapid-firing machine guns – translator's note] without batting an eyelid. Thank God this didn't happen. Could it be that this devil-may-care attitude led to the many rams taking place in 1941?

We began to harass Captain Kazmin with written requests for transfer to the front. He remained silent for a while, but then gathered all of us together and rapped out, 'There is an order from the *narcom*: no one leaves the reserve units. Our duty is to train crews for the front. No reduction in the flying program, but completion in the shortest possible time! We'll work day and night at maximum load.'

We provided the 'load'. The young, tough, zealous-to-fly instructors settled down in the instructor's seat at the crack of dawn; cadet flyers barely had time to exchange places with each other in the pilot seat. And when the tanks were running out of fuel, we would taxi to the refuelling spot directly from the landing run and, gesticulating on the way from the top hatch, demand a fuel truck be brought immediately. This would happen over and over again until the last drop of fuel was used up – take-offs and flights continued until the last sunbeam disappeared. In a flying day I would manage to do up to thirty or even thirty-five landings. The night shifts were no less hard.

But at the beginning of July, despite the commander's predictions, came the order that should have been expected: to form a squadron from permanent and casual personnel, incorporate it into the regiment and send it to the front. Tokunov was appointed squadron commander, Serguey Evdokimov his deputy; the instructors were to be flight commanders. The rest of the complement was to be taken from the casual personnel. Navigators were selected on the same principles. I failed to find my way into the squadron. Tokunov wanted to take me but Kazmin wouldn't let me go. He kept muttering, 'Who will I work with?' The best aircraft were given to Tokunov, although even they were pretty much worn out. We were left with old, early model machines – but there was still a chance to make them fly.

Tokunov's squadron took off one quiet and clear morning, flew over the aerodrome in a farewell formation, set course westwards and vanished in grey mist. Forever and aye. In a month it would be no more. The squadron commander himself was killed in action on 26 July. Only a very few of the guys managed to get back to our positions from the depths of German-occupied territory. Fine combat flyers, brave fellows! They were propelled into action in small groups or as single planes, in clear weather, with no escort at all, to strike at distant targets and enemy forces on the front line. They were thrown across air space swarming with German fighter planes. The odds were long and no other result could be expected. Certainly without sacrifices there would be no victory in this war that had caught us napping. The real question is: were these the sacrifices we should have made?

The front line was getting closer and closer. Front-line aviation regiments pressed by the enemy began to land on aerodromes around Voronezh. The parking areas were crammed, and it became crowded in the sky as well. It was time to move away. At the end of August Kazmin led the squadron of the reserve regiment to Buzuluk, beyond the Volga. The town, which still preserved traces of the quiet, out-of-the-way life of the Russian provinces, seethed and bustled, overflowing with Air Force people who were followed, one way or another, by their families and numerous relatives – wives, kinsfolk and the children of those who were still at the front and those who had already died over there. Our smartest pilots contrived to get their wives and brides into their planes at night in deep secrecy, without the knowledge of the commanders. In light dresses, with almost no luggage and wrapped in plane covers, the women would literally grow numb at frosty altitudes, but even though they knew beforehand the ordeal that awaited them, they went without hesitation.

The buildings of Buzuluk (nearly all of them were wooden huts with extensions and shacks built on) were tightly packed with these un-expected guests. It was impossible to see how these people lived and were going to live with no job, resources, food. Married officers would take home meagre rations supplied in the dry messes to share with wives and kids, but occasionally during flights everything would grow dark before the eyes of flyers burdened with large families, or they would feel giddy because of their emaciation. And maybe this was why planes began to crash more often. One winter night in 1941 Vasya Skaldin hit the ground from high altitude. He hadn't even tried to bail out.

Endless files concerning flyers, navigators, wireless operators who had lost their planes and their destroyed regiments began to come to us from the front. There were some who had managed to return from across the front line on foot – some with their crews, some on their own having lost their comrades in aerial combat, during clumsy forced landings, or to German captivity. Crowds of men from the rear who had not tried front-line life and were craving real and not official word of the war listened attentively to the stories of their experiences, full of dramatic tension. The accounts weighed heavily and oppressively upon our souls. It seemed that the same thing was going to happen to all who dared to take off into front-line skies, and that only a very few, like these lucky ones, would manage to survive and get back to our side of the front.

We grew depressed: where was our glorious army, and where was the Air Force? Was it true that they had run out of spirit and strength? No, that couldn't be! We knew everything the newspapers were writing and the public radio system was broadcasting, what the political commissars were 'bringing home to us'. But the real spirit of war was brought to us by the courageous and desperate guys who had returned from the front; who had come to know the taste of combat success in the fight against the foe but had also taken their share of hard and bitter blows from the dreadful force that had won complete mastery of the sky and was press-ing our troops eastwards. No wonder a gloomy tone dominated these guys' mood. Their combat records included quite a number of heroic acts and exploits in front-line skies, but failures and defeats tend to influence human feelings a lot more than successes and victories.

Time went by, but obviously not all of those who had managed to get out of the furnace of combat could shed the after-effects of combat overload. Some of them were in no hurry to get back to the front and were looking for positions in flying schools, various training centres and at headquarters: they had already had more than enough impressions of war to last them all their lives.

Pavel Korchagin – a flight commander from Tokunov's squadron, a companion of mine on evening walks during our recent time in Voronezh – also came back from the front. A strong and sturdy, swarthy man with the build of a boxer, iron muscles and a stubborn character, he was a fine, brave flyer who had lasted longer than the rest of Tokunov's group. Now he appeared to be without spirit, broken, deprived of his former enviable dashing appearance and self-confidence. One evening we were sitting at supper in my tiny rented 'cell' where I had invited Pavel to stay the night. A little bit tipsy, staring past me with a far-away look, taking long pauses and forcing out every word, he was remembering details of that last aerial battle on 18 August (you don't say! – it was Air Force Day). The fight in which Messers [a common nickname for Messerschmitt 109 fighter planes – translator's note] shot up his aircraft and set it ablaze, and then, making a circle, machine-gunned him as he hung on his parachute and followed him with fire down to the tree tops. He wasn't killed, only wounded: Pasha was left standing. He and the other survivors were about 100, or maybe even 300 kilometres from our positions – no one knew for sure. Scattered, retreating and surrounded, groups of our troops still defended themselves from the Germans in the forest mazes of Polesie [a province in Belorussia known for its thick forests – translator's note], but the main forces held the line somewhere far beyond the Dniepr, near the River Desna [a tributary of Dniepr – translator's note]. He managed to change into rustic, cast-off clothes and – moving day and night, away from main roads, under cover of forests and swamps – he reached Soviet forces on the fourth day, but he still had to fight his way east with them in heavy battles as the front moved. No one else from his crew came back. His boys had surely perished while still in the air, otherwise they would have managed to bail out of the burning plane. All this experience had left noticeable traces on Pasha's personality. But time was merciful and he soon regained his previous temper, spirit and self-confidence. He resumed flying and didn't lag behind in climbing the ladder, but flew in a reserve regiment training airmen for the front.

It would be putting it mildly to say that I felt ill at ease in front of Pasha, in front of Tokunov's guys, and when I compared myself with all who had been killed or were still fighting at the front – I felt ashamed of my completely safe war service far from the front line. I felt it was almost despicable. And I wasn't the only one. Nothing had managed to shake our determination to find a way to the front. To tell the truth, some of the guys, especially married ones, didn't pester anyone, didn't write applications and looked west with no enthusiasm. But they also knew their job well and worked for the front and for victory with all their might. Their position was as follows: they wouldn't ask for it, but if they were sent they would go into combat without batting an eyelid and would fight gallantly, no worse than those who were dreaming of battle.

Putting common sense aside, I was looking for justification for my impulses. The Germans already stood near Moscow and Leningrad. How could we – the Air Force men who saw the defence of the Fatherland as their first and sacred duty – shirk in the rear? Dnepropetrovsk had already been captured by the enemy. You could go mad trying to imagine what it was like in there. My mother, father, brother were left in the city. Where were they? What was happening to them? Meanwhile I, a jaunty military airman, commander of a formidable combat plane, remained in complete safety and absolutely beyond the reach of the Germans, for they were unable even to fly as far as here. No doubt someone had to train airmen, bring new crews up to strength, prepare them for the front – they were badly needed there. But there were ageing instructors – old experienced sky-dogs. There were quite a few of them at the front but they were also needed in flying schools and reserve regiments, and we – the youngsters – belonged over there in combat.

Autumn was sliding deeper into winter and flying weather was becoming really precious. One more aerodrome – for ferry operations – was set up outside the town on the opposite side from the training ones. There they stored Il-4 planes dispatched from the aircraft works in Komsomolsk-on-Amur [a city in the Far East of Russia – translator's note] and front-line flyers arriving on transport planes or trains flew brand-new aircraft to their regiments. But once the job of ferrying a small group of planes was entrusted to our instructor crews. And mine was among them. The way I saw it, it was a rare, and perhaps the only, God-given opportunity to break away to the front. Could they really not let me stay once I got there? I don't know how or why I gave my plan away; most likely my overly animated mood did it, or maybe my suitcase, which was slightly bigger than those of the others – apparently it was big enough not for a trip but for moving house! Whatever the case, when I was already sitting in the cockpit eagerly awaiting the signal to start engines a messenger jumped up on my plane's wing and yelled into my ear, 'Melnikov has cancelled your flight. Another crew will fly the plane.' My heart sank. Melnikov was the regiment commander. Who had incited him to take such a decision and how? The Chief of Staff, Major Govorukha, stood at the edge of the aerodrome. Hearing my puzzled question, he squinted his eyes in a cunning expression, gave me a wink and said slowly, with a spiteful and revealing smile, 'Ain't no fools here.'

Snow fell, alternating with rain; an early frost was taking hold before its time. Suddenly Captain Shevtsov appeared in the regiment. He examined flight records, talked to people, tested night-flying techniques. He was interested not only in the casual staff but in the permanent personnel too. Speculation was rife. There was a hint as to his intentions: the captain had significant authority to select flyers and navigators for the special night-time, long-range bomber regiment headed by Major Tikhonov. Both the regiment's status and its commander's name were shrouded in a kind of mystery and inscrutability that intrigued everyone immensely.

Shevtsov was going to test two or three airmen in our squadron, including Kazmin. Why Kazmin it was unclear. There was no way he would be taken away from the squadron. How could it survive without him? I had nothing to attract Shevtsov. The captain flicked through my flying log-book without any interest and put it aside into the pile of the ones he didn't need. But he had the look of a kind-hearted and approachable man, and, having selected a convenient moment, I went to him and begged him to at least make a night flight with me. 'What have you got to lose, Comrade Captain?'

'All right, I'll do it,' he smiled. It seemed to me that this was said with some kind of indulgence, almost with a feeling of pity for me. In any case, with no serious intentions. And what could be of interest in a junior lieutenant unknown to him?

The following night, having done a flight with someone else, he came up to my aircraft. The weather was calm. The moon had already set. The clouds were high.

'You know what? Let's do a run into the training area,' he said, somewhat prosaically. 'You show me what you can do and I'll watch.'

In my mind I scanned the whole program, missing no detail, and then I demonstrated all I could do in the zone. The flight went by in silence. When the propellers stopped turning he stretched his hand to me and said, 'You'll join Tikhonov.'

He said it positively, as if it was a decision made. I was overwhelmed by unprecedented joy – everything rejoiced inside me. But time went by and nobody called me or asked for me. A rumour spread that some paperwork about the selected men had arrived at headquarters. But the commanders remained silent. Someone told me in secret that Melnikov was blocking it because he didn't want to let the instructors go. But a day later new information came through: there had been a message from General Gorbatsevich – he demanded I be released immediately. This man was the chief of the long-range bomber command – there was no one superior to him.

I went to see Melnikov without an invitation. The 'Prince of Silver' [the title of a nineteenth-century Russian poem – translator's note], as we had nicknamed our commander because of his prematurely grey hair, met me on the doorstep and flew into a rage on the spot. I noticed on his desk, and read upside-down, a telegram bearing my surname and a stern warning about insubordination. I didn't get to say the words I had prepared for the conversation: I listened silently as Melnikov cursed everything, arguing with himself and invisible opponents. At last he exploded and threw me out of his office, bidding me farewell with the blessing, 'To hell with you!'

At headquarters I found out that at dawn the next morning a TB-3 which had stayed overnight would head off to Tikhonov's location from the ferry operations aerodrome. A flyer (a senior lieutenant from the ferry operations airbase) and a navigator from the permanent staff would get on it. I didn't even bother to pick up my documents – it was too late and there was no point. I put on my overall, threw my trench coat on my shoulder, grabbed my trunk of underwear and rushed into the pre-dawn darkness and to the aerodrome. The TB-3 which was on its way from the Far East region of Russia still stood there, not yet warmed-up.

CHAPTER TWO

Night is for the Elite

Tikhonov's regiment hadn't completed the staffing process, but it was already operating at full tilt. Despite very difficult weather conditions, the planes went out on combat missions day and night. The commander set our group to fighting straight away. He ordered several flyers who had had long breaks between piloting to make one circular training flight with an instructor; I was to make two. I was told that Tikhonov had asked Shevtsov about me with some displeasure: 'Who's this you've sent me?' Although Shevtsov stood up for me he failed to allay the commander's doubts. That was why Tikhonov ordered me to make two flights with an instructor instead of flying independently, just in case. The squadron commander, Captain Chernichenko, got into the front cockpit. I had the feeling that I would be kicked out with no hesitation if I made the slightest error. What then?

Snow was falling slowly. Visibility barely extended halfway down the airstrip. I took off, made a box outlining the clouds, then closed for landing and touched down. I repeated the manoeuvre. Chernichenko said nothing.

'One more?'

'No, that's enough.'

'Should I get myself ready for a sortie?'

'No rush. You'll be told.' Yes, he was right to be non-committal. Chernichenko had nothing to do with making the final call. In this regiment only Tikhonov assigned tasks and took decisions – the rest of us carried just them out. Now there were more crews than planes and the intensity of flying could be increased. The commander decided to do just that: some crews operated in daylight, some at night, all in the same planes. I felt that there was no chance of night flights for me. All right, let it be daytime, then, as long as I got some time in the air.

The situation at the fronts was desperate. There was a catastrophic shortage of strike aircraft – short-range bombers, ground-attack planes and long-range bombers and fighters had to shoulder their duties too. Forget about night raids on the enemy's deep rear while the Germans were pressing on the outskirts of Moscow and, having captured the central areas of Russia, were advancing eastwards. Our crews were reaching Warsaw, the Baltic shore and even further, just for reconnaissance and only by day, hiding in the clouds and dropping below their lower edge only over short stretches. They would take off towards the end of one night and land at the beginning of the next. Poland and the Baltic shores were not close by. These flights were made by order of General Headquarters and the crews were chosen for their top-level skills – Kononenko, Shevtsov, Lomov, Kusnetsov ...

The commander was apparently waiting for better weather before he would send me, not considering the fact that conditions would then also be easier for the German fighter pilots, to say nothing of the anti-aircraft artillery. And they would have more of an advantage than I. When it came, the good weather appeared unexpectedly. The railway junction of Vyazma was fixed as the strike target for me and Senior Lieutenant Pavel Radchuk. To make a sortie to such a target in clear weather was a risky business, to put it mildly. Vyazma was well protected by both fighter planes and anti-aircraft guns, and there were only two of us. But trains loaded with matériel, fuel and ammunition were gathering there and the schedule of operations was dictated not by weather but by military necessity. It was good enough for me, but why was Radchuk to fly in the daytime? He was a very experienced flyer, had worked as a test pilot at an aircraft works – such a man should have been saved for night operations. It was clear to me that Radchuk also knew his worth, but he went out on the daytime sortie without complaint. I held position to his right and behind him, and I saw his navigator, Khroustalev, by the machine gun as he leaned over the gunsight in the front cockpit – he was measuring the wind strength. There was not a cloud around. All our hopes would rest on our machine-gun fire should enemy fighter planes be encountered – and, of course, on manoeuvring and switching to contour flying if we could. Such a mission needed to be escorted by at least a flight of fighter planes according to the old regulations. But forget about that. There were not enough of them to beat off the fascist bombers, let alone carry out other duties.

We approached the front line. From left to right all along the horizon Russian villages were burning, twinkling with fire and drowning in smoke. Who set them ablaze? The Germans? Our troops? What would our poor peasants do, finding themselves out in this cruel frost and having lost everything? It was impossible to imagine the Germans in a village in the heart of Russia, near Moscow itself.

I glanced at the map: the curve of the long strip of fires precisely repeated the front line. The gunners and the navigator were at the machine guns (Dvoevka – an aerodrome full of enemy fighter planes – was a bit south of Vyazma). I pressed my plane closer to Radchuk's. It would be easier for two of us to beat them off: it would mean six barrels anyway. Time dragged slowly on but eventually we approached the target. The outlines of the railway junction came into view from far away. Volodya Samosudov began to measure the wind. We were still flying calmly and establishing our attack heading. I lagged behind the leader a little bit – we were setting our targets independently. The whole space around us was densely peppered with grey, smoky puffs. There were more and more of them: shells were bursting nearby, very close in fact – sometimes ahead of us, sometimes to the side. They were zeroing in! But when you are on an attack heading you don't move – otherwise the bombs fall off target.

'Volodya, do you see the target?'

'I can see everything, commander. All the tracks are full of trains. Don't miss!' The flak guns hit thicker and thicker; the plane was crossed by the smoky traces of shell bursts. I could hardly wait to drop our bombs.

'Go for it!' Volodya shouted. I felt light jolts as the bombs released, the smell of the ignited pyro cartridges reaching me. That's it; now I was free. I turned sharply right, changed my banking angle, lost altitude and increased speed, trying to find the shortest way to flee the zone of flak fire. The bombs had hit on target and now, following Khroustalev's batch, fires started on the station tracks and our weapons exploded too. The crew had an excellent view, and as we turned I could also see the scene.

Radchuk was already heading back and I joined him at full speed. The fighter planes should have appeared now, according to the classic scenario. Surely Vyazma ground defence had informed the aerodromes about our planes? Pavel turned a bit to the north, away from Dvoevka. The clarity of the sky was terrifying. Maybe it would be better to switch to buzzing, I thought? We must have been plainly visible at that altitude. But Radchuk didn't lose height. What had got into him? We could already see the front line on the horizon and I was almost confident they wouldn't get us. Someone managed to take a few hasty shots in our direction with flak guns but I believed they could only hit us accidentally now. It seemed the German fighter planes really were frozen to the ground. What else could have stopped them from making short work of us?

Major Tikhonov was pleased with the results of our strike, and seemingly most of all with the fact that we had come back. Our planes were already being prepared for a night sortie but they would be flown by other crews. However, the commander did now begin to entrust me with other tasks: that was the most important thing. By that time the regiment was based near Moscow in Ramenskoye, having flown closer to the front line under the umbrella of the capital's anti-aircraft defences. Unfortunately for those who made sorties at daytime, the clear and frosty weather set in for a long period. The German fighter aircraft rushed about beyond the front line and our losses began to mount. Perforated planes began to return from sorties, with wounded and killed in their cockpits.

The German bombers targeting Moscow at night were based at Smolensk aerodrome. A flight was assigned to hit the base: Radchuk as leader, Anisimov to the right of him, Klotar to the left. Take-off was set for dawn on 24 January. The elderly and highly experienced Senior Lieutenant Vasiliy Anisimov, who had arrived only recently, had managed to take away my crew, having talked Major Tikhonov into it. Anisimov had failed to knit together his own crew, and the old flight commander, who was past his prime, was apparently wary of flying his first combat sortie with novices. It was much easier to snatch a seasoned and well-organised crew from me than from someone else – a junior lieutenant was no match for a senior. Most of all I was worried about not flying with Volodya Samosudov. He was in no position to choose where he went: if he was attached to Anisimov he would have to fly with him from now on. But I had worked hard to get to him into my crew and I didn't want to lose him as navigator. He was a clear head, a man with a decent soul and noble courage. He was also – and in addition to his many other good human qualities – a real musical genius: he played the *bayan* [a variety of accordion – translator's note] superbly. He carried this huge mother-of-pearl and gold-plated, glittering marvel with him everywhere in a massive black case. Volodya had perfect pitch, fine musical taste and good though undeveloped skills. His fingers ran over the closely spaced rows of multi-coloured buttons producing complicated, clear, harmonious sounds. How he had captivated everyone at the recent New Year's Eve party in Sasovo! We rang in 1942 with pain and hope. Those who were not in the air that night gathered towards midnight at a narrow table. Division commander Colonel Loginov turned up too. Just days before he had taken our regiment under his charge, along with the so-called 'Bitskiy group', which consisted mainly of Aeroflot pilots (Bitskiy was one of them). They called themselves a group, in civilian style, rather than a regiment, as if preserving their free spirit, although theirs was actually an ordinary 750th DBAP [long-range bomber regiment – translator's note] incorporated into Loginov's division.

The division commander had recently served with Major Tikhonov in the Far East of Russia, knew him well, like many others from that area who had become airmen in our regiment, and maybe for this reason he preferred their company on New Year's Eve. The celebration was not a joyful one. And why would it be? Although the Germans had been thrown back from the outskirts of Moscow and were creeping slowly westwards, they still had a grip on Rzhev, Vyazma, Orel and Kursk. Severe ordeals awaited each of us.

Loyal toasts were made, with food hastily eaten between them, and the party would have gone on in the same depressing way if Volodya's *bayan* had not struck up. Then everything changed: everyone froze in silent fascination and gave himself up to his emotions and thoughts. People enjoyed the music, joined in with singing and demanded Volodya play more and more – and he did. The head of the Operations Department rushed into the room from time to time to whisper something in the regiment commander's ear. The latter nodded, made some comments and the man from headquarters disappeared. Then the commander left for the CP [command post – translator's note].

Some crews were in the air and a new group was preparing to take off. The weather was nasty – low clouds, snowfalls, ice-overs. Captain Shevtsov had left the night before on combat duties with Captain Uroutin and hadn't returned. His plane was found damaged by shell splinters on the outskirts of a small village in the area of Shatsk, a stone's throw from our aerodrome. He had transmitted what information he could via his radio but failed to make it home. I felt really sorry for this kind-hearted and thoroughly decent captain. I almost worshipped him – the previous autumn he had been the one who hadn't passed me over or waved me aside but had included me in the new group for Tikhonov's regiment. The squadron commander, Vasiliy Shevtsov, was buried as a major: the order for his promotion had arrived on the day of his death.

The New Year's Eve celebrations were behind us. Volodya, who had given us unexpected joy that night, soared in the eyes of those who were lucky enough to listen to him and I was proud that I had such a special friend and navigator. But now he was to fly with another commander. And although I was assured that it was only for one flight, I felt certain that was not how things would turn out; I was seriously worried. I rushed to the squadron headquarters, which had always been manned by unattached navigators, and found Vasiliy Svertchkov, who wasn't included in any of the crews. True, he had no combat experience, but he knew how to bomb and had even been a bombing instructor. I also found a two-way operator, and locating a machine-gunner among the arms technicians was easier.

There was still the main hurdle to overcome: I had to persuade the commander to give me a plane and to attach it to Radchuk's flight. The squadron commissar, Alexey Tsykin, supported me. My calculations showed that after landing (provided it happened, of course) there would be enough time to get the plane I would use ready for a night sortie. Major Tikhonov thought for a bit, shook his head, but agreed: he allocated the plane's number and its place in the formation – behind and to the right of Anisimov.

A severe frost below −30°C persisted through the night. The stars faded imperceptibly and a blue of pristine clarity spread overhead. The heaped snow creaked resonantly, reaching for the sky like pillars. An anticyclone. Its cloudless domains stretched to infinity, encompassing our targets as well as our base. Heaters had been burning all night under the planes, driving warmth under the engine jackets. In such frost engines usually start with difficulty but mine fired after just half a crank. An ageing, weather-beaten technician helped me warm them up and gave them a run at full revolutions while standing on a wing. Then he adjusted my parachute straps and seatbelt, leaned towards me, unexpectedly kissed me and rolled down the wing. This was the way some of the technicians – those who were older – often blessed the flyers in a kind of fatherly way, for luck.

It was time to take off. Radchuk went first. I could see that one of Anisimov's engines didn't want to start and I taxied for take-off in his stead, taking my place on the right-hand side. Klotar approached the airstrip from the left. He took off, stayed in the air for a short time, then suddenly turned sharply aside and began to close hastily for landing. He had a long-term reputation as a faint-hearted pilot, and on the ground he complained of poor engine performance, but however hard the engines were run under all possible conditions, nothing dodgy was found. Klotar remained on the ground yet again.

Radchuk made another circle over the aerodrome – he was waiting for Anisimov, but the latter wasn't showing up. There was no point in waiting any longer and we set course towards Smolensk. Then we saw the front line. The air was clear and transparent. We peered into the blue, fearing that we might miss enemy fighter planes. I was pressed tightly against Pavel and could see the look of concentration in his profile. I didn't look at the map: it had no calculations on it and, folded several times, it was tucked into the top of my boot. But I knew the general route; I remembered the course bearings. Svertchkov – a smart navigator and skilled bomb-aimer – sat ahead of me. He wouldn't let me down.

In all my previous flying years I'd worked diligently with maps: drawn route lines, measured course bearings, conducted navigation calculations, and always kept my map-case on my left knee. But it seemed to me that in this regiment my older comrades – seasoned flyers – didn't prepare maps themselves and I had not seen any of them carrying a flyer's map-case. 'What's your navigator for?' they would ask me, laughing. They were warm and friendly towards me but slightly patronising, even a bit condescending – kind of 'when you've been around as long as we have you'll know what's what'. I was drawn to them, tried to hang around them, but still kept my distance to a certain extent.

To be honest, on this mission I'd neglected to draft the course not so much because I'd fallen under the influence of someone else's way of doing things, but rather because I had decided there was no point in busying myself with navigation while I was sticking to my place in formation behind Radchuk. He and Khroustalev would surely find the target and bring us home, and my duty was to follow him. That's why I was flying without referring to the map, and everything was going as well as could be. But suddenly Pavel turned his face towards me, leading his plane smoothly into a right turn. Where was he heading? He turned by about 30 degrees and took a direct heading again. There was no two-way connection between us. I showed him a left turn with my hands – that's where we go? My gestures became persistent and rather rude. I even tapped my head with my fist – but Radchuk and Khroustalev just looked at me from time to time, no reaction on their faces.

Then I understood everything – the commander had decided to fly towards Vyazma. In this clear weather with its limitless visibility it would be too risky – nearly madness – to count on an unpunished flight by two bombers over Smolensk, to which there was still a fair distance to fly. It was much more likely we wouldn't make it there. If there were four of us it would be all right, but two of us would be knocked out straight away. Vyazma was closer – in fact it was right next to us now. Its railway station was always full of trains packed with troops and matériel. The new course of action was entirely logical, apart from one detail – we'd been ordered to bomb Smolensk aerodrome and not Vyazma. This was a combat mission following an order, and so there could be no other interpretation. Maybe Radchuk's aircraft had had some kind of malfunction and he couldn't fly further even if he wanted? I didn't know what to think. Radchuk was on a new course and was looking at me sternly, as if demanding that I follow him. But I fell behind a little, turned left and set course for Smolensk. Then I diverted further to the left to get out of harm's way – damned Dvoevka and its Me-109s was to the right again, on the beam of Vyazma. If the Germans came to their senses they wouldn't have far to look – our long, dense, white contrail stretched behind us treacherously.

Suddenly it hit me – I had deserted my commander, hadn't I? God forbid something should happen to him. That sort of caper is never forgiven a wingman in combat. But again I sought to justify my action: 'Our target is Smolensk, not Vyazma!' For a single bomber to be alone under an endless dome of clear sky, deep inside enemy territory, is an absolutely unbelievable scenario. But we still kept making our way further in. If I could just make it to Smolensk. It should have appeared over the horizon by now but I still couldn't see it. Then, at last, the target aerodrome showed up black and became more visible as we got closer. Dark silhouettes of bombers stood stock still on the white field, wing to wing. There were about sixty of them. I was on the attack heading. Anti-aircraft guns began to shoot: fluffy puffs of smoke hung all around me, but this was not the most fearsome opposition I could encounter – please don't let the local fighter planes protecting the aerodrome lift off.

Following the anti-aircraft bursts, Svertchkov reported, with tension in his voice, 'Commander, there's ack-ack!'

'They're not on target. Don't pay attention. Do it like a practice run!' He measured the wind carefully, introduced adjustments to our course, made the last extra turn and, 'Steady as she goes!'

The air was taut and still, the plane steady. The pointers on all the instruments were stationary. To the side I could see shell bursts getting closer and closer. The plane was already brushing the puffs of smoke. For some reason they were black here although they were grey over Vyazma.

'Bombs away!'

Now I had to get carefully out of the line of fire, flying lower so as not to be hanging in full view. Svertchkov and the machine-gunners re-ported: our stick had crossed the aircraft parking area at a slight angle. The planes had caught fire. The navigator said two of them were ablaze, the gunners said three. Shortly after that one of the planes exploded. Maybe it would take out some others too: they were parked quite close together. I managed to glance back for a second – a shapeless cloud of smoke showed black over the white plain.

The Germans from Dvoevka had obviously missed us on our way to Smolensk. Clearly they hadn't expected any stray strikes in such clear and frosty weather, but now they would not let us get away. Had Radchuk escaped in one piece? A sense of alarm began to build, but the sky was still like a sheet of glass, not a fighter in sight. I could see Dvoevka on the horizon, still far in front of me and to the left. Two black dots darted out of a cloud of snowy dust one after another and disap-peared. Messers! They had come for me! I turned towards a large woodland, took it more and more to the right and pressed myself towards the tops of the pine trees. But the Messers were not coming. Where were they? They wouldn't have taken off in hard frost just for an exercise. Who could they be worried about except us? We had to get home as quickly as possible. The world seems to stand still even though we were flying at full speed.

At last the pair of planes appeared at high altitude. They moved slowly towards us but both were sweeping from side to side, as if blind. Apparently the Germans were hampered by the low sun and they didn't see us against the background of the forest. For the time being they were flying far to our left and slightly ahead. I moved further and further away from them to the south and saw them turn back before the front line. Now moving towards us, they entered my back hemisphere, but then they suddenly swung around, heading directly at me. Gradually catching up, the Germans closed in and one of them shot a long machine-gun burst from afar. It missed but a burst from our machine gun had already rushed to meet it. Then – I don't know why – the leading Messer suddenly pulled off and the other followed it. The fighters, as I would notice on later sorties, didn't much like engaging in combat beyond their lines, but this time it was more likely that they were running out of fuel and their aerodrome stood too far behind. This was the end of the engagement.

We crossed the front line and felt at home. But where were we? It was clear that we'd diverted far to the right of our proper course. I turned left sharply – still acting on guesswork. Unfortunately, there was no decent landmark: only forests. A road or a village flashed by and then it was forests again. I pulled my sketchy map from inside my bootleg, but I couldn't match it to anything that was on the ground. Our estimated time of landing was approaching but I could see no landmark that would tell me I was approaching the aerodrome. What the hell was going on? Where were we? I gained altitude, picked up a railway and followed it, hoping to come across at least a large station, a river or a road crossing, but all in vain. I turned the map this way and that but it told me nothing. Through the lower slot in my instrument panel I saw the navigator jumping about in the cockpit, throwing himself now to port, now to starboard. We both swore, but it did no good. We were running out of fuel – it was time to land, even if not at our aerodrome. The two-way operators had spotted an airstrip. It was ours of course, Soviet, but not the one where we were expected. I put the undercarriage down and landed, then turned off the engines. Looking around helplessly, the navigator and I tried to work out where we were. Our ignorance was embarrassing, but what we could do? No one came up to us or showed the least interest. Fighter planes stood nearby under covers and mechanics were working on some of them. I sent a machine-gunner to get some information, tasking him to discreetly find out the aerodrome's name, making it look like a casual chat. We watched him lean towards someone to get a light, start up a chat, gesticulate cheerfully (what an actor!). Soon he climbed up on my wing and reported quietly: 'Khimki.'

Bloody hell, that took the biscuit! Khimki was off my map, north of Moscow, but our aerodrome was south of it. This was what I deserved for preparing the map poorly, for being thoughtless about navigation, for going on this, my first sortie – a combat sortie – so confidently! This lesson stayed with me for the rest of my long flying life. But what about my navigator, Vasiliy? He was alternately throwing his arms out wide and then clutching his head. It was true I'd been setting my own headings, hoping that the navigator was doing the dead reckoning. But he, sticking to the machine gun, was apparently studying the air rather than the watch and compass, and you couldn't blame him for that.

I went to the local commanders and reported that due to long man-oeuvres under pursuit by German fighter planes I had had to choose this aerodrome for landing and I requested a little bit of fuel so that I could return to my aerodrome. An ageing captain with eyes red from sleep-lessness smiled sourly and ordered a fuel truck brought up. They also found a large-scale map of the area; on my way home I didn't take my eyes off it, checking my route against every bush on the ground. We came in for landing when it was already twilight. The airstrip was illuminated by searchlights. The short winter day was already dying. People were bustling around parked planes, getting ready for night sorties. After landing, I hadn't even managed to turn off the engines before someone got up on my wing.

'Off to the take-off point to see the commander!'

'Where is Radchuk?' I yelled in turn.

'He came back long ago.' Thank God for that. It was a load off my mind.

A *polutorka* was waiting for me under the plane. Division commander Loginov, Tikhonov and the deputy regiment commander were pacing nervously by the CP. I went up to Loginov and reported that the order to attack Smolensk aerodrome had been carried out. The commanders exchanged glances. They were very surprised by what I had to say and began to ask me in detail about the flight conditions, the layout of Smolensk aerodrome and the results of the strike. It turned out that our two-way message about completion of the mission had not been received at the CP. Perhaps the low altitude from which the two-way operator tapped it out had impeded transmission. It would have been too risky to turn away from the machine gun to make one more transmission in the danger zone and to wait for a receipt.

The commanders livened up noticeably, but the gloomy expression did not leave their faces. It was only now that I understood it wasn't my crew they'd been expecting at the take-off point – they'd given us up for lost. They'd been waiting for Anisimov. Based on time estimations he could be still in the air, but then the estimated time passed too. Anisimov never came back, taking away my crew with him. I was told that an engine on his plane hadn't wanted to start for quite a while, but at last it fired up. The commander, not losing a minute, hastily taxied to the take-off point, took to the air without pausing and immediately followed his course. At the time Radchuk was turning back from Vyazma and I was still on my way to Smolensk. From that moment Anisimov was never heard of again. Many years would pass before we found out about the last moments of my crew and their new commander in his first combat sortie.

Judging from where they crashed, they were certainly headed for Vyazma. The fighters from Dvoevka, alarmed by Radchuk and even more by my aircraft, which had penetrated deep to the west, managed to get their delicate machines cranked up. They took off for interception exactly at the moment when I was supposed to approach the traverse of Dvoevka on my way back from attacking Smolensk (one may assume the fighters had been warned about it). And that was exactly where Anisimov ran into them: the whole mob attacked him straight away. Only later, having come to their senses, did one pair rush blindly to cut me off but they were too late.

Village people who witnessed this aerial drama saw either five or six Messerschmitts hanging over the bomber, spraying it with machine-gun bursts. Maintaining its course, the plane manoeuvred desperately and returned fire – and apparently it stitched one of them up good and proper, for the fighter went down very steeply, dragging itself towards the aerodrome and trailing smoke. Machine guns kept rapping in the clear sunny sky for quite a while, but then the Il-4 banked steeply and began to lose altitude. Anisimov bailed out. He opened his parachute but was already dead when he hit the ground: there was a bullet in his temple. His pistol lay nearby, tied to the holster by a shoelace. Whose bullet made a hole in his head – his own from the pistol or one from the Messers who were shooting at him as he hung on his parachute straps? The truth remains unknown. Navigator Volodya Samosudov, machine-gunners-cum-two-way operators Nikolay Kamenev and Nikolay Ladnik stayed in the falling plane. Were they still alive at that moment? The Germans pursued to finish them off, but on the Il-4 someone's machine gun was still rapping away. Then it too fell silent. The plane shaved off tops of pine trees and hit a thicket at the edge of a glade where it continued to burn and explode for a long time afterwards.

The body of Anisimov was taken away by the *polizei* [police force made up of collaborators – translator's note]. In the early 1970s one of those men was found; he had managed to see out his time in the Gulag, but he couldn't remember what had been done with the commander's body.

* * *

We didn't get on well with Svertchkov. He was due to move to the Transsiberian aircraft ferry group and indeed he soon disappeared. The machine-gunners didn't really fit into the crew either, and I now had to recruit a new 'army'. I went to headquarters – where else could I go? The reserve of navigators had been totally depleted. Only one remained – Senior Lieutenant Vasiliy Zemskov – but he was the squadron adjutant. He had childishly fat cheeks and was generally a bit chubby for his age (although he was eight years older than me), but he was a very agile and robust fellow, always rushing about and wrangling on the phone. Everyone wanted him to get them vehicles, beds, coupons of one sort or another and God knows what else. But when I asked him to leave all this behind and fly with me, his decision was instant: 'I'm ready!' I also found excellent gunner/radio-operators – Nikolay Chernov and Alexey Nezhentsev. Zemskov handed over his headquarters duties to his assistant – a smart technician who easily swapped the romance of the aerodrome's roar of engines for the corridors of headquarters. Vasiliy arrayed himself in flying 'armour' and provided himself with maps. He turned out to be a superb navigator – he guided the aircraft as if it was travelling along a thread, bombed with no misses, and did all of this with cheerful fervour. It was as though all those flak shells and enemy fighters were never intended for him, and when he dropped bombs he would always say something mischievous.

The long-lived anticyclone was succeeded by a series of bad-weather episodes – heavy clouds swept over and snow fell. The weather kept us close to the ground, exposed us to direct machine-gun and small-calibre artillery fire, but it didn't save us from dangerous encounters with fighter planes. And not only fascist ones. In early February one such meeting nearly ended in disaster for us. Full of battle fervour, we were on our way back from a bombing raid on the Dorogobuzhskiy bridge (which we had hit really well, by the way) when we were caught by a solitary Messerschmitt 109 in a gap between the clouds. Before we could hide, the rascal managed to spray us with bullets but we didn't incur any significant damage. The duel ended there because he couldn't find us again. Clear skies soon returned, but we were already over our own territory and, noticing a flight of I-16 fighter planes, we felt completely safe. The trio approached us smoothly and began to form up with us while they were still at a distance. I decided that the guys had resolved to fly a while as a kind of escort beside the friendly bomber returning from a sortie. But just in case, we gave them a 'friend' signal: waggled our wings and shot out flares. Then we were caught in a hail of bullets: the glass of my windscreen shattered, holes appearing all over the wings and the navigator's cockpit. There was no point engaging in a stupid dog-fight. I yelled to the machine-gunners, 'Send them a burst!', and pressing myself against the armoured back of my seat, abruptly threw the machine into a steep dive down to the very tops of the trees. The *Ishaks* [nickname for I-16 fighter planes: literally, donkey – translator's note] immediately scattered after our machine-gun burst and then, coming to their senses, rushed into pursuit like backyard curs, shooting from afar, but all their fire went wide. When we switched to contour flying they dropped back altogether.

My guys were not hurt, but after landing I had to taxi the machine to the workshop to have the holes patched. Division commander Loginov, who met us at the aerodrome, was outraged, rushed to the phone, tried to find someone, scolded and swore. All in vain. There was not a trace of the *Ishaks*. Most likely the flight was already recording on its account a shared victory over a Heinkel or a Junkers. Well, that sort of thing happened more than once. Not many fighter pilots had seen our planes in the flesh and in their regiments there were no posters of our aircraft because of their secrecy status. For this reason, if our fighter pilots saw a plane of configuration unknown to them they would shoot without hesitation. Perhaps it was done on principle – we would rather down a friendly plane by mistake than let a fascist get through. It was not only fighter pilots who were guilty of this; more often the culprits were anti-aircraft gunners. Actually, it was easier to deal with them if you were flying at high altitude. After the first salvos – which were usually inaccurate or, more precisely, ranging fire – we had enough time to communicate with them using the 'friend' signal. But sometimes a plane flying at low altitude would be downed by the first burst. A handsome guy with light-brown hair, Major Kalinin, nursed his Er-2 [an aircraft rarely used by the Soviet Air Force – translator's note] to our aerodrome on one engine, having been shot up by German fighters. His machine, which was quite unusual in shape (two-keeled, with inverted gull wings), was flying over Kratovo at a height of about 500 metres in full view of the aircraft parking zones when female anti-aircraft gunners from the nearest battery shot it down with the first salvo. What grief they felt later at the cemetery.

Our two worst problems were the weather and the fascist anti-aircraft defence. One late evening the commander ordered us to bomb Rzhev.

Intelligence clarified the situation: the town was crammed with troops. Survivors were retreating from Moscow and fresh troops had arrived from the west with tanks, artillery, ammo. They were still well entrenched, aiming to make a new assault on Moscow. In addition to us, some other planes were supposed to bomb Rzhev that day but all their strikes were done *en echelon*, stretched out – in essence by solitary planes.

In the morning visibility was bad: there was fog and it was snowing. The weather didn't promise to be better over the target and we had to wait. Then the clouds rose slightly and the end of the airstrip became visible. Green flares soared from the CP – it was the signal for take-off. It was impossible to fly under the lower edge of the clouds – sometimes they came down so low we couldn't see the ground. We climbed above the bottom layer but there was no break and we flew by following our time calculations. The last minute of estimated flying time had gone by – it was time to descend to Rzhev. The lower our altitude, the more careful we were in our descent. The clouds suddenly darkened from a height of 1,500 metres – the tops of pine trees became visible. The haze below us was still dense and it was snowing. We crossed a railway leading towards Moscow, then positioned ourselves precisely and headed to Rzhev on a westward course, staying south of the line.

At last Zemskov turned right and we headed for the attack. The altitude was 600 metres, the clouds rushed just above our heads. We darted out to the edge of the town. The bombs were about to be dropped and at this moment a torrent of fire fell upon us. Tracer bullets stretched towards the plane from all sides and intersected not far off – overhead, below ... Chernov and Nezhentsev shot long machine-gun bursts from both sides but the German fire only intensified. There was no escape. I was very tense, expecting a fatal outcome. Would I be able to make it home if anything went wrong? Zemskov could see the jumble of fire as well as me, but it didn't seem to concern him. In heated outbursts he first laughed and then came out with an expression like: 'Oh, look at the bastards run!' At last, nearly at the end of my tether, I heard the long-awaited word – 'Drop!' – and felt the bombs break away from the plane. I turned slightly right and climbed straight up into the clouds. The machine-gunners and the navigator had managed to spot our bombs exploding in a clump of tanks.

'Good!' Zemskov rejoiced. 'We've got one good hit in!' Then he added, after a short pause, 'Let's do one more strike.'

I went cold. 'You've gone out of your mind!' The situation was quite clear: luck was with us on the first run, but we wouldn't get away with a second.

'What was the point of expending a long stick on a short target? One half was enough for them the first time. Let's chuck the other half at them. I wish you had seen them rush about down there! It was fun!' The navigator was right from a bomber's point of view. But this was no target range.

There was nothing else for it. We took a look over our plane and the machine-gunners found several holes in the fuselage. But the engines still roared and the rudders were responsive. Our hit on the target was quite a surprise for the Germans and their fire was hasty. Now they were waiting for us and wouldn't let a chance go by. I descended beneath the clouds again, manoeuvred, rolled myself into a ball and headed for the attack as if pitching down into a maelstrom. They met us with fire more quickly and more furiously than before. We flew at full speed. Chernov and Nezhentsev fired off the last of our last ammo – no point in saving it because in this weather fighter planes sat on the ground. Zemskov made more line-up turns but sat quietly, not cracking jokes now.

'Drop!' he yelled. 'I'm closing the chutes! Go, commander!'

'Aha, now you yell "go!"' The clouds were just above us. Into them fast! I pulled the wheel to me, the machine soared eagerly but luck was against us and we leaped into a broken cloud layer. Having been out of sight for just a moment, I was in full view again, but now speed was slower, momentum lost during the climb. It seemed we were frozen to the spot and they were shooting at us from all sides, as if at a stationary target. Then suddenly it was all behind us. The crew had managed to drop the bombs in the same heap of tanks and vehicles as before. Dense black smoke rose from the site, tongues of fire sparkled. We got out of the clouds and set course for home. We had picked up more holes in the wings but the engines were still working and pulling well. We'd got away this time too. Would it always be the same?

One day Major Tikhonov called me. 'Get the plane ready for tonight. I'll do a flight with you to the aerodrome area.'

I replied, 'Yes, sir!' but I was chilled to the bone: I hadn't flown at night for quite a while – I might bungle it. However, I had no choice but to comply. It was pitch dark. The sky was clouded over. On the ground not a single light was visible, apart from a few tiny ones at the take-off point. I wouldn't be able to see any of them from the air: blacked-out towns and villages didn't give themselves away. The task wasn't complicated: I had to fly in circles. I thought I did the first one quite satisfactorily – I maintained speed and altitude, came in well for landing. Helped by floodlights, I touched the aircraft down carefully, almost next to the landing tee. Tikhonov didn't interfere with the controls, kept silent throughout the whole flight and at the end of the landing run ordered me to taxi to the parking bay. No doubt the commander had his own criteria for assessing flying techniques and I was worried that I would be unable to meet them. In the parking bay I quickly turned off the engines, slipped down the wing, and met the commander who was climbing slowly down the stepladder from the front cockpit. I addressed him in the manner customary on these occasions: 'I'd be honoured to hear your comments.'

'You'll be going on a mission tomorrow night,' he said and walked unhurriedly towards an approaching group of senior commanders. It was such an unexpected joy for me that I barely managed to ask, having caught up with him, if I could do a few training flights myself.

'Go on,' the commander drawled. There was a mood of good humour in his voice and apparently it spread to his comrades for I could hear a lively discussion in the darkness and the lights of cigarettes began to flash.

By this time I was ahead of everyone in the regiment in the number of day combat sorties I had carried out and yet I had never been shot down. Maybe it would be a bit easier at night? In sheer greed I made three more flights. Perhaps they didn't go as neatly as the first one, but I felt confident and ready for night fighting. And for me that was the most important thing I could do at this stage in my flying life.

I would like to believe that it was the humbleness of my origins compared with the background of Tikhonov's 'elite squad' and the combat debut of my crew that broke through the regiment commander's prejudice against young pilots. At the beginning of the new year he accepted under his charge two young crew commanders – the same age as me – Ivan Kouryatnik and Gavriil Lepekhin, who would make their names in action right away and who were not inferior in any regard to the older, seasoned fighters. They were young instructors too. And these flight commanders were followed by new waves of strong and skilled combat airmen: Frantz Rogulskiy, Sasha Romanov, Gleb Bazhenov, Mishka Orlov ... The regiment was being replenished by a new and robust force.

By the end of January 1942 we had relocated to Serpukhov which was to become our main base for nearly two years. Of course we would leave for short periods, moving to a whole variety of aerodromes in order to get closer to areas of action and increase combat intensity – in other words, in order to get in not one but two or even three sorties a night. But because we were based around Moscow, unlike other regiments we were in a position to operate, with no loss of time, near Leningrad today, in the Crimea tomorrow, over East Prussia the next night. And sometimes when we had plenty of hours of darkness the first strike would be in the evening on the northern flank of the Soviet–German front and the last towards morning on its far southern edge.

The long-range bomber was the most manoeuvrable and powerful strike weapon of all. It was a pity, then, that the High Command, especially during the first year of the war, didn't always take into consideration this aircraft's special strengths, often dispersing the bombers' might and using them where other combat forces could have handled the job.

Our aerodrome was very cosy and picturesque. The airstrip lay on a green meadow stretched along a straight bank of the Oka river. Next to it but a bit further along, the aircraft parking bays were scattered in curves and straight lines – some in caponiers, some in the open. The CP and auxiliary earth-houses dug into a slope of the hill were located in front of the central part of the airstrip. The roofs of a large village called Lipitsy were visible behind them on a low rise. Our technicians were lodged there in houses and huts. The flight personnel didn't live so close by, but were housed at the far edge of Serpukhov in a pine wood next to headquarters, where the pre-war buildings of an aviation school still stood.

Life in Serpukhov acquired almost a measured rhythm: we would go to the aerodrome by night and in the morning we would return to our barracks. Rolling across the town, old 3-tonne trucks and creaking *polutorkas* transported us as we held on to each other, standing in the back of a vehicle or sitting on the sides. When the river flooded in spring the regiment would leave to lodge with 'richer' neighbours who had concrete airstrips or we would occasionally oust those who could still operate from earth airstrips. But the floodplain of the Oka would recover relatively quickly and we would be settled back at home by the beginning of summer when the ground was able to bear the weight of heavy aircraft again.

Setting the next mission for combat operations, in which my crew was to take part at night for the first time, Major Tikhonov glanced towards me. After thinking for a bit, he said, 'You'll be flying in tandem with Radchuk.'

'What?' I couldn't restrain myself. 'In formation?'

'Exactly,' the commander replied sternly.

I hadn't expected this. I could have understood if it were a daytime mission. But at night? Nobody in the regiment had flown in formation at night. Well, maybe Tikhonov himself had when he led a squadron from Esel to Berlin. He would form his aircraft into a column of several flights and before entering the coastal zone around Stettin he would have them all scatter to operate independently. That way the commander knew he had brought the whole squadron to the target area. In conditions of radio silence and meagre navigational resources, the safety net provided by a strong leading crew was not out of place. He was apparently thinking along these lines now, wanting to make my mission easier, although neither I nor Zemskov had any cause for concern about our navigational abilities. Radchuk was a seasoned and reliable flyer and commander; as for his crewman, Pasha Khroustalev, if there are navigators made in heaven, he was one.

'Well, there is nothing new for me in night formation flying and Radchuk will not lead us beyond the front line anyway,' I told myself. 'We'll have to switch off our lights there and I'll have to pull away to fly independently.' That's how it went.

A thick, damp haze still enveloped the scene right up to the front line. The lights of the leading plane began to blur and then disappeared in the clouds. At the same moment I turned away, changed altitude, switched off the lights. A bit later I resumed my previous course. The clouds turned out to be broken, and the further we were from the front line, the further apart they became. The ground began to show through the gaps, and we kept a check on our position by noting the curves of rivers and the lines of major roads which showed up against the blackness.

Searchlight beams soon began waving on the horizon, sparks of shells bursting in the sky and flashes of bombs flickering on the ground: long-range bombers were striking German troops and matériel. Occasionally, luminescent bombs blazed up and then faded out above the targets. The geography was now completely clear – we could see Vyazma, even make out Orsha and Mogilev. But we turned to Smolensk – this was our destination. Radchuk was flying somewhere nearby and Uroutin, Kouznetsov, Commissar Choulkov and someone else were in a file ahead of us. Others followed.

We couldn't yet see the whole layout of the town but we could make out the area of the railway junction and we prepared to head for the attack. A concentrated night strike is a wonderful sight. But it's hard to grasp how it works when you're not used to it, and at this point we were heading straight for our target point with no real idea of what awaited us. The searchlights caught us instantly, as one: the well-aimed flak fire came straight at us. We had no choice but to head forward. Shells burst so close to us that we could smell burnt gunpowder, but the time for maintaining attack course hadn't yet passed. We flew absolutely straight, at constant speed and altitude, and I now know that ack-ack gunners can't imagine better conditions than these for aiming their flak. The searchlights dazzled the navigator and impeded his aim but he saw the target – and the bombs exploded right where they should. All of us have reached the target – all at once. I began to manoeuvre and, in order to speed up and break away as soon as possible, I started to descend, but the searchlights wouldn't let us go and the fire didn't let up. The beams swung away from the air defence area and stretched towards us, holding on to our tails. Then the firing began to recede and at last we sailed away.

'Got the bombs right at least, navigator,' I sighed.

Vasya Zemskov became animated. 'The bombs landed well. We passed a big island of fire. We've stoked it up for 'em!'

No one attacked us on the way home: the front line was still obscured by clouds, and only here and there did round white patches of search-lights crawl across them, pushing through from below, and sometimes solitary, unaimed shells would burst off to the side. We'd got away: all well and good. Perhaps that's how war is supposed to go. We live until next time.

We made further combat flights and nearly all followed the same scenario – we got caught by searchlights and drew all the flak onto ourselves. And what about the others? I noticed that when ground fire was concentrating on our aircraft, bombs from other planes would explode most intensely on the targets. It meant they knew how to use the moment, didn't they? Besides, flak didn't arrive with the same intensity from all directions – some areas were less well defended and it was much easier to strike from those points unless such a course of action con-tradicted mission conditions. It didn't do to rush headlong at the target – you needed to look around, choose the direction least under fire, seize the right moment when fire was concentrated on other planes and then go for it.

'Isn't our battle route a bit long?' I wondered. Zemskov agreed with me that it was. I hadn't picked up on all the finer points of the science of combat flying straight away, but I was becoming convinced of its importance in action. Many other airmen realised the same, but others didn't. Some would rush to take off before the rest in order to be the first over the target, reckoning that they would achieve the element of sur-prise – when ground defence, caught unawares, would be able to open only disorderly fire at best. Others preferred to drop bombs in the last wave, hoping that exhausted flak gunners would be unable to maintain organised fire at the end of the engagement – but at that time we had so little force and so many missions that we had not yet been able to exhaust the ground defence. Each of us was right in his own way. None of these principles was likely to be universal, taking into consideration the fact that ground defences were not only built differently at each target, but changed between one raid and another.

The raid on the Minsk railway junction had instilled confidence in my crew: this district had defended itself really well, but we'd managed to get through the whole inferno unscathed, drop our bombs on tracks packed with trains and, having set them ablaze, get away from the target. They had caught us on the way out and given us a good flogging, but it was bearable and they were without serious consequences. As to the fighter planes, the Germans rarely appeared on dark nights and engaged us even less frequently, although a few times they managed to ambush a careless crew on a well-trodden route and send them down in flames.

Overcoming ground defence was the most difficult of all the problems facing night operations. It worried both the crews and our commanders. One day the division commander, Evgeniy Loginov, gathered the flying personnel in the small hall of our barracks and suggested we share our experiences of approaching targets. He told us to describe how we made our anti-flak manoeuvres and how we handled encounters with enemy fighter planes. But to some extent this was a lecture. The meeting was addressed mostly by seasoned flyers who had been through difficult flights in this war and by those who had been in Finland, China and Spain [Soviet airmen who fought in the Winter War, the Sino-Japanese conflicts and the Civil War in Spain – translator's note]. I strained my ears to hear the many-sided conversation but was unable to find in it anything of real importance. Some tried to prove their case to the rest; others put forward their own experience to refute the opinions of their colleagues. The boldest ones put me on my guard most of all. Obviously trying to show their mettle, they talked as if they'd gone through enemy fire paying no attention to it at all, 'defying danger and death itself'. My mind immediately went to sticks of bombs that had fallen far beyond a target or a long way short ...

And then Captain Evgeniy Fedorov – squadron commander of a brother regiment, a Hero of the Soviet Union [the highest military award in the USSR – translator's note] from the time of the Finnish War – addressed the meeting. He was a short, slender man, very handsome, always in a good mood and with a pleasant smile on his kind and amiable face. He was a lot more experienced than many of the others, but what new information could he add after all that had already been said and then said again? Suddenly I understood – here was the man who could give the most important and valuable testimony of all I had heard here. Evgeniy Petrovich didn't thrust his opinion on anyone and argued with no one. He simply told how he handled the approach to a well-defended target.

'I climb up to a height of 500 or 600 metres above the preselected altitude, warm up the engines well, switch the airscrews up to a high pitch so they make less of a roar, switch to descent with minimum vertical and forward speed. The end of the descent needs to coincide with the beginning of a short attack run. At this moment I increase revolutions to the minimum necessary for horizontal flying to enable my navigator to estimate the ground speed and the angle of drift, and I wait until the bombs break away. Then I throttle back again, begin to descend, and leave the flak zone, manoeuvring between the searchlight beams. My gliding flight can hardly be heard with airscrews at high pitch and amidst the general roar of other machines, shooting and bombs bursting on the ground. They have no time to pick us up, even when the plane is flying horizontally on attack course at minimum revolutions. That's all there is to it,' he laughed.

Yes, that was the right way to do it. The point was that ground-defence systems worked like this: sound locators took the bearings of a plane's position and the most powerful searchlight working in synch with it hit the pinpointed target with its beam, almost without fail, right from the moment it switched on. We called it the 'tsar searchlight'. Sometimes there were two or even three of these tsars on the ground. Others, smaller ones were then pointed manually. They would pounce on an illuminated plane by the dozen, like little dogs, and all the flak guns would strike at the very intersection of the light beams where a bomber would be twinkling like a bright little star. Of course they would be searching for aircraft by touch as well, by the roar of engines, by the whizzing of falling bombs, but searchlight operators were rarely lucky amidst the rumbling of guns and bomb bursts, and the flak-gunners would be forced to resort to defensive and unaimed fire or to shoot by guesswork, scattering their shells.

I was absorbed by all that Captain Fedorov had to say. During the next combat sortie (whenever that might be) I would certainly use this knowledge over the target. In the evening I had a chat with Zemskov and did some calculations. It seemed that the higher the bombing altitude was set, the bigger the initial extra height had to be. But all the results of our calculations were within the range between 500 and 800 metres.

On 28 February we headed off to Orsha to attack Balbasovo aero-drome where the bombers targeting Moscow were based. Under our fuselages we had RRABs – rotating cluster bombs. These were huge and clumsy cylinders with blunt ends, tightly stuffed with small-calibre splinter-demolition or incendiary bombs. They were tightly closed with lids and securely bound by steel belts weakened by incisions. Stabilisers, twisted like ships' propellers, were equipped with hinges and tied with cables. After leaving its clamps such a bomb loosed its cables, opened its stabilisers and rushed towards the target, rotating furiously. The centrifugal forces of its internal filling pressed on the sides of the cylinder until the notched belts couldn't hold out any more. They broke at a given altitude and then the small bombs flew out of the wide-open case in all directions, covering large areas of the ground with explosions. An aircraft didn't need many of these weapons. One successful fire-bomb hitting a wing or fuselage where the fuel tanks were located would easily set fire to or blow up the plane in question – and its neighbours would get their share. But in addition to the RRABs, we also carried 100kg high-explosive bombs. We had to make two approaches because the difference between the aiming angles required for the two different bombs was too big to discharge them all on one run: the RRABs need to be dropped at a steeper angle than the 100kg devices.

We had already bombed Orsha and its aerodrome a few times and the ground defence in this district had been strengthened between one raid and the next, reorganised beyond all recognition. That day the ground defence at Balbasovo looked impregnable: a whole forest of searchlight beams was sweeping the skies, high-calibre flak shells repeatedly bursting in thick clouds at bombing altitude.

We closed in at excess altitude and, as had been arranged, began to descend with our engines muted. But our calculations turned out to be wrong: I lost altitude too early, my speed falling dangerously low and the engines cooling down too much. I had to switch the engines to maximum revolutions and approach the target sneakily, just as I had done on previous missions. It was a moonlit night and this probably undermined the searchlight operators' confidence somewhat. Whatever the case, they caught us late and the anti-aircraft fire was forceful but dispersed. Fires blazed in various parts of the aerodrome: the regiment was already coming to the end of the bombing mission. We closed in for a second pass from another direction, a direction more convenient from our point of view. This time everything went according to our calculations.

It was strange to be sitting in a gliding plane. We were enveloped by a kind of mysterious calm; instead of the usual roaring we heard the hissing of air in the propellers and over the wings. We had already entered the ground-fire and searchlight zone but we were untouched; it was as if we were invisible, even though, just like before, white beams stretched up from the ground, swaying in the sky, and heavy shells burst here, there and everywhere. We headed towards the target, not so much flying as crawling, stealing up to it. Zemskov, giving course corrections, even began to whisper. This was ridiculous and I asked him, deliberately loudly, 'Why are you whispering, Vasya?'

'For the same reason you are.' It turns out that in the silence of the flight I hadn't even noticed how I had muted my voice. We both laughed and then fell silent.

We took up attack course. Zemskov laid the whole batch of bombs across the area where aircraft were parked. With the snow cover lit by the moon and by burning aircraft the target was as clear as day. New fires appeared as our bombs hit the ground. The searchlight beams began to rush about even faster, the air twinkling even more densely with exploding shells, but it was all off target, disorderly and chaotic. Again we descended at the minimum possible speed. This time we hung around in the flak too long and barely escaped the boiling pot. I was running out of patience. I wanted to step on the gas and break away to freedom as soon as possible, although we were still undetected. When we reached an altitude of about 1,000 metres and it seemed to me that we were on the edge of the danger zone, I abruptly revved up to the limit and switched the propellers to low pitch. The engines immediately let out a high-pitched roar and we jerked forwards. At the same moment the tail of our plane was caught by a good dozen searchlights and shell bursts began to dance furiously around us. I threw the plane from side to side, increasing the angle of descent to give more speed, but the searchlight beams leaned lower and lower, following us, and the flak got closer and closer. Then suddenly the shooting ceased and there was silence, although the searchlights still wouldn't leave us alone. An anxious thought: what's up, why have they stopped shooting? 'Chernov,' I yelled, 'watch the air!'

I glanced back and left. Then I gasped: the black hulk of a twin-engine Messerschmitt 110 was hanging above us, quite close. It seemed that Chernov had headed him off, sending a long burst into his belly out of his ShKAS, but the Messer still managed to shoot a powerful column of fire from all his nose ports. It pierced the body of our plane with a roar. Shedding altitude sharply, I stalled into a steep left turn. I even turned down the revs to reduce my turn radius, but I could already see that my instrument panel had been smashed to pieces and the centre section was full of holes. When the ground seemed quite close I revved up both engines. The left one was no longer putting out maximum revolutions but the load on the elevator had grown immensely – the plane was turning up its nose. But something even worse was happening too – in the front cockpit Vasya Zemskov gave a groan and then fell silent.

'What's our speed? Can we hold out in the air or are we going to crash now? Maybe it'd be better to land somewhere before we drop? Chernov, Nezhentsev, what's on your instruments?'

'Altitude 200, speed 240. We'll be OK!'

'Where's the fighter plane?'

'Burning on the ground!' A fire was indeed blazing behind us and to the right. Only aircraft burn that way. It was our kill. Chernov had aimed well, but I guessed that such a massive lump as a Messerschmitt 110 could not be downed that easily, even by a very long burst of fire. Nikolay most likely killed the pilot.

'Vasya, what's happened to you?' I asked Zemskov at last.

'I'm wounded in the back. Can't get up. My arms and legs won't move. Set course at 80.' He gave me the return bearing to the aerodrome from memory.

A magnetic compass – a device as big as a saucepan – stood on the floor of my cockpit, next to my left foot. It was undamaged and I took the prescribed bearing. Then I looked at the map, concluding that if I turned about 20 degrees right to where the front line bulged towards us, we would be able to get over our territory 15 minutes earlier – if we could only hold out that long. It was further away from our aerodrome but closer to our troops. I made the alteration to our heading and gained altitude while it was possible to do so, not yet knowing what difficulties were in store for us. It was about 350 kilometres to the front line – almost an hour and a half of flying in my shot-up machine. The two-way operators kept providing me with altitude and speed readings. I was not worried about the flight plan but I no longer had the strength to hold the control wheel in climb position. I had to take my foot off a pedal and pressed my knee against the wheel. The altitude reading rose to 4,000 metres. I decided not to go higher because that would make it difficult for Zemskov to breathe. As it was, he was not doing well. He spoke calmly, trying to help me with advice, asking about the plane and the crew, but I told him to take it easy, tried to convince him that we were flying no worse than the others and would be home soon. The halfway mark passed, and it seemed to me that we were already out of danger – our aerodrome and the longed-for touchdown were in front of us. If we could just cross the front line and make an extra turn, there would be around half an hour's flying time left.

Like hell! Our right engine, which had been buzzing smooth and sure, suddenly gave a slight quiver and then the blades of its propeller stiffened and stopped. It had jammed! There was no oil. That meant the oil-tank had been pierced. How could I have known without the temperature and oil-pressure gauges, which were smashed at the same time as the instrument panel, that such a disaster was about to happen? And what would I have done anyway? I could have turned the engine off, couldn't I? But that would have made the situation even worse – the rotating propeller would have created unnecessary resistance. There was nothing else for it: I reduced speed a bit and began to descend slowly on one poorly operating engine. Zemskov was worried and tried to convince me that his situation was hopeless, that it would be better to abandon the plane. But I replied that we were still flying not falling and would be in flight until altitude was completely lost; when the ground was close we would do the right thing and land together.

The two-way operators were still reporting the altitude and speed but their voices became more and more muffled: the generator had stopped along with the right engine. Now we were holding out on only one battery, and that went flat very quickly in the frost. The altitude was 1,500 metres. Now there was another problem: the left engine coughed and began to stall – losing power, the propeller spun like a windmill. Fuel? Of course, fuel! I turned on the reserve array and closed the stop-cocks on the fuel tanks I had been operating from. The engine choked and coughed, but it started and began to pull again. It turned out the fuel tanks were leaking as well, but the fuel gauges had been smashed so I didn't know. There was very little fuel in the reserve tanks. I tried turning on one more array. The engine kept working, so we went with it. I knew the front line should be somewhere in the vicinity, but I couldn't be sure of its location because there were no fires or even shots to pinpoint it. I just wished someone would shoot! The middle of the night. The front seemed to be asleep. It couldn't be that I'd miscalculated. If the front line was drawn correctly on the map, we were now over our own territory. The altitude was 400 metres. I had to get ready to land. We flew on, now over tracts of forest, now over wide clearings. We would land at the next clearing we came to. I gave the order: 'Chernov, Nezhentsev, abandon plane!'

I could barely hear them but they seemed to have understood me: they said something but after another moment they did not answer my calls any more. That meant they had bailed out. I kept dragging on. I saw a large white field ahead amidst the blackness of the woods and beyond it there was forest again. I just couldn't let the plane go that far. My altitude was no more than 200 metres, maybe even 100. I didn't drop the undercarriage because it would have been easy to turn the plane upside down on this unfamiliar snow-covered expanse. We would have to land on our belly. The glade seemed to be smooth and white. I reduced the revolutions of the sole remaining engine, approached the snow cover, and turned on the headlight – but it didn't work. I'd have to come in by the seat of my pants. Don't let me get it wrong! How far were we from the snow? The white plain distorted my perception of height. Luckily the top of a solitary small tree rushed past under my right wing. The ground was just below. I turned off the engine and pulled the control wheel towards me. The plane, which had limited air resistance because the undercarriage was still up and the flaps lowered, flew over the virgin whiteness for a long time. Then it descended slowly and I felt that it was just about to touch the ground.

A shower of snow covered us. We came to a sharp and bumpy stop after a few seconds. Then stillness. The snow slowly settled. It was a clear moonlit night and there was no one around. I rushed to the engines. Everything seemed in order – no fire, no smoke, no smouldering. Now I darted to Zemskov via the upper hatch (I had to knock it out). He was lying on his back in an uncomfortable position. His head was thrown back on the seat. He was completely motionless – he couldn't even wiggle his fingers. I hadn't a clue where his injuries were.

'Vasya, where are you wounded?'

'My back . . .' I opened his overalls wide, lifted up his back a little bit, squeezed my hand under his shirt. There were no traces of blood but I guessed that splinters had pierced his spine and that was why he was paralysed. Zemskov asked where we had landed.

'On our side, I think.' I was still not sure. What if I'd miscalculated? Maybe I'd have to drag Zemskov into the woods while there was still time. But it became clear from the first attempt to lift him up that it would be impossible for me to drag Vasya's immobile body through the upper chute: only one man could get through it vertically, pushing himself up with his arms. Zemskov felt my helplessness and implored, almost begged me, 'Vasiliy, shoot me, I beg you. I won't be able to live anyway. And then go. Otherwise you'll perish too.' It was just as well he said that. To remove temptation I took away his pistol and ammo, put it in my pocket and reassured him that we would wait here and see what happened. Then I pulled out a parachute, spread it over the cockpit, put his body and head in a more comfortable position and decided to have a look in the two-way operators' compartment for the machine gun: it might prove useful. At that moment I noticed a lonely figure approaching us from the left across the deep snow. Who was he? A long trench coat, a hat pulled far down, a rifle in his right hand. Only his outline was visible and I could see neither his face nor the details of his clothing. He stood for a while by the keel of the plane. Then he walked slowly along the fuselage, went around the left wing and came up to the front cockpit. I was becoming more and more convinced that the soldier was one of ours. 'Halt, who goes there?' I swiftly leaped out of the cockpit pointing my TT [Second World War officer's pistol of Soviet design – translator's note] at him. He was taken aback, kept silent for a bit and then calmly said, 'I'm Red Army.' The soldier had no doubt discerned the red stars on the keel and the fuselage and was certain that this was a friendly plane. That's why he was behaving so calmly. Now all my doubts were dispelled too.

In the meantime armed men on skis were approaching us from three sides. They were cavalry from General Belov's regiment. Even with their help Zemskov was only pulled from the cockpit with great difficulty. We tied two pairs of skis together, laid him on them and slowly dragged him to the village. From there a *polutorka* took him to a field hospital in Meshovsk. In the morning, before heading off to my unit, I visited him. He lay on a high bed and could turn only his eyes. When he saw me, Vasya became agitated and asked me to take him with me. I calmed him as best I could. Then I dropped in on the surgeon. 'He won't last long – his wounds are too severe,' he said. 'And we can't do anything for him. We're going to call an ambulance plane. Maybe they will ease his suffering for a while in Moscow.' But he wouldn't have to fly to Moscow. The news soon reached the regiment: Senior Lieutenant Zemskov had died.

Chernov and Nezhentsev made their separate ways to Serpukhov, sometimes on foot, sometimes catching a lift in motor vehicles or on carts. But the authorities at the base were not expecting us to come back and had already moved our gear into storage. It appeared that the dogfight near Orsha had not gone unnoticed, and since our crew hadn't come back from the mission, our downed plane had been recorded as another combat loss.

The crew was quickly re-formed. A new navigator appeared on the scene: Senior Lieutenant Alexey Vasiliev. He was a tall, broad-shouldered man, the heavy features of his broad face slightly speckled with pockmarks. He was ten years older than me. From our first meeting he adopted a kind of patronising manner. It didn't offend me, but I have to admit it didn't make me happy either. The whole regiment already knew his irrepressible noisy cheerfulness and generous bold nature. He loved to sing loudly and laugh uproariously, regardless of the time or place. In 1941 Vasiliev had fought somewhere in the south on short-range bombers but all his crew perished and only he managed to survive. He didn't like to discuss what had happened and seemed to be trying to wipe this tragedy from his memory by indulging in expressions of joy that often seemed feigned.

Before graduating just before the war from a navigators' school, Vasiliev was the chef of the Riviera restaurant in Rostov. Despite his new career as an Air Force navigator, he never forgot his skills as a chef, cooked with a passion and took pride in it. In his trunk there was always a crisply starched chef's cap as high as an Easter cake. Sometimes Alexey would mount it on the balding crown of his head in order to feast his eyes upon his reflection in a mirror. When the regiment filled the air-men's mess after a combat mission, Vasiliev would disappear into the kitchen, dress up in his chef's outfit and then suddenly appear in the hall, ceremoniously carrying towards our table on the straight fingers of his outspread hands a large tray covered with dishes he had cooked himself, in which even common vegetables surrounding skilfully cooked meats were carved into the shapes of fantastic flowers and figurines. His pro-gress would be accompanied by cheerful jokes from all sides of the hall but these would be countered by salty sallies from Vasiliev himself. The kitchen-based female admirers of the 'master of the culinary arts' would contrive to add 'on their own behalf' an extra 100 grams or so of vodka to the front-line regulation 100 grams to which the flying personnel were entitled after a mission. At these moments the 'master' was in perfect bliss. He was also a skilled navigator. He had a propensity for visual positioning, having preserved this skill from his time in short-range front-line aviation, but Alexey was also proficient in radionavigation and was a most accomplished bomb-aimer. To my amazement he would become unrecognisable in flight: he would tense up completely, sometimes become nervous, grow angry and swear at any minor malfunction in the aircraft equipment or any unforeseen complication. A cheery fellow on the ground, he wouldn't make a single joke in the air and wouldn't respond to mine. One might have thought he had some hidden lack of confidence in, or even distrust of, me as a flyer, but he never agreed to fly in other crews.

One dark spring night while approaching our aerodrome we were caught by a couple of Moscow ground defence's searchlights. They had obviously decided to check if we were a friendly plane. At that time Messerschmitt 110s used to penetrate quite frequently into the area where long-range bombers were stationed, and not without success: occasionally they would down some idler, having successfully sneaked up on them. In friendly searchlights we were supposed to send a pre-arranged signal and a combination of flares meaning 'friend'. Vasiliev tried to make the signal but the flare gun would only click and the bloody cartridges wouldn't ignite, despite being replaced. The searchlights held us tight, handing us over from one to another, waiting for a signal, but we were dumb. They were not satisfied with the conventional flashing of aircraft lights. Vasiliev, shaking with anger, was swearing in despair, but the flares didn't want to take off. They're liable to shoot us by accident this way, I thought. And at that very instant a dull explosion resounded in the cockpit. The plane was lit up by red fire and through a slot in the instrument panel I could see the navigator's shadow rushing madly about. They must have hit the cockpit direct.

'Alesha [diminutive for Alexey – translator's note],' I shouted, 'Alesha, are you all right?' Vasiliev was wheezing, lit up in the red glow, but he didn't speak. He didn't answer me until the fire was extinguished. It turned out that he had hurled the accursed flare gun into the corner and it snapped into action right there. Alexey had barely been able to catch the burning flare which was jumping about from one side of the cockpit to the other like the Devil. His hands were badly burned through his gloves and his map-case was caught in the flames too. We were lucky to get away. A burning flare inside a plane is no joke.

CHAPTER THREE

Travelling in Time

This work was interrupted by a new and unexpected task. Klotar was on the scene again. Having lost any hope of pushing him into a combat mission, and maybe hoping in time to suppress his fear of the enemy, the regiment commander gave him the task of test-flying aircraft after maintenance work and engine replacement. The regiment was working very intensely; the combat airmen were getting tired and simply had no time to test fly their planes. But Klotar's fear extended to ordinary flying tasks too. Every flight caused him great suffering and was a pain in the neck for all those who were involved in getting him into the air. He would take off fairly well and somehow stay in the air but then land really poorly: sometimes he would drop the unfortunate machine after levelling out high up, sometimes jab it into the ground at speed. Two days earlier he had been sent to the town of Monino near Moscow to ferry an aircraft repaired there to our aerodrome. Suddenly we received a phone call from the head of the repair plant: Klotar had banked his plane during take-off, collided with a tractor and killed the driver. In addition the plane had incurred a lot of damage. 'Go to Monino as soon as possible,' the commander ordered me. 'You'll ferry the plane with Klotar's crew. It'll be ready by the time you're there.'

I got into my overall, put on my high fur boots and left. I rolled into Moscow on a passing *polutorka* in the evening twilight. And the deeper I travelled into the city, the more agitated I became. Everything I saw stunned and shocked me. I'd known that the whole of Moscow, now quite depopulated, was under blackout, cordoned off by barricades and tank traps, that flak guns and machine guns had been set up on roofs and barrage balloons were floating in the skies. But no stretch of the imagination could be enough to conceive the true scene in all its details. Maybe the heavy feeling inside me was intensified by the fact that only a year earlier, one winter Sunday filled with city lights and shining shop windows, I was in a huge taxi (then standard in the capital) with a cheerful gang of my new friends and their girlfriends, riding on the breeze along the wide Moscow streets towards the railway station to bid farewell before my departure for Voronezh. A flood of people who seemed to me exceptionally attractive and vivacious, sharing our lust for life, passed by outside the cab windows. There was so much tangible joy, even happiness, in the air that it seemed it would always be like this and that nothing could extinguish the mood. In those minutes, which I would long remember, I was love-struck, perhaps with some of those women or with all of them or maybe with the whole world. I was sorry to be leaving Moscow and my friends that evening, but it was time to return to my squadron, my flying brotherhood, and to flying itself, which had become a spiritual need for me.

And now there was neither light nor sound in the streets, which were drowned in black gloom. Only the occasional military truck suddenly appeared out of the darkness with its tiny blue slivers of headlights, which did not light up the road but only just made themselves visible. The vehicles passed by, forcing their way through the snow-drifted streets and immediately disappeared into the impenetrable darkness. There was no one around. Then a patrolman appeared. Covering the light of his torch, thin as a knitting needle, with his hands, he meticulously checked my documents, peered into my face and asked something or other. Then the street was deserted again – impregnable darkness, dead silence. Despite everything, having thrown back a million-strong fascist force from her walls the previous December, stern and gloomy Moscow, bristling behind her camouflage shields and curtained windows, continued to live and work. The city felt completely confident.

It would be hard to reach Monino that evening, and what was the point with night looming? Maybe Fedya, my father's brother, would be at home in Verhnyaya Maslovka [a Moscow street – translator's note]. I headed there. My father was the eldest child in my grandfather's family and Uncle Fedya was the youngest, the thirteenth. There was no man in the world who was closer to me in soul and spirit than my Uncle Fedya. But his flat was locked and Fedya – a complete civilian, an artist who had been in the military reserve – was already somewhere on the Southern Front in the Crimea, serving in the Black Sea Navy. A pity: seeing him had always been a great joy for me.

I stayed overnight at his neighbour's place. We drank tea and I was swamped by memories. I remembered my days as a student at the university's workers' faculty. I should add that the experience didn't meet my aspirations and at the same time I was working as a literary contributor on the provincial youth newspaper. One day towards the end of the course the faculty's Comsomol [Young Communist League – translator's note] members were advised of a special draft into the Air Force. Such an opportunity had not been on my list of possible options for the future since I reckoned that although I had a huge desire to fly, I probably lacked some of the other requisite qualities. I was quite puny and had none of the athletic features commonly attributed to the 'knights of the aerial ocean'. Back then the Air Force not only shone with a halo of heroism and glory but also had the aura of a kind of exclusiveness, although what mostly showed through this aura were the shadows of dramatic events. People of a rational turn of mind did not actually think that joining the Air Force was a harbinger of a happy destiny.

Many Comsomol students responded to the call. Long queues stretched out from the doctors' rooms. Guys with broad shoulders and tight biceps stood out. If these were future flyers, how could I possibly expect to become one of them? But the knights began to fail the medical examinations, sometimes at one doctor's room, sometimes at another's, and I started to notice that I was examined more thoroughly than the rest and slapped on the back quite approvingly. To my surprise I was classified airworthy with no restrictions. Well, well. I was the only guy from the workers' faculty who'd made it through. It seemed that right at that moment everything which had been troubling me floated away. Here it was – the bluebird of happiness. To fly, just fly! To hell with everything else! All my life I had been destined for this. It was time to go all the way, no holding back.

At home the news was greeted with shock. My father went dumb. My mother was alarmed – but found a loophole: 'They won't take you. They can't. You're only sixteen.'

'No, sixteen and a half!' On the surface everything was quiet, but by night I would hear my mother crying and my father trying to calm her down.

My credential committee session seemed to go smoothly too, but suddenly someone said, 'You won't get in, buddy. Only those turning seventeen this year will be enlisted. As for you – not till next year.' I was horrified. It was now only five miserable days till my birthday. Attempts at persuasion would fail. What could I do? How could I get around the regulations? The church records! I remembered my mother saying that at my christening my date of birth had been written down old-style as 23 December [that is 23 December by the old Julian calendar; in 1918 Russia adopted the thirteen-day faster, 'new-style' Gregorian calendar – editor's note]. It appeared that the priest, a conservative soul, might actually be my saviour. Being on my guard against countermeasures, and saying nothing to anyone, I rummaged through all the documents at home and found that priceless piece of paper. Darting into the credential committee office I slapped it on the desk. The captain – the chairman – examined the birth certificate and glancing at me (I was petrified by this time) pronounced, 'Now this is a different story!'

My father and mother saw me off without showing their true emotions, but I knew what was happening in their hearts. My affectionate and kind-hearted younger brother Zhenya [diminutive of Evgeniy – translator's note], who was very strongly attached to me, stood with his blue eyes wide open, not knowing how to react to my departure. Who could imagine at that moment that ten years later when I, having survived the war, became a regiment commander, Zhenya, after seeing out the war in the infantry, would join my crew as a gunner/radio-operator. All went well until one night when we found ourselves in a bad situation during take-off. I had no time to think about either myself or my brother, but I did remember our mother: what would happen to her if we both crashed? In the event everything turned out fine: I managed to take off but I decided then and there not to take Zhenya flying with me again. I transferred him to another crew.

As I left to join the Air Force our neighbours poured out into the yard and headed towards me with hugs and tears. They'd known me as just an ordinary boy and hadn't noticed that I'd grown up. I remember how I walked past them, waving my hands in farewell and nearly crying myself.

My time as a cadet in Voroshilovgrad Military Flyers' School encompassed the glorious years 1936 to 1938. The cadets' imagination was captured by cascades of distinguished aviation records – the great flights of crews led by Chkalov, Gromov, Grizodubova, Kokkinaki [famous Soviet test flyers who carried out long-range and intercontinental flights – translator's note], and before that, the landing at the North Pole by Papanin's expedition. Soviet airmen fought against Fascists in Spain and smashed the Japanese in China and in the Far East of Russia, near Lake Khasan. My God, real life was passing us by: we were flying circles over our school and would miss out on everything! But the time went quickly. I graduated at the age of nineteen, screwed the red junior lieutenant's cubes to the blue badges on my collar and was ready to rush into the great life of the Air Force. Yes, that's actually how it all turned out.

*   *   *

The director of the Monino plant met me suspiciously. From his point of view I was no match for Klotar and since he, a seasoned wolf of the air and a senior lieutenant, had ruined the plane, what could he hope for in trusting it to a boyish-looking junior lieutenant, and in this gloomy weather too? He grabbed the telephone straight away, rang Tikhonov, and having been assured there was no mistake, ordered the crew be given access to the plane. It was already running: back then people worked around the clock, not wasting a minute.

I found Klotar depressed and downcast, sitting all alone in a gloomy room in the garrison guesthouse. The rest of the crew were squeezed into a small neighbouring room: Klotar knew how to keep his crewmates at a distance. Deigning to confide in me, he told me about his sorrows and even began to confess to his failures. I understood now that it would be impossible to drag him back to the steering column. 'All right,' I rounded off the chat, 'gather up the crew and off to the plane. You go in the front cockpit with the navigator.' By nightfall we were home. I don't know what kind of order the regiment commander issued but Klotar soon disappeared quietly and unnoticed. He didn't have to worry about finding a place: the head-of-staff, Tsoglin – whom Klotar had most liked to hang around, delighting his patron with his copy-book hand – secured him a new assignment and supplied him with the most complimentary references.

For many years no one knew anything about Klotar but then the true course of events became clear. Having somewhat recovered from his shocks at the front, he first found himself in the position of head-of-staff of a front-line air force regiment and then rose higher. Apparently he managed to get at his personal file and having 'fixed it up', he made it work for him. A year later, from the position of senior assistant to an army aviation department head, Klotar was enrolled to study at the Air Force Academy. We finished the war and he graduated from the academy. Two years later he graduated from another one. He rose rapidly in rank: appointments were repeatedly conferred on him ahead of schedule because of his 'front-line feats'. In his personal file were nearly 100 records of successful combat missions and his ribbons certainly instilled respect among those who had been at the front and among his superiors. He began to behave with self-assurance and pride, and his judgements were blunt and unchangeable. He began to believe totally in his new, inextinguishable star, and he stopped at nothing in climbing up the steep military career ladder. It seemed nothing could check his progress.

But in the early 1960s at Air Force General Headquarters Klotar once came across Colonel Tsykin face to face. Taken aback, and fearing that he had made a mistake, Tsykin cautiously inquired if this man was Klotar and if he was, how could such a metamorphosis have occurred? Bursting with bureaucratic indignation, Klotar was about to put this colonel who had overstepped the mark in his place, but at the next moment he gave in, surrendering completely. Adopting a delicate and ingratiating tone he pointed out that he fully understood the reasons for Tsykin's feelings about him, but so much time had passed since the war and there was no reason to bring up the unpleasant events of those days: he implored the colonel, appealing to his better nature, to let bygones be bygones. 'No, Klotar, it's not going to happen. I'm going to do my best to find out where those general's shoulder badges and decorations came from,' Tsykin assured him. Applying to the senior commanders he requested that this puzzle be investigated. It didn't take long: everything was unearthed very quickly – the original documents were still intact and living memory was not yet faded. Klotar was dismissed from his position as Chief of Staff of the Soviet Forces' Air Force Group in Germany and was sacked from the armed forces.

CHAPTER FOUR

Pirates and Hunters

At last we had our own aircraft – and a new one too. Vasiliev and I were getting ready for our first combat mission. He was a straightforward and stubborn man and he regarded some tactical tricks with distrust – he wouldn't hear of flying over a target area with muted engines at low speed and with a short run-up to boot. Of course my last sortie with Zemskov had put him on his guard when all this inventiveness ended in the loss of a plane and the death of a navigator. But I stuck to my guns. He eventually yielded and began to do the necessary calculations. Everything was set up for the first target we would hit together – the Dno railway station. It was considered formidable, but unlike other possible targets it was classified as only 'moderately dangerous' – just right for a first go.

We approached from Ilmen. The station was already on fire and the latest pair of candle bombs was hanging over it – we had to hurry before they went out. We lined up with them smoothly and hissed downwards. Amidst powerful but dispersed flak and searchlights anxiously sweeping the sky we managed to find our way quietly to the target, make the strike and, manoeuvring between the beams, get away unnoticed. The time went by terribly slowly, just as it had over Orsha, but my nerves didn't fail me and I felt I was doing my job sensibly. Outside I could see bombs exploding on the railway tracks more and more densely. The fires illuminated the hellish scene of the station's agonising death. Fountains of exploding material flew out of the immobilised lines of wagons. It was obvious that more than one regiment had been at work here. The enemy flak was uncoordinated, at lucky moments striking en masse at spotlit planes, but it failed to deal with some while pouncing on others.

Vasiliev had not shown any signs of doubt before the bombs were dropped, but after the chutes were closed he boiled over: 'Why the hell are you hanging around here, get out fast!'

'Patience, Alekha, otherwise we'll stuff everything up.' We got out safely: not a single aimed shot reached the plane. Alexey had dropped the whole stick of bombs on the trains and had hit some buildings with its tail. Something flared up down there.

'Looks like we hit their fuel,' he rattled off. I felt our first success had cheered my navigator up, but he wasn't letting his emotions get the better of him. Apparently he now believed in the wisdom of a noiseless approach to the target.

The bomber pilots were not always able to assess accurately the effect of their strikes. It was not too difficult to determine what had happened if a fire flared up or a major explosion occurred – it could be said with certainty that the bombs had smashed something serious and done a lot of damage. But if the fires from high-explosive bombs died out immediately after the flash of their own explosions, our spirits would fall: it meant we hadn't hit anything significant. Did a lack of fire always mean the bomb had failed to reach a significant target? In fact what looked like the 'blank' in a batch might do much more damage than the explosion in the aforementioned fuel tank that had sent the crew into exultation. For example, once in Smolensk someone dropped bombs off the aerodrome and neither fire nor explosion followed. This incident might have been forgotten but then an intelligence report arrived – under those bombs, which had hit some residential buildings, about 200 Luftwaffe flying and technical personnel had perished! A major award awaited the author of the deed but he could not be found. Something similar happened on 3 May 1943 in Minsk: it took the Germans three days to bury their dead airmen.

The geographical area of our strikes was expanding. Night after night we bombed railway junctions – Pskov, Bryansk, Smolensk, Bryansk again and Kharkov. We struck in whole divisions and at short intervals delivered blows at bomber aerodromes in Luga, Orsha ... On a good night at high altitude the fires, especially at stations, were visible from 100, 200 and even 300 kilometres away. They blazed for a long time. But bloody hell, although we were fighting the Germans, the names of the targets were all Russian! They were beyond the reach of front-line aircraft and for this reason they passed to us. German place names would have suited us long-rangers, but, having suffered a major defeat near Moscow, the Germans were gathering and concentrating their forces in new strategic directions. The 'far meridians' would be too much for us. The south was the most obvious target. The prelude to Stalingrad was under way.

My crew was in action every night. And although no two sorties were identical in complexity and result, all had something in common and they eventually lost their individual colour. Nevertheless, some would stay in the memory more firmly than others, like the one that occurred at the end of April 1942 when Vasiliev dropped three half-tonners from the outer release clamps on Staraya Russa station. At the same time two 100kg explosives hanging from the inner clamps and meant for the second approach broke away but didn't make it to the ground; they landed on the slightly open bomb doors and were more likely to explode inside the plane than fall further.

The radio-operators reported that things were not right. The detonator locking pins had broken off, the safety catches had unscrewed under pressure of the headwind funnelled through slits and, huddled one against another with their stings exposed, the bombs were pointing their noses at the front wall. Now the least knock would be enough to make them slide forward a little and smack into it, sending an impressive high-altitude explosion into the starlit night. What could we do? We swept the edge of the target once, then twice, hoping to get rid of our night-marish load, but the shutters were stuck. We headed home and while enemy territory was still under us we pressed with all our might on the opening levers of the bomb bays, but all in vain. We would have to think about how we were going to land.

'Guys,' I told the radio-operators, 'the bombs have to be fastened so they don't fall off during landing or even worse slide forward.' As yet I had no idea how that might be done, but I fully understood the danger of the task to which I was condemning the radio-operators. However, Chernov and Nezhentsev were already working in the bomb bays, feeling with their whole bodies what it meant to let go with their hands or miss when grabbing on as they climbed up and down the sheer structure. All the while the icy wind penetrated the plane. We were all conscious of what the landing would inevitably entail if the bombs were not fastened. No way would we abandon the plane – it was brand new – because of some cable caught in the bomb bay gearing linkage.

Ropes cut from aircraft covers were brought into play and lines were found in the toolbox; soldiers' belts came in handy as well. Nezhentsev was at work hanging above the bombs, Chernov securing him by holding him on a leash. Alexey not only fastened the bombs but also wrapped them in aircraft covers so that they couldn't knock against each other and would be less inclined to slip on the bare duralumin. He did all he could, but would his efforts hold out during landing? We needed to come down as gently as possible but that was by no means guaranteed despite best efforts. And now we got some more news: our home aerodrome couldn't receive us because it was closed by fog and we were ordered to fly to Ramenskoye dispersal field. I warned Ramenskoye that we had bombs in our bays which had come off their clamps and made my presence clear with flares and flashing sidelights.

I don't know whether they had managed to get everyone landed or had dispersed them to other landing zones and aerodromes, but no one was in our way as we touched down. The radio-operators were next to the bombs, holding them by straps and sashes. I handled the landing well: the plane rolled smoothly for a long way with me barely touching the brakes. At the end of the landing run when the speed had dropped I turned right so as not to impede the touchdown of other bombers. Then I taxied to a remote spot and stopped the engines. Armourers were already running towards the plane: it was their party now. I led the crew as far away as possible for a smoke.

Those dispersal airfields were unbearable. But what choice did we have? Because of fog crawling out of the Oka our airfield on the flood-plain in Serpukhov was unusable more often than any other right up to morning when the crews returned from sorties. Sometimes the Germans would appear, drop anti-personnel frog mines and dig up the airstrip. Then red flares would soar and radiograms would be tapped out sending everyone to neighbouring sites. We would come back by midday at best, but sometimes it was evening or even night-time before we returned, just in time to head off on another mission. People would crowd into the dispersal fields and there was no chance to rest or to eat properly. On top of that, the Luftwaffe would try to take advantage of the opportunity such overcrowding offered. The Germans were afraid to fly in large groups, fearing Moscow air defence, and marauded mostly one at a time. Apparently they had not forgotten the visit they made when, having missed our take-off for a raid on the fascist headquarters in Poltava (where, by the way, Hitler himself was still present), they turned up out of the blue at nightfall in a group of twelve Heinkel 111s. Having haphazardly dropped their bombs on an empty aerodrome, they were only six when they made it home: one was cut-off by flak gunners from the aerodrome; another was knocked over by an I-16 fighter that had come from nowhere; four more were taken by the large-calibre guns of Moscow air defence. Against these losses the Germans' success didn't look impressive: two technicians were killed, another wounded; a passer-by was killed in a neighbouring village; and one LaGG-3 was damaged in the parking area of a fighter-plane squadron.

Now single German planes would fly along our routes and above our aerodromes like ghosts – sometimes mingling with our planes, sidelights switched on, sometimes turning their lights off just before attacking. On one of those nights when I was set to land at Ramenskoye, keeping my distance behind another plane which was ahead of me in the circle, one more aircraft, barely distinguishable as a black silhouette on the right of the plane ahead, appeared from nowhere. It was flying quietly, keeping to the left, but why the hell did it have no lights? I thought, it's one of those cheeky chaps who has to be first to land. He's about to cut the corner of the third circle, overtake everyone and turn on his lights over the airstrip before the searchlights and touchdown. The one who comes after him (perhaps me) will be driven out for another circuit.

Then suddenly fiery tracer bullets reached towards my leader from the plane on the right. The leader immediately returned fire (he'd obviously been watching out) and my gunners added their share too. All sidelights went out within the circle. I wasn't hanging about and descended into free space, although closer to the ground. They switched off the ground lights at the end of the airstrip and dozens of planes found themselves in the darkness, not able to see each other. Please don't let's smash into each other! But after a minute the aerodrome was through the panic and came back to life. Everyone gradually closed in for landing, crowding and impeding each other, their wings sometimes visible, sometimes dissolving into the dark again. The German didn't reveal himself again but he was detected over another aerodrome – there he unsuccessfully strafed the ground landing lights and attacked two or three crews. But he was obviously rather timid. Having flown too far into enemy territory and, moreover, into the very heart of Moscow air defence, he was shooting from afar, hastily and inaccurately. He was definitely a 'fat goose' with a gun turret, to all appearances a Heinkel. Maybe he was not marauding on his own?

Whether it was that plane or another, one 'goose' got his come-uppance: as the German hunted our planes which were circling for landing, Lieutenant Korovitsyn lay in wait for him in his Il-4 and gave it to him till he burst into flames and crashed right there. A royal catch! But the German raids were not always unsuccessful. In early June 1942 pilot Tsygankov, who had just returned from only his second combat sortie, was shot down over Serpukhov aerodrome. A Messerschmitt 110 attacked Major Lomov in his first attack but he managed to get away, darted to ground and hedge-hopped to another airfield. At the same moment the German came across Tsygankov and shot him down point blank.

Sometimes someone would unsuspectingly bring guests home on his own tail, becoming a victim of his own negligence. That's what happened to Bronnikov. A young and sensible flyer, well battle-seasoned and seemingly cognisant of all the intricacies of night combat, he had disregarded one lesson: he must have seen, but hadn't paid attention to, a plane following on his heels with its sidelights turned on, just like his. Bronnikov wasn't the only pilot returning from the combat mission – the whole regiment was coming back. But just before the aerodrome boundary where the planes were gathering for landing his 'wingman' closed in to about 100 metres and sent a thick stream of bullets and shells into Bronnikov. It was a Messerschmitt 110. Bronnikov sort of tripped: his plane stooped on one wing, dropped its nose and hit the ground. All this happened instantly. Tikhonov immediately sent us off to other aerodromes and we, returning towards midday, came in for landing over a still smoking machine. It was a shockingly simple end – he hadn't expected it, hadn't thought about it, yet he had found death on his own doorstep. And he had known very well how to 'check the papers'. Turn aside suddenly: if your unfamiliar companion follows, he's a German; one of ours will know the road home and won't stay on your tail. Then you think about how to get rid of that German – either go away to the dark side of the horizon and hide your exhaust flames with a wing, or dive down and turn sharply to meet him. Such a manoeuvre had rescued many of us. It had come to my assistance a few times.

In early July 1942 Popel was pounced on in an ambush beyond the Oka river. Mysterious light signals used to flash in a thick, dark forest on the opposite side of the river to our aerodrome. They were visible from the ground, even from the river bank and from the regimental command post. When an armed party rushed towards the lights or they were strafed from the air by machine guns, they would disappear, but later they would turn up again. There were rumours that they were German spotters. We didn't really believe in the spotters because they hadn't been nailed even once, but we knew invisible Messerschmitt 110s were flying over the forest, knew it for sure. As he was preparing for landing Captain Popel went too far towards the forest and was caught there. The whole crew died. I still remember that no-longer-young captain, a handsome, stocky man with a thick, well-groomed, dark chestnut beard. Sometimes in a card game his friends among the older generation of airmen would, giggling and joking, offer to raise against his beard, but he protected and cherished it and would never expose it to the risk of being publicly shaved off. However, towards summer, just before the tragedy, he upped and shaved it without provocation. His friends took his death hard, but they didn't wonder about the reasons for it; grief stricken, seeing in it the sinister finger of fate, they repeated time and again, 'What did he shave his beard for?'

Popel's navigator Major Kovalev was outstanding too. He knew the combat trade having been seasoned back in the wars of the Thirties. But he hadn't always been lucky in flying, and others hadn't always been lucky with him either. Kovalev was always changing commanders and no more than a month earlier had suddenly been assigned to my crew. It had to happen that once, while we were approaching the front line, the astro hatch fastener broke off: the lid had warped and got stuck. A stream of air from the headwind blew into the cockpit and Kovalev demanded an immediate return to the aerodrome. But it was a clear night, the bombs were in their compartments and we were halfway to the target. We argued for a long while but the plane kept flying along its course. He flew into a rage but I wouldn't give in; I said that I wasn't going to land with bombs on board and wouldn't turn back before I had dropped them on the target. The stream of air from the front cockpit was hitting me too and I was well aware that the navigator was feeling much worse discomfort, but I also knew that he could work in it, especially if he moved to the front of the cockpit. The evening was warm but I decided not to take on too much altitude, so as not to expose us to cold airstreams. Nevertheless, Kovalev kept growling. We didn't reach the main target (I failed to out-argue him), but I got to the alternative one, which was closer and had even more teeth. We did our bombing by the book (he was a great aimer), came through the flak intact and turned for home. Kovalev remained silent all the way back. We would never meet again in a plane. He preferred Popel over all the pilots, having refused to try many. And now ...

Popel's crew – or to be precise the gunner/radio-operators – must have slipped up. The night wasn't that dark. The Germans disliked pitch darkness and, until they got radar, would stay away from a fight in the dark. The rear hemisphere, the only area from which an attack could be launched, was guarded by machine-gunners and no one else, and judging from the fact that they didn't get a shot off, they were not watching the air at that moment. One yawn and what a price.

Night visits by the Germans were rare, however. Most often they would appear towards morning when the regiments were back from missions. The Germans obviously took into account our fatigue after many hours' flight, full of struggle against flak gunners and fighter planes, and the better visibility offered by the dawn. One dawn, not yet touched by the rays of the sun, having swallowed a dry canteen breakfast on the run at a dispersal field, we pulled the zips of our overalls up to our chins and turned up our fur collars, leaned against each other right under a wing on engine covers and instantly fell asleep. Suddenly we heard the firing of machine guns, the roar of cannon and excited shouts. What the hell ... ? I opened my eyes and saw the familiar black silhouette of a Messerschmitt 110 approaching the aerodrome at low altitude in the greyish sky. It was as if I was watching it on a cinema screen. The multicoloured traces of bullets and shells stretched towards him from all sides but flew past, and he was coming in a straight line as if spellbound, sometimes tilting to one side or the other, but without having to avoid fire, as though all the chaos on the aerodrome didn't concern him.

Sleep was banished in a second. Without waiting for the gunners to wake up I darted into their cockpit, turned a machine gun towards the Messerschmitt and began to chase it with the gunsight. My God, how tiny it was, negligibly small, like an ant creeping quickly between the disproportionally thick rings of the gunsight. Was it really possible to hit it? I managed to fix it in the sights and pressed the trigger once, twice, a third time. The ShKAS was shaking with effort but the bullets were flying past. I made a correction but missed again. Those banging away with their guns from other angles were no more successful. The Messer flew over the parking areas and airfield intact on its westward course. Obviously it was time for him to go home after his night-time marauding and he had decided at the last minute to have a look at our aerodrome.

Maybe our flak gunners or even fighter pilots would be lucky enough to intercept him somewhere en route to the front. But was it possible that our own plane was also seen in the enemy's gunsight as a mere point, a fly racing through the endless skies? I have to admit our bomber, flying over a hot target, had always seemed to me an excessively huge colossus taking up half the sky with its wings and attracting all the shells. But more than once I had left the zone of fire unscathed, with a gloating, triumphant feeling of relief, marvelling at the dullness of the German flak gunners who had not managed to hit such a huge target. Apparently not everything was simple for either side in this confrontation.

The Germans marauding by night over Soviet Air Force stationing areas were 'pirates' in our terminology. We used the same way of operating but delicately called it 'free hunting'. Volunteer hunters could always be found. On a clear moonlit night when the regiment was winding down at the parking bays the commander would allow the planes to be refuelled, the bombs to be hung and ammunition to be replenished. Then there would be a 'walkabout' to the fascist side. Suitable targets were always found – an operating airfield motionlessly waiting out the night or a train rolling along between stations or even a night-time column of troops marching down a highway towards the front.

It was easy to deal with targets on wheels: we would close in at low altitude at an acute angle to the length of the target with no rush, make dummy runs or even release the first pair of bombs for ranging – just as over the training ground – and often manage to strafe it with machine guns. The Germans would return fire of course, or to be more precise, try to frighten us off, for they had no searchlights and it wasn't that easy to pinpoint a plane in the night skies.

It was harder to blend into an ordinary group of planes flying around the vicinity of German airbases. They listened attentively to the skies and if an unfamiliar sound was detected the situation would change instantly: their planes would disappear somewhere, the aerodrome would sink into darkness and machine guns and flak would begin to shoot from the ground. There could be no question of striking unexpectedly – it was better to stay out of that storm of fire. But we had a trick in reserve that sometimes worked. On the approach to an aerodrome the propeller of one engine would be set on low pitch and the airscrew of another on high pitch. The first one, almost at maximum revolutions, would produce high notes, but the other, raking the air with wide blades at a steep angle, would reduce revolutions and begin a bass roar. The duet sounded harmonious – the plane would produce a howling sound exactly like a flying Junkers.

I was unlucky with aerodromes. Towards morning they would quiet down, displaying no sign of life, and any kind of sneak attack inevitably ended up with outbursts of ack-ack activity in a fight in which Lady Luck promised no joy to a solitary plane. But those who flew out earlier sometimes had a chance to join a circle of enemy planes as an equal, to get up close to a German and strafe him with a machine gun. This was usually as far as it would go: the aerodrome would show its teeth and our planes would have to get out. Once or twice some of the most reckless guys – Alexander Shaposhnikov, Nikolay Tarelkin, Sasha Romanov and others – would have more luck. But even they, while shooting up the Germans, would manage to cop it from the enemy's ring-mounted machine guns.

In general it was not a bomber's business to shoot down planes and our hunters preferred, having got behind a German coming in for landing, to imitate as naturally as possible an exit for another turn, so that having positioned themselves above an aerodrome, they could stretch a series of bombs across a landing strip or even through parking bays from low altitude. This kind of hit had to be the spontaneous action of a 'soloist', and there were many complications in organising it. Often the results were modest and sometimes even unknown. Something smashed, something burned, but what? And was it always worth taking the risk?

Then suddenly a real combat Messerschmitt 110 appeared above our parking area! It had been captured somewhere, hale and hearty. When our Division commander Evgeniy Fedorovich Loginov found out about it he insisted on having this trophy handed over to him. Engineers examined the German plane, put it in order, drew red stars on it instead of its original crosses and after that Loginov did a bit of flying in it. He passed it on to Vyacheslav Opalev – a flyer from a fraternal regiment. Slava [diminutive of Vyacheslav – translator's note] quickly tamed it and by night, together with his navigator Zhenya Okorokov, he began to visit the German airfields. There he would generally queue up behind a plane coming in for landing and at the moment when his man, having switched on his landing lights, was completely absorbed in touching down, he would strike from above right in the neck with all four barrels.

The burning German would dig his nose into the ground then and there, and Slava would disappear. He prudently changed target aerodromes from flight to flight, and he managed to shoot down quite a few planes this way. But the Germans pricked up their ears, began to watch the behaviour of the planes near them and to demand proof of identity by prearranged signals. Slava, feeling it wouldn't do to ask for trouble, would move on to another aerodrome, and sometimes instead of an aerial attack he would resort to a low-flying raid against planes on the ground.

Everything was going as well as he could hope until one dawn when, on his way back home from another successful raid, he found himself under fire from our own flak gunners in the Tula region. And would you believe it, they got him with their first salvo! He had to bail out. The village people who ran up to the men who had bailed out of a fascist plane handled them roughly – because of the fire the plane's original crosses began to show through the stars. The locals didn't want to accept the flyers' desperate attempts to explain themselves until Slava Opalev (a most refined and well-bred man) deafened them with some choice Russian swear words. The villagers were taken aback and stopped immediately, recognising them as friends. Then they wouldn't stop apologising, tending to the men with lotions, feeding and treating them to the local hooch until evening when their commanders flew over to pick them up.

Opalev switched back to an Il-4 but didn't fly much longer. One dark night in the spring of 1943, coming back from a combat mission in a shot-up plane with a burning engine and gradually losing altitude, he managed to drag himself across the front line and, almost gliding over ground, he ordered his crew to bail out, intending to be the last to leave it. But a village suddenly came into view in the path of the plane's possible fall. While he was dragging it past, the altitude for jumping ran out: his parachute didn't have time to open. The peasants buried him on the bank of the Belichka river near the village of Mashkino, Kursk Province.

Division commander Loginov remained attached to the idea of free hunting, developing it further, and soon began to raise a special new regiment of hunter-blockaders in American A-20G aircraft (also called 'Bostons'). These light, twin-engine machines with powerful stationary artillery armament in the nose of the fuselage (installed by our specialists, by the way), with the bomb bays well loaded, were just the thing for blockading the enemy fighter planes' aerodromes, neutralising anti-aircraft batteries and aerial hunting. But the Bostons were slow in coming and the regiment could not be formed quickly. Among the very few who were first to master the aircraft and begin operating with it was Ivan Kouryatnik, my messmate from flying school, an extremely modest, quiet bloke, always kind-hearted and affable, who treated everyone the same, no matter who they were. All his tremendous will and inner strength burst forth when he flew in combat. Once Ivan was over a German aerodrome he wouldn't let anyone take off while we were pounding a target nearby. Flak guns would also fall silent under his fire.

Our technicians thought the world of him, treating him with absolute faith and something approaching adoration. Without asking anyone's permission, they traced out 'Ivan Kouryatnik' in large golden letters along the fuselage of his Boston. It looked less like a name than a symbol. Ivan was regarded so highly in the division that recognition of his combat merits expressed in such an unusual form shocked no one and was accepted as standing perfectly to reason. We would not have let anyone else get away with it.

Ivan fought on till the end of the war. He fought the same way as he worked – the peasant way: quietly, thoroughly and honestly. He was to fly across the front line 310 times and never seemed to make a mistake – he never caught fire, never bailed out, never lost anyone. This was an incredible record for a combat airman. Even when a propeller came off a crankshaft over East Prussia, Ivan managed to fly his plane to Serpukhov as if nothing had happened. After the war he became a regiment commander. His regiment was a robust one – better than many others. But in the summer of 1953 as Ivan was leading a formation in a long-range, four-engine bomber someone collided with him during a turn. No one managed to bail out of the broken craft. Lieutenant Colonel Ivan Kouryatnik was thirty-three years old.

But let's return to the frosty days of early 1942. Once, coming into the flying personnel's dormitory, I was stunned, unable to believe my eyes: on an unmade soldier's cot which was crammed into a compact row of similar ones, and smiling with difficulty through the rictus of weariness, sat Serguey Kazmin. In astonishment I breathed, 'Good day, Comrade Captain! How did you get here?' He held out his hand to me, moved over a little and without answering the question said, 'Sit down. Tell me what's been happening.' He was still in a fur-lined jacket and an army deerstalker. His trunk and tightly packed rucksack stood next to him. Obviously he had just sat down after his journey and after giving his report to his commanders, and he didn't know yet how to start his new life. I myself couldn't think what to say first, but I managed to galvanise myself and began to tell him about our way of life, about the commanders and flyers, about everything that had happened to me.

Nobody was paying attention to us. Flyers and navigators were crowded around a table in the far corner of the room and there was a deafening clatter of dominoes accompanied by the laughter of players' supporters – a natural period of psychological relaxation before a combat flight. 'Well, and what's it like behind the front line, over the targets?' Kazmin wanted to know everything in detail. I told him. He listened very attentively with a severe and seemingly passionless expression on his face which didn't change even in moments of relaxation. Suddenly I caught myself with the crazy idea that my ex-commander, whom I'd obeyed for nearly two years, hanging on his every word and idea – the man who had instilled in me everything necessary to my current role – now needed my small experience and advice. Not even the faint shadow of even a vague feeling of pride came over me. On the contrary, I was very much afraid of accidentally slipping into a jaunty tone, inadvertently flashing with derring-do or, most of all, exaggerating all the hazards and surprises of the real circumstances of combat flights about which he knew nothing. And Serguey Kazmin himself wasn't the sort not to sense the slightest insincerity in the very first false note or gesture. Had I lost self-control even for a second he would have broken off our conversation instantly.

'Comrade Captain, how did you end up in this regiment?' I asked finally.

'Oh, the usual way. Called me up to the headquarters and handed me my orders. It seems the Air Force Administration demanded it. I handed the squadron over and headed off here.' The clatter of dominoes suddenly stopped; the buzz of the barracks gradually settled down. Everyone wandered off to his bed and fell quiet.

'You go and take a nap before night comes. You're going to be flying tonight.'

But sleep wouldn't come. Kazmin's arrival hadn't only disturbed me, it had alarmed me too. How was he going to fight? Would everything be all right? What was the point of diverting him – no longer a young commander and the most experienced and professional instructor – from the job that the front depended so much upon him doing right in his squadron, from which he'd been turning out new crews for combat regiments and in which there were many superbly trained flying instructors and flight commanders, full of the vigour of youth, any of whom could have taken the place of Kazmin in Tikhonov's regiment? This was no fault of my friends who had stayed in Buzuluk and seen their commander off to the front, but ... Apparently, although Major Tikhonov had already begun, albeit very cautiously and circumspectly for now, to accept young reinforcements under his command, he still had a propensity for the air force's old buffalos.

But Serguey Pavlovich was a true soldier. A day later he took off for his first combat mission as if nothing was wrong, as if it was a regular flight in his own squadron, and that way daily combat operations became routine for him. He found himself at the intersection of searchlights more than once, came under heavy fire from the ground, and during two or three daytime flights he spun like a top, shooting back under tracer from Messers and dodged them. He was still flying in various planes, but then two or three brand new ones were flown to the regiment and one was allocated to him. With an almost childish grin he suddenly shared something with me, like it was his innermost secret: 'You know, there's an autopilot in my machine. What a luxury!' He was going to the aerodrome with his crew and I tagged along. Yes, this wonder was installed in only one machine in the regiment and Kazmin had got it. In the pilot's cabin, between the instrument panel which had been slightly cut away from below and the control pedals, a bulky, wall-to-wall, flat black panel with a multitude of nickel-plated levers had been fitted. I studied it for quite a while, trying to understand the role of each by label, and Serguey, standing on the wing next to me as I sat in the cockpit, waited patiently for me to get familiarised with it. Then he told me in detail how to switch on and tune the automatic pilot when flying. It was quite a simple operation and easy to remember.

'Let's go for a fly – you'll get an idea how special it is to sit in a machine with your hands off controls.' Yeah, right! For all its merits, the Il-4's directional stability left much to be desired. The controls could not be left for a second: with the most ideal neutral setting of the elevator a machine with no one at the controls would unhesitatingly and arbitrarily climb, or, if it felt like it, would drop down at high speed. It cheekily dragged at the pilot's hands and would wear him out during extended flights. Serguey had already had time to fly with this novelty, enjoying the unheard-of comfort, and, not hiding his delight, he wanted to share it with me. Who else could he show it to? He hadn't yet found new friends among his peers, nor was he looking for them.

I gained 500 metres in one circle, lined the plane up with the airstrip and, having set the course, bank and latitude channels, began to turn them on one after another. The machine jerked slightly each time and as I flicked the last switch, I suddenly felt that it had been caught and was tightly held by some other force, rigid and masterful, totally unlike a human one. I carefully relaxed my hands, took my feet off the pedals and put them on the floor. Amazing – the plane was flying itself!

Kazmin was rejoicing in the front cockpit: 'Terrific, isn't it?' I'll say! I tried to overpower the monster but in vain! I even felt a bit put out because of the realisation that something in the plane was rudely resisting me, bending me to its will. I was comforted only by the autopilot's manual over-ride. One movement and it would strip the invisible monster of all its strength. From then on Kazmin would only go on a combat mission with the autopilot turned on and wouldn't let anyone else fly his machine.

CHAPTER FIVE

Under the Wing of High Command

During those days of March 1942 we found out about the transforma-tion of the Long-Range Bomber Command [Dal'nebombardirovochnaya Aviatsiya – DBA] into the Long-Range Bomber Air Force [Aviatsiya Dal'nego Deistviya – ADD]. There are quite a few statements in the post-war literature that neither an ADD as such nor anything like it had ever existed before in our Air Force. Some authors (especially those who came from civil aviation) erred out of ignorance; others did it quite intentionally, to secure themselves a historic role in organising the ADD. In reality at the outbreak of war there were five heavy bomber corps, three detached air divisions and one detached long-range bomber regiment – which together included about 1,000 aircraft with compre-hensively trained crews. This was the Air Force of the Supreme Command of the Red Army, assigned to strike at the most important military-industrial and political centres in the enemy's far rear. And although the first sorties in accordance with its main operational mission were carried out with the aim of destroying the military sites of Danzig, Königsberg, Warsaw, Cracow and Katowice, from the very beginning the war introduced important corrections to the principles of combat use of the DBA, forcing it to transfer its efforts to strike enemy troops in the near-front zone.

By noon of the first day of the German invasion, the front-line air force had lost about 1,200 planes. The losses kept growing during the following days. The DBA, having deeper-placed bases, hadn't experi-enced enemy strikes on its aerodromes. But at the same time it was suffering huge losses in the air, having been drawn into fighting against enemy panzer groups and field troops – the planes combined into small groups directed at small targets, in the daytime, from low altitude, with no fighter escort. The centralised control of the DBA's forces was disrupted. The commanders of front-line troops in whose operational areas the long-range bombers were based would draw them into combat at their own discretion, thus making up for the disastrous shortage of front-line assault aircraft.

The Stavka was alarmed by the growing, unaffordable losses in the DBA, and at the beginning of July 1941 demanded it be used from now on only from high altitudes and at night-time, and by day only with an escort of fighters and only after there had been some preliminary neutralising of enemy anti-aircraft artillery. Scheduling of missions fell to the head of General Staff, but the General Staff managed to carry out only two aerial operations and the situation didn't change for the better.

The DBA lost more than two-thirds of its combat strength during the first six months of the war. The corps departments were already disbanded and only seven weakened divisions remained in the ranks. There was now a real threat that these forces would be lost too. Only resolute measures could save the DBA. On 5 March 1942 by decree of the State Defence Committee it was reorganised into the ADD and placed under the command of the Stavka. From now on no one could dispose of a single plane without the permission of the Stavka. General Golovanov, who later became the Chief Marshal of the Air Force, was appointed as ADD commander.

Long-range bombing operations now became massive strikes by crack groups on the most important targets at night-time. The aircraft fleet began to be intensively replenished: three plants worked for us at full swing, some civilian planes were converted for combat use and several regiments were gradually armed with American machines sent through the Lend-Lease agreement. The network of radionavigation points and beacons was expanded, simplifying night-time navigation. Two flying schools in Central Asia not only replenished ADD losses but also provided crews for new regiments.

We felt the strength of the long-range bomber command being revived with renewed quality. In the hands of the Supreme Command the ADD became the most far-reaching and powerful striking force. Enormous credit for this must go to Alexander Evgenievich Golovanov – a man of great energy and common sense. By the summer of 1943 the ADD consisted of eight aviation corps and its strength again reached more than 1,000 planes and crews.

But the depth of our raids had already begun to grow noticeably by those spring days of 1942. Foreseeing sorties on remote targets, the regiment commander drew up a list of crews for combat activity in all weather conditions over the whole flying radius. At the head of the list was Major Tikhonov with his crew. My surname appeared seventeenth – last, so as not to bump out a captain. I was glad of this recognition.

One of our first remote targets was a Hitlerite command post at Angerburg – a small town in East Prussia where intelligence reports had indicated Hitler himself was residing. The mission was set up unexpectedly and that evening, 27 May, we took off from the Kratovo aerodrome (ours in Serpukhov was still drying out). It was to be a serious ordeal. Although Tikhonov had picked the strongest crews for this task not all of them managed to force their way through the storm front that blocked our path on the final stage of the route. The turbulence was severe, like being thrown against a stone wall. The bursts of lightning dazzled us, but it was during these very moments that I was able to find gaps in the cloudy labyrinth. After that it got a bit easier. The fading thunderstorms were wandering over Angerburg and the planes were diving into them like ghosts among cliffs, looking for signs of the town in the gaps. It was extremely hard to pinpoint the microscopic target whose exact location was not known even to the intelligence service. Luminescent bombs were floating among the clouds, failing to highlight anything the crews were looking for. I guess that if Hitler had been there that night he wouldn't have had to hide at all.

Explosions from the bombs dropped by other planes were distracting and they tempted us to stick our own in too. Vasiliev was rushing here and there, changing course. At last under a stray illumination bomb he noticed something like the target, turned to the attack and dropped his bombs. A minute later some more sticks landed there too. To all appearances that was it – the target.

It took us half the night to get back to our territory. The thunderstorms had gone away; the clouds had disappeared. The dawn met us too early, before the front line. A clear blue sky shone, the sun was straight in our eyes from the horizon, and in front of us and all around stretched an endless snowy plain of fog. We tuned our two-ways for reception and asked for bearings. An hour had gone; another was going by, but the 'landscape' under us was still the same, only the sun had got higher. Vasiliev was nervous: there was nothing he could fix his eyes on. 'Is it really fog?' he kept asking me. I began to have my doubts too: maybe it was only a thin layer of clouds 300 to 400 metres thick and underneath there was open ground with landmarks. We descended to the upper edge; the altitude was 800 metres.

'It's fog, Alesha, real fog.'

'You check it, make sure. Perhaps it's not fog at all.' He really wanted to see the ground.

'And what about the surface topography here?'

'There's no elevations here,' he cut in without hesitation. He knew how to apply pressure. All right then ...

I warned the crew to be all eyes watching for the ground and set up a gradual descent at 2 to 3 metres a second. We seemed to be flying in thick milk. The altitude was getting lower and lower, but it was still a long way to the 100 metre mark below which I was not prepared to go. There was watchful silence in the cockpits. I kept my eyes on the instruments, sensing the whole machine through the control wheel. Suddenly it began to grow dark very quickly and everyone yelled, nearly in unison: 'Ground!' We were still among wisps of fog but the tops of birches and village roofs were already flashing under the propellers. They had come into view much earlier than I had expected; the elevation was not as low as we thought. I gave it full gas at once and sent the roaring plane into a climb. A huge church cross swelled before my eyes at the last moment and, barely clearing the very top of it, we disappeared into the fog. I felt the whole crew sigh with me.

The sun was still shining brightly above the fog. Around us lay a white desert, but such a nice, peaceful and welcoming one. It's not as if I didn't know what searching for the ground under fog commonly leads to, but I had yielded to persuasion – it had been my own fault. Then at last the fog began to grow thinner, and the ground opened up distinctly in the clear and transparent air. Vasiliev had been worried for no reason – we hadn't deviated at all, had passed Moscow from the east and come out at our aerodrome. Several more crews landed after us. Only two were still in the air Kazmin and Tarelkin. I inquired about them with the land-based radio-operators – there had been no communication with Kazmin and Tarelkin had asked to land on a dispersal field. Quite a bit of time went by but there was still no news. No one had seen either burning or falling planes that night. Telephones were silent. There was no news from partisans, and POWs in the German camps wouldn't hear anything about Kazmin or his crewmen till the very end of the war …

Had the automatic pilot let Serguey down? That appliance was supposed to be turned off in turbulent clouds. The powerful steering controls reacted to the turbulence of stormy air instantaneously and tried to hold the plane on a straight course, but the structure of the plane underwent enormous strain as a result and his machine might not have been able to handle it. It would endure the ordeal of turbulence much easier in the pilot's hands, and even then it couldn't be guaranteed to come through without serious after-effects. Maybe his plane had encountered enemy fire en route or over the target, picked up a large shell or bumped into a stray interceptor. Lots of things could happen in the wartime sky. A simple engine failure – a more than common event – sometimes became a real drama with a tragic epilogue over enemy territory. Serguey's death on that confused night was undoubted. There remained only guesses as to what had actually happened, inescapable pain, and the memory of him.

In the muddle of unclear and incomplete two-way messages it had seemed to us that Nikolay Tarelkin was asking to land on a dispersal field. Later all became clear: there had a been a report of the completion of the mission and an engine failure, but all the rest had been a misunderstanding. He, like Kazmin, hadn't returned.

Nikolay was also one of us, from Voronezh. He was a skinny man, very tall, with a big forehead and fine features. No pre-war acquaintance joined us in friendship, but we were drawn together in the front-line regiment. He was a man of inborn nobility and decency – that was the verdict of all who knew him. The young flyers were a mocking and cynical crowd, but even they didn't dare direct dubious jokes at the purity and openness of relations which had drawn together Nikolay and the very modest and pretty Zoechka, who worked in the regimental office and had become his wife just before the war. It hadn't been a year since their wedding day, and now a tragedy like this.

A whole week went by without a scrap of news. The people of the regiment had begun to get used to the idea that both crews had perished. Once the prescribed time had passed, one of the staff clerks, or 'nails' as they were called, with no unnecessary emotion and not uttering a word of sympathy, scratched out in longhand on letter-headed sheets the news that they hadn't come back from a combat mission and sent it to Zoya Ivanovna and Vera Nikolayevna Kazmina, and to the mothers and wives of six more men. The clerk ended with a full stop, driving the unfortunate women into bitter agony, tortured by uncertainty and by hope for a miracle and the men's return. Then two weeks later a brief message arrived: Tarelkin had advised his location and asked for help in getting out.

What had happened to Tarelkin and his crew became clear later. Half an hour from the target an oily trail crept across his aircraft's wing behind the right engine. It didn't seem dangerous to Tarelkin, and having decided that he would somehow make it back to his own territory, he stayed on course. But half an hour after completion of the mission the engine stalled. The altitude began to drop slowly. If this continued there would be no chance of making it to the front. The commander ordered that everything unnecessary be thrown overboard, but there was nothing unnecessary on board – just tarpaulins, the toolbox, ammo, radio and oxygen cylinders. The plane didn't react to the lightening of the load and by dawn the ground was just below. It was too late to bail out and when a lake flashed ahead of them Tarelkin turned slightly towards it and smoothly touched the water. Raising waves and clouds of spray the plane slid towards the shore but came to a halt on a sandbank 1 ½ metres short. The crew quickly left the machine and went deep into the forest. Tarelkin led them eastwards. Opochka was somewhere nearby; further south on the railway was Idritsa. They would have to cross the most dangerous line – the Novosokol'niki–Leningrad trunk road. The front line was even further, on the Velikiye Louki meridian, and followed the river Lovat. It was about 120 kilometres away if you went in a straight line.

Having walked quite a distance, machine-gunner Afanasiy Terekhin decided to go back to the plane to pick up the special food rations and never made it back to his comrades. No one had thought about these rations (a plywood crate full of chocolate, biscuits and tinned food) except for Terekhin – a man from the Bryansk forests and a former village school teacher, the most senior of the crew in age and experience of life. He clearly didn't put too much trust in the wisdom of his young commander and fellow travellers marching on foot across enemy-occupied territory. I guess he was tempted not so much by the rations as by the prospect of walking on his own, which could be less dangerous than travelling in a group where a chance mistake by one could cost the others their lives.

At the end of May the forest in that area gets flooded by water, small creeks and rivers bursting their banks, and the spring that year, after a winter of heavy snows, was especially wet. They were a strong crew, and they walked as hard as they could, without stopping, but their daily rate of progress was still insignificant. They chose the drier places to spend the night and slept on brushwood. They ate whatever they could get their hands on – the springtime forest wasn't too generous in terms of bush tucker. Their footwear was wet through; their clothes turned into rags. Then they came out onto the railway – its length was thick with guards walking up and down. They had to wait for night-time and then under cover they crossed that barrier as well. Now there was more woodland and marshes, kilometres of gruelling walking, sometimes wading supported on sticks or on planks lashed together, sometimes floating on logs.

The Lovat showed up on the eighth day, flashing from behind a thicket. Were they saved? As they looked for a crossing point the flyers were spotted from our side and a boat was sent to pick them up. Ragged, unshaven and starving, they were at last among friends, at home. But the befuddling, limitless joy that gripped them was short-lived. After arriving at headquarters they were disarmed and convoyed to an NKVD [People's Commissariat for Internal Affairs – translator's note] camp set up to check the political reliability of those who returned from behind the enemy lines. Many such camps had been established since December 1941 and by the summer of 1942 the NKVD had managed to fill them.

Several days passed before Tarelkin somehow contrived to send a message to the outside world.

Major Tikhonov located an aerodrome next to the camp and ordered the squadron commander, Captain Galkin, provided with all possible authority, to fly immediately to ferry the crew back to the regiment. But he was to run into the wrong sort of people. Despite all his requests, arguments and tough language, the camp commanders were not going to yield to Galkin. He brandished documents, swore and cursed, but it was all in vain: 'It's not permitted. There is an order!'

Finally, seeing that his efforts were useless, Galkin talked the camp commandant into letting Tarelkin and his navigator Dedushkin at least walk him to the plane. He had asked for Mitrofanov as well but the guy (apparently because he was a junior officer) was flatly refused. Tarelkin and Dedushkin headed towards the aerodrome alongside Galkin under armed escort. On the way the instruction came in a whisper: after the engines were tested, at a sign from Galkin they were to dash into the lower hatch of the radio-operators' cabin.

At the sight of the plane the escorts were overwhelmed. Apparently they had never seen a flying machine in their lives, much less such a big one and so close up. And when Galkin turned on the engines the soldiers were taken completely aback. The rest happened like a flash of lightning. Well-built though they were, Tarelkin and Dedushkin still disappeared through the hatch instantly. At that moment the engines roared and Galkin, having turned the aircraft's tail slightly towards the escorts, showered them with dust and went for the take-off. By nightfall the rejoicing regiment was greeting Tarelkin and Dedushkin. I felt Nikolay cheer up when he saw me. We fell on each other's necks, mumbled something and slapped each other's shoulders. Then I walked him to the dormitory to restore their already cancelled residence permits.

Two or three days after their escape a camp representative accompanied by an armed escort arrived at our regiment and demanded the immediate return of the escapees. The commander resolutely refused and in the face of the representative's officiousness, threw him out of headquarters. The man would not calm down and stuck his nose into the dormitory, but he was met on the porch by flyers who advised him to leave in order to avoid trouble. The jailer backed off and, threatening reprisals, disappeared.

The story of Tarelkin and Dedushkin's escape from the NKVD camp reached General Golovanov and seriously alarmed him. He decided he had to interfere in this delicate and dangerous case. As for the chances of finding themselves in such a camp, the flying personnel of long-range bomber command had a lot of 'advantages' in this regard: our crews were larger than those in other branches of the Air Force and we had to operate much deeper into the enemy's territory. Taking into account the fact that the combat personnel of the ADD were not big in number and that literally every crew mattered to the Stavka, the commander's worry was understandable: any continuation of this practice could have badly affected the combat capacity of the long-range bomber force.

Golovanov applied to Stalin with a bold request – to allow ADD crews to be referred directly to him at headquarters after crossing the front line. He assured Stalin that he vouched for them and took personal responsibility for their reliability. I don't know if Golovanov's past service in high positions in the NKVD in the 1920s and early 1930s played a part, but Stalin agreed (albeit not immediately), and the important exemption for pilots and navigators from the ADD came into force, although it didn't apply to those who came back after escaping captivity.

*   *   *

By summer 1942 the situation on all fronts had become so desperate that the ADD couldn't worry too much about remote targets. All forces were thrown not only into the destruction of military sites located at an operational depth from the front line but also into striking at enemy troops concentrated on the front line near river-crossings and in fortified districts – in other words, to act as front-line bombers and ground-attack aircraft. The latter operated only during the day, they were still at short strength and we had to help them out. However, the power of our strikes was somewhat greater than theirs. We were assigned small targets and the front line near which our own troops were located was very close. Fortunately the men on the ground were careful to make themselves visible with fires and flares. Our work was meticulous and, of course, low altitude; this made us an ideal target for the enemy's small-calibre artillery, which had 'been fruitful and multiplied'. We couldn't avoid combat losses. And the aircraft, which were getting no rest, would sometimes take cruel revenge for our unintentional, unwilling coercion – cases of engine failure in the air entailing consequences no less dangerous than shell damage became more frequent. Once even I got my share.

It happened in May after a powerful pinpoint bombardment, excellently illuminated by candle-bombs, of a railway junction in Kharkov, on which we brought the whole weight of the division to bear. We had already got a long way away from it and left Voronezh abeam behind us when my bomber's left engine resonantly banged, shuddered and caught fire. The night was clear but dark and a flame was shooting from the engine, even though it was turned off. The blaze dazzled me, preventing me from recognising anything in the vicinity. No operating aerodromes were visible but we had to land as soon as possible.

'Alesha,' I said, 'if you get me to Voronezh I'll find the aerodrome with my eyes closed. I know this whole area. I'm a native.' At last I caught sight of the familiar outline of the blacked-out city and straight off, without seeing the airstrip, I began to close in for landing. Only when I got nearer did I make out several dimly guttering oil lights. But there was no reaction on the ground to our red flares. I landed by guesswork because there were no signal lights on the ground, illuminating my way with the aircraft's landing lights. It turned out that the aerodrome had been closed after the return of the fighter planes which had beaten off a German evening raid on the city, and there were no plans for anyone else to land or take off there that night. Fortunately there were some people on the parking areas and they helped us put out the fire. There was a clear reason for the blaze: a cylinder had been torn out of the crank case along with the bolts. We were lucky it had happened over our territory; what if it had failed deep behind enemy lines?

By morning the Germans had again pounced on Voronezh. We were awoken in the huge barracks where we stayed overnight on plank bunks not so much by exploding bombs and the weapons cannonade as by the staccato banging of the barrack-dwellers' jackboots. Wearing whatever came to hand, they were flying out through all the doors and windows like water out of a fire hose. But we were so wedded to sleep that after only lifting our heads and glancing at each other we closed our eyes again. The windows were rattling, plaster was falling down, but the sounds of combat didn't disturb us.

On 13 July the whole division was thrown into alarm: General Loginov hadn't come back from a mission. The regiments were bombing gatherings of enemy troops at a ford on the river Don near Korotoyak. There was a lot of fire from both the ground and the air. The bomb load of most of the planes consisted of RRABs [rotating cluster bombs] stuffed with ceramic balls filled with an incendiary mixture. They would scatter over large areas, some flaring up after colliding in the air before heading for the ground as a stream of bright-white fire. Those that reached the ground intact would split up there, forming a number of high-temperature, unquenchable sources of fire. But in return we were getting our share of trouble from the ground: we were striking from low altitude and weapons of all calibres had something to shoot at. It wasn't easy to break through to the target point unscathed, and had a shell splinter or a bullet hit the RRABs hanging on the lower clamps, they would have flared up instantly, enveloping the whole plane in fire. Because of this, and the heightened drag of these awkward lumps, we hated carrying them, preferring to use ordinary bombs. But the RRABs were an effective weapon and had to be considered.

That night Loginov took off in the first echelon of the division's battle formations on board squadron commander Major Uroutin's plane. The division's commander should have been at the command post when it was in the air. All the information about the operation and aerial conditions was concentrated there and combat operations could only be run from the post. In quickly changing flight conditions, his decisions were awaited not only by the crews but by the ADD commander and the Stavka in Moscow. When he was a regiment commander Evgeniy Loginov used to fly combat missions as a pilot, though it wasn't simple for him to do so even back then. And just try doing it as division commander! In fact he'd been flying on commander's business day and night, and he'd been doing it superbly. He took a fancy to pilot an unusual plane – a sport monoplane UT-2. He used to approach the aerodrome, turn off his engine about 500 metres over the starting line, and in gliding flight, twirling spirals and figures of eight until at the very last moment, he would suddenly align the plane to land exactly at the landing T. The whole aerodrome would have its eyes glued to this ballet. But what was the point of having the division commander on combat flights? He was the commander on the ground but only a common ordinary flyer in the air in the combat echelons. That was why division commanders, gradually losing their night-flight skills, rarely flew combat missions at the control wheel and only after a considerable break. When there was a need for the commander to have a look at the organisation of a strike and assess its real results (which had become a commander's duty after direct orders from the head of the ADD), sometimes he would resort to putting the most experienced and reliable crew into the plane.

Mikhail Uroutin's crew was such a one, considered nearly the most skilful and invulnerable in the division. Having taken his place at the control wheel in the navigator's cockpit, the division commander would simultaneously examine the flying skills and combat practice of the plane commander and his crew. It was a serious exam and the crew would do their best to pass it without any slips.

Uroutin went straight at the target as if not noticing the dreadful attack and dropped off his RRABs, covering the target with a dome of fire. Obviously wishing to show the division commander the scene of destruction in living detail, he bravely reduced the altitude, which was low anyway, turned around for a second approach and found himself under candle-bombs that had suddenly ignited above him. The plane, illuminated from above, was clearly visible in the German ack-ack gunsights and they didn't miss their chance. The plane shook, caught fire and went down at an angle. Uroutin gave the order to jump. It would have been easiest for the navigator, Major Matsepras, to bail out first, but he conceded this right to the general – he opened the hatch and helped him out. Persuading him to leave the aircraft ate up a few precious seconds. The radio-operators and Uroutin followed but Matsepras – no longer young and not distinguished for his sporting prowess – apparently didn't have enough altitude.

While Loginov was hanging on the straps he caught a bullet, but a glancing one that went right through. His landing was unsuccessful – straight into some bushes. The general rolled up his parachute and hid. There was fighting around him. He had to analyse the situation, but the main thing he understood straight away was that he would only be able to move in the dark. He would tend his wounds during the day and look for a road ahead. By the end of the third night he came out onto the Don and swam across. A patrol on our side met him not very respectfully, to put it mildly. It would have been a surprise if they had greeted him politely: a scruffy character swims over from the German side and insists he's a Soviet general! But soon an order came via front-line communications to assist the crew of a shot-down bomber that had had a general on board. The unusual prisoner didn't take offence and he and his guards parted on friendly terms.

Evgeniy Loginov soon shrugged off this really quite ordinary wartime drama and became absorbed again in his command duties. The survivors – Uroutin, Garankin and Sharikov – made it home too. Only Matsepras, who most likely hadn't managed to leave the plane, perished.

* * *

I don't know if there is still a village named Pakhanok near Kursk but at the beginning of the summer of 1942 it certainly existed. There in a grove near its outskirts German tanks were gathering. Setting up the task of destroying them, the regiment commander unexpectedly put me forward for the job.

'You'll go first. Find the grove and mark it up with RRABs and incendiary bombs. Captain Doubyago will be your navigator. There'll be no candle-bombs.

'Clarify the situation with the chief of intelligence,' he finished. But the chief of intelligence, as always, had no more information than he had put before the commander the previous day. So, having marked the desired grove with crosses on large-scale maps and chosen other more reliable landmarks, we were ready for the operation.

The RRABs were on the outside clamps, bombs inside. The radio-operators took a couple of 8kg AO-8 splinter bombs with them into the cockpit, just in case, as they had done a few times before. Sometimes en route to a target when a German searchlight suddenly shot up ahead of us and began to swing its beam under our nose trying to catch the plane and light it up for the flak gunners, the navigator would take good aim and at his command the radio-operators would drop the bombs onto the lower end of the beam, directly through the lower access door. It was fun, for the waggling light beam would suddenly come to a standstill and shine into nowhere at some absurd angle. It was easy to imagine a frightened searchlight crew bolting from the bomb, not having had time to turn off the machinery. We would laugh with all our hearts and prepare a new bomb for the next passing searchlight.

We took off for Pakhanok at dawn and approached the target in twilight. We matched the map to the surrounding landmarks – there was no doubt: in front of us was the very grove where the tanks should be. But there was not the least sign of life. Our bombers were just about to come over and there was no target! My nerves were at breaking point. I was swearing and by now losing all hope, shedding altitude and circling the grove. With my eyes fixed on it I clearly distinguished the tops of the trees but there was nothing under them. The area was silent, enveloped in the evening gloom as if falling into an early, peaceful sleep. No way could I drop bombs on this peaceful paradise! 'You never know,' I thought, 'the intelligence guys could have got confused this time too, or the tanks, foreseeing a strike, have upped and gone.' I called Nezhentsev, a two-way-operator/machine-gunner. 'Get your bomb ready, will you?'

The navigator changed course towards the presumed target and the bomb at his command (just in case) slipped. Oh God, what had we started! I gasped, like I had fallen into an ice-hole. A hail of flak gun traces instantly soared up from the grove, enveloping the plane in small-calibre shells. 'Vasya, get out, get out fast!' Ivan Lavrentievich yelled.

I didn't need his exhortation to encourage me into action: I was already rushing away from that hell's kitchen at full speed. Still, the Germans' hearts had skipped a beat: they couldn't handle one pathetic bomb. We couldn't drop the RRABs: our altitude was too low for them and they wouldn't have time to open up. We gained the necessary 500 metres and in the stream of bombers that had arrived, we smashed up the tank nest. The flak spurting out of it now gave everyone a good pointer. The grove was being transformed before our eyes: smoke was pouring out of it, tongues of flame were bursting through the trees, explosions were flaring up. By the second approach the fireworks from the cannon had died down and the incendiary bombs were starting one new blaze after another. Of course it was impossible to smash such a target in one raid. We repeated our visit to Pakhanok twice, alternating it with raids on a similar tank grouping in the vicinity of the village of Frolovka near Mtsensk.

CHAPTER SIX

Downed Behind Enemy Lines

No matter how high the demand for ADD strikes on German troops near the front line, the most important military targets in the far rear of Germany itself were still asking for it. By now we felt it was time to hit them.

Many years afterwards I found out from Alexander Evgenievich Golovanov that Stalin had tasked him with a strike on Berlin on the first anniversary of the German invasion of the USSR. But Golovanov replied that the shortest and brightest nights occur right in the last third of June and our planes would have to negotiate significant areas during daylight to carry out such a raid, something the fascist aircraft would be sure to exploit. Golovanov requested the raid be shifted to the end of August. The arguments were sound, and Stalin, having thought it over, agreed, albeit unwillingly. But it was not just the 'white nights' that worried the ADD commander – would we manage to reach Berlin from the airfields around Moscow; would intermediate aerodromes be available near the front line for the heavy bombers; and would fighter planes be able to give cover as we crossed the front line en route to the target? There were many questions and they would all have to be resolved in a matter of two to three months.

A series of strikes on Königsberg was suggested and then, a bit later, on Danzig. A large group of crews was taken under the control of a special engineering team. They studied fuel consumption and flight and engine performance under various conditions. All the data were subjected to thorough scrutiny – analysed, compared, summarised. In a long list of ADD crews ranked according to how far they could travel on a load of fuel, mine came fifth, although I had never competed with anyone and had never taken any measures to save fuel. Sticking to the strict rules of any long-range flight, I'd always preferred to remain at the altitude most comfortable for the engines – 4,500 metres. I'd never resorted to weakening the fuel mixture in pursuit of distance, and had managed to do without afterburning or the second gear of the super-charger.

At this time a new device was installed under the visors of the pilot's cockpits – a gauge for working out the fuel mixture. Being deficient in principle and primitive in engineering it was incredibly inaccurate and could betray the credulous: sensible flyers rejected it out of hand. We believed that there was nothing more reliable than using the colour of the exhaust flames as a guide to adjusting the mixture: I knew a barely visible bluish tint meant the engines were getting the healthiest feed.

Then our aircraft were fitted with suspended tanks: now they were really something. Each pair of streamlined, light-yellow cigars made of tarred cardboard contained enough fuel for an hour and a half of flying. After the fuel was consumed, the tanks were jettisoned. But not many of us managed to dry them out completely. Imperfections in the fuel feed meant the petrol would be sucked out unevenly, emptying one tank first and sometimes leaving the other nearly full. After sucking air the engines would cut out unexpectedly and abruptly, the plane would begin to shudder and we had to switch quickly to the main tanks. It was impossible to monitor the fall in fuel pressure but the suspended tanks did give an extra 40 to 50 minutes' flying time and this was usually enough to reach the target and make it home.

On the eve of 21 July I was on my way to Königsberg again. By evening we were crossing the front line north of Velikiye Louki and heading deeper into enemy-occupied territory. Two days earlier we had been moving along exactly the same route when, somewhere over Lithuania in the dark, we came across thick thunderstorm clouds. Negotiating their jumbled piles we managed to find our way through, flying around the thunderheads, which were flashing with fire. Man-oeuvring between searchlight beams and shell bursts, we broke through to the centre of Königsberg. Our target was down there and Vasiliev didn't miss. We saw large-calibre flak guns desperately firing from the city's outskirts and from warships scattered all over the harbour, densely peppering a huge area with explosions. Even after the strike it took us a while to escape to freedom, avoiding the searchlight beams with our engines muted. But the fire from the ground was nervous and confused, and the searchlights seemed unable to grab hold of anyone – they would slip over the fuselage and lose their target straight away. This section of the German anti-aircraft defence seemed to be sitting its first exam. In the city fires flared, bright splashes flashed out from explosions, but it turned out not to be a very powerful strike – few of our bombs had managed to reach their targets. That night most of us dropped our weapons on secondary targets.

The weather did not promise to be much better on this second Königsberg raid either. No hazardous phenomena had shown up before the front line on the charts but the meteorologists warned us that powerful thunderstorm fronts were possible over and to east of the Baltic coast. In fact German anti-aircraft artillery and fighter planes were not the main threat on our way to targets. During the summer months there was nothing more dangerous than night-time atmospheric storms raging behind the front line. It was impossible to get used to them – they were always frightening. You might think that because we had synoptic charts, nothing could have been simpler than plotting routes to avoid the worst of the weather. If a storm front was in the way, why didn't we shift take-off time by a few hours or postpone it till the next night? But our charts only contained information about the area up to the front line. Beyond it there was a blank desert. Meteorological data was as strictly confidential for the warring sides as the contents of operational documents. And conducting meteorological reconnaissance deep behind enemy lines was completely out of the question. A lone scout flying along the route of a forthcoming combat flight would definitely become the prey of enemy fighters. Besides, daytime weather doesn't guarantee at all what will happen at night. It had been simple in peaceful pre-war times: if a thunderstorm had been forecast – cancel; if you came across it en route – turn back. During a combat flight decisions were based on different criteria. Even in battle anyone has the right to turn back. However, before making that decision we had to try everything possible to break through to the target. But where and when do you reach the point beyond which lies calamity or even death – and how do you not step over it inadvertently? The struggle could have various outcomes: some crews managed to force their way to the target and, already knowing where the thunderstorms were, took alternative routes home. Others, not able to find a gap between the thunderheads, came back to their aerodrome without carrying out their mission or bombed a secondary target. Still others abandoned their broken planes or stayed with them till the end. It was a very difficult decision to return to your aerodrome with your bombs intact. A sense of guilt weighed on your soul and gave no peace. Some non-flying but vigilant officials cast a cold eye on the unlucky guy. And God forbid such thunderstorms or even fiercer ones came your way the next night – you'd battle them to the end but you wouldn't bring your bombs home again.

... Our altitude was 4,500 metres. The air was calm and didn't give any hint that storms lay ahead. But then the stars began to dim almost imperceptibly before suddenly disappearing behind a dense shroud of clouds: a black wall of foul weather showed up ahead of us. It appeared immediately behind the front line, much earlier than the weather-forecasters had promised. We moved deeper and deeper into the cloudy wilderness and peered into the black, looking for passageways through. We rushed towards the least gap, but then a new wall would grow up in our path. The engines dragged the machine forward – you can't stop an aircraft to have a good look around! It was tossed from one wing to the other, thrown up and down for hundreds of metres. The clouds were filled with fire and they flashed all around us. Vasiliev was silent; he was looking for gaps and plotting our chaotic course. It would have been better to head back but we were wedged so deeply into this raging beast that returning might have cost us more dear than forging ahead. It seemed we were just about to overcome the last obstacle and break out into free space, but then the plane lurched again repeatedly with an increasingly dangerous intensity. I used the elevators to smooth things out as best I could, but by now it seemed to me that the plane was falling under the power of this terrifying expression of nature. A mysterious force pressed me into the seat, sinking my head into my shoulders. Then it threw me upwards so that my weight was on the seatbelts. At last, after a drop of nearly half a kilometre, the machine shot up again abruptly, a metallic crack resounded, the engines stalled and one end of a snapped cable began to whirl around the cockpit. Traction disappeared from the control wheel. Bloody hell! I swore loud and colourfully. For a moment my strength left me, my hands hung at my sides, my head fell back against the headrest. This was it! The end! But the next moment I pulled myself together.

'Jump, everybody jump!' I yelled over the onboard intercom. 'Leave the plane, Alesha!' I repeated vehemently. 'Jump!'

'What's happened? Aaagghh!' His cries didn't stop.

'Jump, Alesha, jump!' He continued shouting something but the plane, losing balance, listing and changing angle, was flying downwards, losing precious altitude. There was no point staying. Opening the canopy and fighting against the shifting G-forces, I scrambled over the right board with great difficulty and broke away from the aircraft. Its huge body flashed in front of my eyes; it was without its left wing console and tail unit.

I was falling on my back and didn't reach for the parachute ring straight away, trying to distance myself from the plane, although it had instantly disappeared from sight. When I could delay no longer I suddenly felt that I was caught in a very strong and fast centrifugal motion. My head and legs were making wide circles and I had lost all sense of bearing and timing. I was in a spin. I remembered my parachute instructors' training: stretch your arm out and wait. Opening a parachute during a spin meant death. Then the spinning stopped and I began to fall with my head down. I quickly found the ring and pulled it forcefully. The white cloth soared behind my spread legs like a candle. If only it would fill up in time! A powerful jerk caught me by the shoulders, turning me head over heels, and at exactly the same moment I punched through the tree tops and glided sideways, plunging into a forest bog up to my shoulder blades. The landing was rough – it knocked all the air out of my chest. I wouldn't have survived a landing at that speed on firm ground.

Choking and gasping I caught my breath with difficulty. I moved my hands and legs – I was in one piece. It was pitch dark. Rain was falling; lightning was tearing the sky apart above the tree tops. The parachute cupola had caught on some branches. I wanted to lie down and have a rest but suddenly a thought struck me – the Germans might be quite close. I couldn't afford to make a mistake and had to find my way to our lines at any cost. A fallen tree trunk was under my head. I dragged myself onto it, moved to firm ground, released myself from the parachute straps, pulled the dome down and sank it in the bog.

I was wearing fur-lined boots and overalls. Beneath the overalls was a soldier's blouse with no badges. I had my TT [Soviet-made pistol – translator's note] on a belt too, so as not to lose it in the event of a bail-out. I had no identity papers, only some spare ammo (in addition to that inside the pistol), a watch, a knife, a tiny compass and some matches.

The fire from my burning plane was gleaming through dense, black thicket, now fading, now flaring up. Pushing aside the bushes and splashing through the flooded forest I set out towards it but soon stopped by a small creek. At that moment I came back to my senses: an exploded and burning plane in this unknown forest could have attracted the attention of both the Germans and the *polizei*. An encounter with them would mean certain death. It was unlikely that anyone remained in the plane – there'd been enough time to abandon it. But where were Alexey, Chernov, Nezhentsev? What had happened to them?

Having struck a match, I got out my compass and took a bearing to the east. Flashes of lightning lit up the forest from time to time and I had a chance to establish the course I should follow for the next 5 to 10 kilometres. When I glanced back, having gone just a bit further, there was no longer any fire: either it had been extinguished by the water of the bog or it was obscured by the woods. It was past midnight when I reached the edge of the forest. Just in front of me within a broad glade the lightning flashes revealed the huts of a village stretched out in a line. Who lived here? I didn't dare step into the open field and decided to wait till dawn so that I could observe it first from afar. Thoughts were flashing through my mind one after another, mixing with and contradicting each other: 'This is occupied territory but there must be Russian people in it, mustn't there? I need to find someone (just one person!) and find out everything from him without witnesses. I'll be able to cope with one person if something happens. But pursuit may follow. The pistol is my only hope. But what if ... ?' Captivity was out of the question. They wouldn't take me alive. I had my pistol under my blouse to ensure that didn't happen.

Time dragged agonisingly slowly. The storms calmed and the rain eased, but I made no discoveries in the first grey light of dawn. Crouching down, I walked up to the bushes along the side of the village through the forest thicket: there was no smoke, no sound. No man nor dog, nor even hen. It was after eight. There was a small, poor hut closer to the forest than the rest; bent over, I sneaked up to it. As it turned out, it was the only occupied dwelling in the whole village. A shaggy old man, abandoned by everyone, lived there with his deranged grandson. Seeing a stranger suddenly appear in front of him the old man was astounded rather than scared. Wet fur clothes, hair stuck to forehead, pistol in hand ... I was aware of my appearance and I knew that to get the old man on side I would have to begin with explanations rather than questions. This kind-hearted individual prompted no fear in me and he treated me with trust. He'd heard a loud explosion the previous night and now he linked it to my arrival. 'The residents who are younger,' he told me, 'have joined the partisans, and women, the elderly and children have gone in all directions, either to towns or big villages. Some have hidden in the forest but some have managed to get across the front line over to our side.'

'And where are the Germans?' At last I asked an impatient question.

'The Germans? They don't live here. They used to come here on horses or in tanks. They would plunder what they liked, shoot or take with them the menfolk who, in their opinion, looked suspicious and leave again. Now they drive past: they've looted all they can and emptied the village. But sometimes they rush in, scatter all over the place, rummage around the huts looking for partisans staying overnight, and pass on. Our men, the Reds, come around as well.' (That was what he said: 'The Reds'!) 'More often they move through Rassvet and Broutovo if there are no Germans. If they come across them a battle starts up. The Germans sometimes lodge in Broutovo and have a small commandant's office. It's not far away and Rassvet is just next door.'

I couldn't understand how our men had been getting to this area, but if I was lucky enough to come across them I would be safe. Still, there was more chance of coming across the Germans: this was their territory. Maybe, rather than tempt fate, it would be better to go deeper into the woodland and press eastwards through it? But how could I cross the front line, given there were troops nearby? What if I encountered open space and German emplacements? I asked the old man if he had any clothes and footwear he would exchange for my overalls, fur-lined jack-boots and breeches. He began to bustle about, obviously tempted by my luxurious gear, and soon found a pair of boots which were falling apart and scraped but fitted my feet. I had string for laces, also using it to tie up the soles which were falling off, tightly bound the legs of my breeches and got ready for a long march. The old man solicitously folded up the overall and jackboots, wrapped them in rags and stuffed them up the chimney, shoving odds and ends in on top of them.

Through the dormer window, as if from an observation post, he showed me two roads to the villages where he said 'The Reds' could sometimes be found. Broutovo, obscured by distance and forest, was on the right-hand side and I would have to cross a bridge to get to it. It was dangerous. The roofs of Rassvet were clearly visible straight ahead. There was a byroad leading to it and it was bordered by an arc of forest on the left.

I said goodbye to the old man and dived straight into the thicket, not letting Rassvet out of my sight. The clouds had gone and the sun peeped out. My boots were making loud smacking sounds but they stayed firmly on my feet. Suddenly a pair of horse-drawn carts appeared on the road. I froze behind branches, scrutinising the unhurried approach of the strange procession. About a dozen armed men sat on the carts. I looked at them closely. Bloody hell, they were Germans and there were other people with them. *Polizei*? It felt as though they were all looking towards me and could see me clearly through the undergrowth. But the carts jolted past and turned left by the old man's village of Chernoushka, apparently towards Broutovo. I felt tingles run down my spine.

It was already past midday when I approached Rassvet. Unlike Chernoushka, it was a large village – the mysterious one where 'The Reds' were sometimes to be found but which the fascists had just left. Without leaving the forest I observed the village for quite a while, thinking about how I could approach it unnoticed. Maybe I should wait till night? There were people in the village – someone walked down the street, others were working in their backyards. At last, having closely examined the nearest house, I headed for it along a narrow footpath overgrown by corn on both sides.

There were two older women and a girl of about fifteen in the house. Noticing me, they froze and fell silent. There was no reaction to my 'hello'. And it didn't come later either. I got nothing out of them except 'we don't know' and 'we haven't seen anyone here'. The silence was heavy and I was becoming desperate. It had been easier with the old man: my flying outfit had worked in my favour on the first contact. This time I had revealed myself to strangers in a quite different guise. I would have to go into the forest again and then who knew what might happen. I thought it unlikely that the women would remain silent about my visit, but who would they tell? The Germans? The *polizei*? The partisans? There was no sign of 'The Reds' in the village. Suddenly a shadow flickered at the window closest to the door. 'Oh, Uncle Vanya,' the girl said rapidly and instantly slipped across the threshold before I had time to react. Here was the moment of truth. Who was Uncle Vanya? Clearly he was Russian not German, but he could be even worse than German – *polizei*. There was no way to tell on the spot. A small window behind me looked out on the forest. With an imperceptible movement I opened the lower hook which held the shutters. My pistol and the window – I had nothing else.

I didn't have long to wait. Two or three minutes later soldier's jackboots clattered loudly and heavily in the inner porch. I thrust the window open and released the safety catch of my TT. The women gasped and pressed themselves against the walls. The door squealed sharply and opened. A tall and fine-looking junior lieutenant strapped about with belts froze on the threshold, looking at my slightly raised pistol. A rifle barrel was pointing at me from behind his back. There could be no masquerade here. I lowered the pistol and lay it on a bench. The junior lieutenant stepped into the room. He was Platoon Commander Safonov of the 953rd Rifle Regiment of the 3rd Shock Army. His platoon was with him.

I told the commander all that had happened and at this point my hostesses raised a hue and cry, pulling smoking pots out of the stove, urging me to take some food and rest. Safonov believed my story despite the fact that I had not a single identity paper on me.

'What are we going to do now?' He asked a pertinent question.

'It would be best if you help me to cross the front line,' I said.

'But we are on a combat mission. We have to keep going.'

'No problem. Take me along, commander. I won't be a burden to you. The TT is not much of a cannon but it can still be of some use.'

'Don't worry, if there's action there'll be weapons.' And so it was settled.

The platoon was stretched out along the road. It seemed to me that it moved in disunity, in a disorganised mass, but then I began to realise it was divided into distinct tactical groups. The densest one, in which Safonov and I walked side by side, was the assault group. I shared my observations with him. 'The Germans have just rolled out of this village.'

'They're always sneaking away. There are not many of them here – no benefit for them to be drawn into combat.'

The strain of the recent events began to ease and I felt my left knee joint begin to ache badly – it swelled up and began to impede walking. My landing in the forest was still making itself felt but I managed to walk with the platoon without falling behind. I soon found out something about the type of warfare our troops had been waging in this German-occupied area. Safonov wasn't talkative but he disclosed a little of the essence of events. In this woody terrain, where the front line wasn't marked with opposing trenches and had been inactive since winter, our subdivisions and units had been penetrating into the German rear and waging guerrilla warfare. They would sometimes slay a fascist garrison, wipe out a military column or destroy a railway station with all its trains and then pull back to our side across the front line. This time they had been charged with the task of attacking a German headquarters located in Yukhovo.

Our route lay via Chernoushka and I asked Safonov to go deeper into the forest to search for our fallen aircraft. We stretched out in a line and were just about to enter the thicket when armed men appeared from behind the bushes as if from underground. They were partisans – a small group of about twenty. Apparently they had been observing us closely from afar, lying quiet, and only when they were confident that we were friends did they come out to meet us. They knew Safonov well and some of the others too. Having heard a plane explode in the forest the previous night, the detachment had begun a search at dawn but had not managed so far to locate signs of a fire. We all went deeper into the forest. We could see only a few metres ahead. But then a creek crossed our path – apparently the same one I'd encountered the night before. We followed it but failed to find any traces of the night's events.

Day was giving way to night and Safonov was losing time. Leaving the forest behind, the platoon headed off to carry out its mission. It began to rain again. In twilight, and already very wet, we came to the river Loknya and stopped at a small abandoned farmstead on its banks. Towards night a storm broke out. It began to rain really hard and the downpour continued for several days. Engaging the Germans in such weather, after fording the swollen river and storming enemy troops who were sheltered in houses, would almost certainly have been suicide for the platoon. The enforced delay turned out to be just what I needed – my aching knee and ribs were demanding a rest. At night I could hear the familiar buzzing of Il-4 bomber engines; they were pulling westwards one after another. Would many of them manage to find their way to the distant targets?

On the fourth day the sun emerged. Close to evening in the farmstead we heard the sentries hailing someone, then excited voices and the tramping of feet. A *starshiy politruk* [senior political commissar – a military rank for political officers in the Red Army in the early stages of the Second World War, equivalent to a captain at the time – translator's note], all hung about with weapons, noisily entered the room where Safonov and I were staying. It seemed he was now in charge. *Starshiy Politruk* Stankevich had brought a battalion equipped with heavy weapons, a radio set and sappers. Black-haired, sharp-eyed and quick in his movements, first he asked Safonov about me; I sensed that the new commander was very much displeased at the arrival of such an unexpected recruit. Then he and I had a conversation which Safonov summed up: 'There'll be action. Losses are inevitable and I'm not entitled to risk the life of a combat airman. You are needed over there – in your plane, in your regiment. So tomorrow they'll walk you across the front line.'

We took off in 'battle order': one soldier ahead of me, another behind, just as we'd been instructed. But when the farmstead disappeared from sight around a turn in the road, we began to walk alongside each other, quietly chatting. Their rifles were thrown behind their shoulders. I asked the soldiers to walk through the forest once again to search for my plane. We set off in a new direction, sometimes walking apart calling to each other, sometimes coming together, but the new search yielded nothing. There was just a little bit of light left. We turned east, crossed the outskirts of Chernoushka once again and, having emerged onto a deserted forest footpath, headed towards the Lovat. The soldiers were marching ahead of me. They barked warnings from time to time: 'Mine!' I would immediately freeze and ask, 'Where?' They would giggle and show me some small hump or tussock just a step or two from my boots. Now I did my best to follow precisely in the steps of my guides.

By evening we were on the banks of the Lovat, facing thick woods on the opposite side. The soldiers whistled the prearranged signal. The trees began to move and a boat was launched. Soon we were in our own territory. The next day I was required to have a detailed conversation about my experiences at the headquarters of the 3rd Shock Army. The men from the *Osobyi Otdel* [Special Department – translator's note] of the counterespionage service, which was called SMERSH [abbreviation of 'Death to Spies' – translator's note], could be distinguished from aviation officers by their way of asking tricky questions. I managed not to raise any doubts in my interlocutors' minds, but they were not yet in a hurry to let me return to my regiment. Apparently inquiries were still in progress.

There was someone else in the little shed where I was allocated overnight lodging and I was on my guard. My neighbour was too unusual. To put it better, he was scary. A deserter? A bandit? He wouldn't be under guard for no reason. 'You'll spend the night with him,' my escort told me. 'He's just been transported down here. They say, he's an airman as well.' I approached the man and was horrified by his appearance: he was unshaven and scratched all over; his blouse was torn to shreds and his bleeding body was visible through the rags. Instead of trousers he was wearing undershorts. Fresh wounds were bleeding on his bare feet, which were plastered all over with mud. He sat with his head hanging and breathed heavily. 'What are you standing there for?' I turned on the soldier who had brought me. 'He needs help!'

A medic came in and lit a lamp. With my assistance he helped the poor fellow have a wash and swabbed and bandaged his wounds. They brought him linen and clothing, fed him and put him to bed. He was Lieutenant Ivan Doushkin, a flyer from a sister long-range bomber division. His 'odyssey' had been a bit more serious than mine.

Back on that ill-starred night he was also on his way to Königsberg. Having passed through thunderclouds a bit to the north of my route and flown noticeably further than I had managed, Doushkin was torn out of his seat by turbulence in one of many powerful drops of several hundred metres. The back of his head broke through the canopy and he found himself outside his aircraft. All he could do was open his parachute.

He didn't see where his plane fell, didn't hear the sound of it falling, and wasted no time before heading off towards our territory. Bypassing roads and settlements, fearing any encounter with people, Doushkin kept moving east day after day, guessing the direction by occasional landmarks, thus following a winding path and unintentionally making his journey longer. Again and again he came across forest brakes, heaps of tree trunks, creeks, marshes. He got around some of them but had to force his way through others. The forest fed him with what it could. At the beginning of his march Doushkin had encountered either a creek swollen by heavy showers or a forest lake. It was impossible to ford this obstacle in fur-lined boots and with his fur overalls on his shoulders. Ivan constructed a kind of raft out of a small log and some branches, broke off a punt pole and, having stacked his flying gear and trousers at the stern so as not to get them wet, he set off on his voyage, pushing himself along with the pole. But after travelling just a little way the raft gave a lurch, listed and overturned. The overalls, jackboots and trousers went down to the bottom. Ivan fell into the water and swam to the opposite bank. He was wearing just his blouse and underpants and had lost all his equipment except the pistol on his officer's belt. The way forward through this wild, overgrown woodland flooded by the spring thaw was a huge test of his willpower and endurance. He reached the Lovat in the daytime and waited for night before swimming across the river. There he was picked up. Doushkin's identity papers, wet though they were, had survived and this had saved him from unnecessary interrogation. They gave him time to recover and treated his wounds.

Graduates of Voroshilovgrad's school for pilots, 1938. Vasiliy Reshetnikov is on the right in the upper row.

Vasiliy with his cousin Fedor Reshetnikov, 1939.

Seated: Alexey S. Vasiliev (left) and Vasiliy Reshetnikov; standing: Alexey G. Nezhentsev (left) and Nikolay B. Chernov, May 1942.

Vasiliy Reshetnikov (left) and A. Kusnetsov. Their planes were wrecked by thunderstorms, Reshetnikov's in July 1942, Kusnetsov's in August the same year.

Georgi K. Zhukov and
Alexander E. Golovanov, 1943.

Vasiliy G. Tikhonov,
Evgeniy F. Loginov,
Alexander I. Shaposhnikov,
May 1942.

After a successful bombing raid.

From left to right: Nikolay Tarelkin, Serguey Dedushkin, Nikolay Mitrofanov, Afanasiy Terekhin, March 1942.

Vasiliy Reshetnikov, in August 1942 when he returned to the regiment having been downed after his plane was wrecked by a thunderstorm.

The Il-4 bomber. Until the arrival of the B-25, which was supplied via the Lend-Lease programme, the Il-4 remained the main workhorse of the Soviet long-range air force. Its two M-88 engines allowed it to carry up to 2500kg of bombs and it could fly up to 4000 kilometres.

An Il-4 bomber. It was less reliable and more difficult to maintain than its German counterpart, the He-111 but it was relatively easy to manufacture and around forty new aircraft were turned out every month. A total of 5256 Il-4s were built.

Dusk – time for take-off.

Heating up the engines in winter. The engines and the cockpit are covered. The hot air from the gas jet is directed into the carburettor inlets.

Preparing 500kg bombs for hanging on the Il-4 which is standing in the background.

Ten 100kg bombs lie in a row, waiting to be hung in the bomb bay of an Il-4.

An Il-4 taxiing. The navigator has his hatch open so he can help the pilot to manoeuvre.

At last some news came from our side (apparently from ADD head-quarters). They issued us with tolerable soldier's boots and black puttees, provided us with some grub for the road in the form of dry rations and handed us travel documents. They also dressed Vanya [Ivan – translator's note] in well-washed soldier's trousers and blouse. It took us two days to reach Bologiye, sometimes travelling on foot, sometimes on passing carts, and finally on a freight train. A passenger train heading for Moscow wasn't much faster.

When we reached Moscow's October station Ivan categorically refused to walk across the city, embarrassed by his appearance which was undeniably made frightening by the traces of his recent, though bandaged, wounds. 'No,' he insisted, 'how will I get by in Moscow like this? Let's wait till evening and then somehow ...'

There was no money in our pockets and there was no hope of getting a lift. What could we do? In the square by the station we saw a huge comfortable ZIS [Soviet car marque, *Zavod Imeni Stalina* or Stalin Plant – translator's note] glittering with varnish and nickel-plating. I took a chance and asked the driver if he would give us a lift to the Petrovskiy Palace. 'We haven't actually got any money ...' At these words the driver's eyes screwed up and he swung towards me with a cheeky smirk (for which I'd have loved to punch him in the nose). 'But we've got some grub,' I went on. The smile vanished and an expression of interest appeared. Our ration packs still contained a couple of pieces of lard, a loaf of stale bread and a briquette of pea concentrate. The driver glanced at all this luxury, incredible for the time, silently grabbed the pack and opened the back door of the car. Sprawled out on velvet cushions, Ivan and I felt rather like kings. Unfortunately the palace wasn't far away and the ride was a short one.

As we arrived, all those who happened to be by the front stairs of ADD headquarters pulled themselves up and respectfully stood to atten-tion, expecting the car to contain a high-ranking passenger. Seeing us, they craned their necks and dropped their jaws. And only when they found out who we were did they pick us up and lead us to the com-manders. Immediately transport was called to give us a lift: a light vehicle drove up from Monino [an airfield near Moscow – translator's note] and my commander sent a U-2 [a light Soviet-made biplane, later nicknamed 'Charlie Bedcheck' by the Americans during the Korean War – translator's note] to pick me up.

Vanya and I had become such good friends during the few days we'd spent together that it was hard to go our own ways. There was so much magnetism, kindness and sense of humour in this fascinating man that I felt exceptionally happy in his company and all the miseries of our life on the road had been imperceptibly smoothed out by his presence. We stood for a while, hugging one another and patting each other on the shoulders. Then he got into a black runabout and left. I crossed the Leningrad motorway, came out onto the airfield and ran towards the waiting U-2.

I was driven direct from the plane to the regiment commander. Tikhonov came out to meet me, hugged and kissed me. He then sat me next to him. The commander questioned me about everything that had happened, cheered me up and finally presented me with a bottle of fine wine and ordered me to get my likeness recorded, just as I was, by the regimental photographer before I returned to the dormitory.

The regiment's welcome was noisy. Flyers, navigators – both my contemporaries and senior commanders – poured out of their rooms. I was patted and tousled all over. The greatest curiosity was aroused by my puttees – everyone wanted to find out how I had become so good at wrapping my legs. After the questions – 'How was it?' and 'What happened?' – someone managed to collect glasses from all the rooms and my bottle of wine was distributed into them in eyedropper doses.

Nikolay Tarelkin was not among those who gathered in the dormitory. I asked about him and the answers came back – 'He's missing', 'Hasn't come back'. I was told that Nikolay had been grief stricken by my disappearance and two days later he himself had vanished without a trace. Back on that night of 23 July Tarelkin took off to bomb the German troops at the Don river-crossings near Konstantinovka, not far from Rostov. The day before that, after a short trip to Buzuluk where his wife Zoya then lived, he'd done a bit of flight practice around the airfield, and then he was given a combat mission for the first time since the Angerburg drama which he had come out of so well. He took off with his unfailing navigator Dedushkin and new gunner/radio-operators to replace Mitrofanov and Terekhin. The night was pitch dark and thunderstorms were raging above the Don. Only four crews out of the regiment broke through to their targets. Tarelkin's was among them. Unintentionally they struck from an altitude much lower than had been assigned. No one knew if he broke through the ground defence or what happened after that. The other crews had only seen a burning plane go down at a shallow angle and another – apparently a large one – explode on the ground at a bend in the river near Zadonsk. Only Tarelkin never made it home. Back then no traces of him could be found. Nothing turned up later either.

Barren beds stood in the dormitory room where Vasiliev and I used to live. Our trunks were kept in the storeroom, our identity papers at headquarters. I quickly put my camp life in order and began trying to get myself a new crew. But then Matsevich – the regimental surgeon, a very agile, cheerful and jocular man – popped in to see me. He was always around, knew the flying personnel very well, and in matters of health could see straight through all of us.

He didn't like the look of me. Matsevich felt something in my ribs and took me with him to the town clinic. There he discovered I had two fractures of my lower right ribs. I could have flown with these injuries, but after Matsevich's report the commander ordered me sent to our divisional rest home for a couple of weeks. The old-fashioned former country estate with its mezzanine, columns, and carvings round the doors and windows was situated in an unusually beautiful and scenic spot on a high bank of the Oka river, several kilometres away from the airfield. Cosy rooms, young nurses, calm, whiteness, care ... a miracle! And around the place there was a bright forest with a wealth of mush-rooms.

Those who had managed to make it home after wandering on foot behind enemy lines, those who were having their healing wounds cared for, those whose health was failing because of the sleepless strain of combat life were gathered there. I encountered quite a few familiar faces but the most welcome was Captain Alexander Kouznetsov, one of the best flyers in our regiment. Flight after flight he returned to the aero-drome in one piece. Shells and bullets seemed to avoid him. He'd been the first in the regiment (most likely in the whole division) to complete 100 combat sorties, and the regiment was just about to celebrate this event with a banquet. The canteen was fragrant with flowers and decorated with placards honouring the hero; a festive bustle filled the hall. But Kouznetsov went out on another flight – the second in one night. His friends had tried to talk him out of it, urging him to give it a miss ('You never know what's going to happen – you could spoil the party this way!'). But he was adamant and took off with the others for his 101st mission.

The friendly words of caution, just like Kouznetsov's stubbornness, had no bearing in logic on the events that followed but they provided an excuse for many to say sadly time and again, 'You don't say! We did tell him!' Alexander carried out the combat mission as accurately as always and had already crossed the front line on his way back when he plunged his plane into some storm clouds over Gzhatsk. Who knows why it happened. Had he been flying slightly to one side he would have sneaked through, but luck wasn't with him this time. The plane crunched and fell apart. The radio-operator fell out, opened his parachute and survived. Navigator Kiryukhin and machine-gunner Dikayev crashed. Kouznetsov himself was seriously injured. Apparently he hadn't adjusted the hip straps of his harness properly and they turned out to be loose. During the dynamic jerk after the parachute opened, one of the straps pinched his crotch. It was a dangerous injury and Kouznetsov was in pain for a long time. During a medical examination doctors detected other ailments which he had skilfully disguised up to this point. The upshot was that Kouznetsov had to give up the pilot's seat.

Sometimes with him but mostly on my own I would stand on the balcony seeing aircraft off on combat missions and welcoming them at dawn. The aerodrome was plainly visible from the high ground and from the outside its life seemed to be mysterious and full of surprises. From time to time the Germans would come over. They would do some shooting, drop two or three bombs and disappear. The ack-ack would bang away after them for quite a while but then it too would calm down. If the bombs had fallen outside the aerodrome landing would continue. But sometimes they would explode on target and everyone would be sent off to another airfield while ours sank into darkness. A watchful calm would settle over it.

A little further east, next to the main aerodrome and also on the bank of the Oka, a fake airfield copying the layout of the main one in almost every detail gleamed invitingly with landing strip lights, but it never tempted the Germans. Once, however, coming back home from a combat mission in heavy and impenetrable rain, Pavel Petrovich Radchuk ended up there. Searching for his aerodrome, at long last he noticed the lights of a landing T flickering in the torrential rain. He reduced throttle, managed to drop the undercarriage and landed. The plane smashed through sand dunes and riverside scrub, ran into a small gully and, raising its tail, stood on its nose. Pavel Petrovich was embarrassed although no one reproached him or even joked at his expense – his authority as an airman and a fighter was too high for this mistake to touch him. After all, nothing particularly bad had happened: the plane was rolled to the parking bay, fixed up and sent off for a flight a couple of days later. There were many false aerodromes set up back then – nearly every division had one. The Germans noticed this obsession and, their sense of humour not yet exhausted, flew over our neighbour's fake in a small but tight formation, dropped a wooden bomb on it and went straight from there to shatter the operating one according to all rules of engagement!

The enemy built us quite a few fake targets too – and displayed a high level of engineering skill in the process. In general we suffered no inconvenience from them, but once when a large group of ADD regiments approached Bobruisk aerodrome the Germans dropped a bunch of candle-bombs above its fake twin and a few minutes later staged several explosions and a couple of fires. The leader of the group responsible for illumination, thinking that someone had jumped the queue, took the bait and dropped his candle-bombs over the spot where the German ones were still shining. Others added their share too and the rest ran on automatic. Trusting their leader and tempted by the excellent illumination of the target, the striking echelon, no longer bothering with precise positioning, pounced on the 'aerodrome' and there were a few more fires and explosions, which were in fact staged by the Germans. Flak guns fired, searchlight beams crossed the skies, but the real operating aerodrome full of planes, to protect which this whole carnival had been set in train, remained quiet and dark, showing no signs of life. It was unscathed.

As it turned out later, quite a few of the navigators and plane commanders had had some doubt about the validity of the target, but the whole spectacle was so immense and effective that any suspicion of the possibility of a mass error evaporated. The herd instinct inherent in us all and the habit of unanimity taught over many years didn't fail this time. Could anyone imagine leaving the main group, flying a bit further and giving the real target a work over while everyone else was so enthusiastically pounding another spot? No one wanted to trust either the aerial photographs or the intelligence reports. But there was no choice. The bombers had to visit Bobruisk once more. This time we performed properly and the real aerodrome burned and exploded for real.

My ribs were giving me no more trouble and it was time to move back to the regiment. For my retraining the commander chose a small out-of-the-way aerodrome somewhere beyond Gous-Khroustalnoye. I went over the training area once, practised take-off and landing, and felt my former flying skills had come back. I was in full combat form.

Petr Arkhipov – a navigator – was the first to join my new crew. He was sturdy and well built, moderately tall and fair haired with a handsome, kind and manly face. He was a bit older than I. He had already made several harrowing flights but then suddenly left his crew and requested a transfer to any other one. It seemed he had been fortunate in his commander – a seasoned and experienced pilot, a 'Russian fairy-tale knight', Major Sourov. His height, gaze and commanding conduct were simply admirable. But it had been beyond Petr's power to drive this luminary onto a shooting target – he would be doing his best to slip past it sideways. And when the navigator, not having reached the target aimed for, refused to drop the bombs, the major grabbed the handle of the emergency drop himself and got rid of them in two movements, explaining to the 'halfwit' in a didactic tone, 'Remember, you blockhead, they don't shoot cardboard from down there ...'

Once, pleading poor engine performance, Sourov ordered Arkhipov to dump the bombs into the Oka river, within our own territory. Arkhipov, feeling that the rhythm of the flight was in fact quite normal, urged the commander to go at least beyond the front line or as a last resort to land with the bombs, for there was no real danger. But Sourov got rid of the bombs this time too, without his navigator. No engine faults were detected on the ground, and this time Arkhipov mutinied. As for Sourov, he somehow managed a painless exit from the regiment.

It was amazing but Tikhonov – a strict commander and a man of principle –was sometimes inexplicably indulgent towards 'luminaries'. As far as I can remember the very same Sourov had come to us for a short probation period but Tikhonov, using his privilege, had gone and got him included in the regiment's core establishment. More than one notable guest flyer had joined us to pick up combat experience but they were more trouble than they were worth. Having had a little taste of war, many of them strove impatiently to get out of it as fast as they could. But there were also serious and practical probationers. There was a period when navigators, trainers, instructors and department heads from flying schools and colleges began to frequent the regiment. Those admitted to flying took part in operations; others studied war experiences based on headquarters documentation. Tikhonov sat probationers next to me quite a few times. Once I flew with a Major Kompan, a flying school instructor. Having heard and read plenty about how our warriors when going into attack at the front would always shout 'For the Motherland! For Stalin!', he dropped my bombs somewhere over Orel with this war cry, just at the moment when the plane was turning round. 'What did you go and do?' I yelled in despair. Having lost my temper I cursed him foully all the way back to the ground, but he kept assuring me stubbornly that the bombs had exploded on the railway station tracks. They couldn't have got there. The radio-operators knew better: the bombs had fallen on the city.

By the time I was mustering my new crew Nikolay Mitrofanov had returned from an NKVD camp. Had he come back a bit earlier he would have joined his former crew – Tarelkin's – and who knows, he could have died along with him, but now he was assigned to me. This, however, didn't in any way increase his chances of a happier fate.

Afanasiy Terekhin appeared over the horizon too. His lone trip across enemy-occupied territory wasn't distinguished by impetuosity. Terekhin marched in no hurry, thinking over his every step. His in-flight crew rations released him from the necessity of popping into villages but he obtained information from people he came across. He spent his nights in the forest, or sometimes in village bath-huts. Once he ran into a *polizei* detachment and, firing back at them, hid in the forest. He was tracked down by partisans who, learning the circumstances of Terekhin's odyssey, help him cross the front line to our side. The filters of the special NKVD camps were waiting for him on our side. Having freed himself of the suspicion of being 'unreliable', Terekhin aroused the commanders' interest with his intellectual maturity and erudition, and he was suddenly offered the position of the camp's radio platoon commander. No objections were raised. His new career took off and soon Afanasiy was appointed company *politruk*. The only problem was that his Communist party membership card was still with his regiment. It was kind of awkward to have a political commissar without a party membership card, and they had to give him a week's leave to return to the regiment to pick up it and his gear. But things didn't turn out that way. The regiment commander immediately took him in hand and appointed him machine-gunner in Sasha Romanov's crew. The NKVD camp men kept quiet, remembering that it was better not to mess with Tikhonov, and it seemed the loss wasn't really a big deal for them. As a result Terekhin fought in the regiment till the end of the war.

My crew was also reinforced by an aerial gunner. Vasya Shtefourko joined us, a young, chubby-faced chap with big blue eyes and an ingenuous smile on his plump lips. His whole countenance shone with childish spontaneity, cordiality and trustworthiness – few men can manage that. He knew his trade, held out valiantly when fighting in the air, and was a willing and diligent lad.

My first sortie with the new crew was, of course, to Vyazma railway junction – our firing range as we called it. This target always provided really good experience for both novices and crews rehabilitating after a break from combat flying. It lay not far off, gave heavy fire and, because it was always crammed with trains, readily burned and blew up.

CHAPTER SEVEN

Old Debts

At that difficult time nearly the whole Air Force was thrown into the Stalingrad defence operation. In the south the enemy avalanche, drawing in powerful reserves from all directions, was moving heavily and menacingly towards the banks of the Volga. It had to be stopped at any cost. Seemingly there was no more important task than this one. But the ADD commander, mindful of Stalin's demands and his debt to him, removed from the Stalingrad missions just over 200 hand-picked crews and directed them at Berlin, Bucharest, Warsaw, Stettin, Königsberg and Danzig.

August 1942 was hot and the night-time thunderstorms – sometimes single ones, sometimes in clusters – were still the main obstacle and a deadly torment to us on our way to those remote cities. Berlin did not open itself up to every one of our planes and certainly not to all of us at once. Of course it was the most important and the most prestigious target, although on the scale of difficulty some of the others were no easier. Because of orders known only to our commanders, our targets changed from flight to flight. We raided the closer targets from our base airfields but would fly to the most remote ones via intermediate airstrips near the front. Initially I was assigned Königsberg again. My old and exuberant acquaintance hadn't changed much, but it had gained more firepower, would meet me earlier and wouldn't waste flak shells. We floundered in thunderstorms over half of the way there and I remember them better than all the fire from ground and naval batteries. The ack-ack fire, for all its might, was of relatively short duration. The city was barely visible. It lay in darkness because the searchlights hampered visibility and not all the candle-bombs could find their way to it. But Arkhipov pinpointed the target, managed to aim and let off a salvo.

Our encounter with Warsaw was different. The city was as bright as day under dozens of illuminating bombs. Not only streets and squares but also house roofs and church spires were visible in the transparent air. The flak artillery fired with all its might but all by guesswork and at random without actually spotting its targets. Searchlight beams swayed monotonously and indecisively, not landing on anyone. It seemed the city had accepted its doom and was defending itself unwillingly, as if begging for mercy. Arkhipov set us on our attack heading and led us towards the central train station, which was our assigned target. Its tracks, crammed to the limit with German troop trains, were visible through the shroud of fire and smoke. Our bombs sank through the air, hitting the ground and making it glitter with the white fire of explosions. We retired quietly, as if from a training ground. We kept glancing back and could see Warsaw burning for quite a while. The dotted lines of exploding bombs and the auroras of major explosions still flashed in various parts of the city.

Even Budapest didn't fire at us like a capital city: it was much weaker than some provincial cities, let alone Danzig and Königsberg. That night Budapest was scary not for its ground defence but for the wild raging of thunderstorms over the Carpathians, blocking our way to the targets. It was terrifying to approach the wall of fire with its torrents of water and snow. I was just about to turn back but then decided to divert a bit to the right and it seemed to me that a gap loomed ahead. Had I known what was going to happen I wouldn't have gone into it. It led us even further off course and drew us into a brutal ordeal in which the plane seemed about to cave in. Then conditions became easier and we suddenly entered free space. Budapest peeped out from the moon-washed mist. It was already being bombed, although very few of our aircraft had managed to break through the thundery walls. The ground defence started up: artillery fire came from large-calibre guns over a wide area and searchlights smeared the sky from one end to the other, their confused tangle of beams looking like long paint brushes.

We'd lost a fair bit of time on the detour around the thunderstorm and now I could only wonder in alarm whether I would actually manage to make it back to our territory. For quite a while my fuel tanks had been less than half full. There was still a fair way to fly to Budapest – about 20 minutes – plus 20 minutes to return to the spot I was at now. No, no more flying forward. I wavered. I turned sharply back and yelled to the navigator, 'Petya [Petr – translator's note], it's better to miss Budapest than the front line! Look for another good target!'

'Commander, where the hell will I find a good one? The ones there are not worth our bombs. We'll find what we need on the way back.'

Yes, he was right. I looked at the map, then at the ground. There was absolute calm down there. Lights were on in the cities. Most likely everyone was sleeping. I couldn't stop tapping the fuel gauge and counting the kilometres, minutes and litres. It would be great to get rid of the bombs now but they were already assigned to Kovel, where there was a whole spider of railways along which the Germans were moving their troops and matériel from west to east and south. The Carpathian storm front had thinned out a little and we pierced it in almost a straight line. At last we reached Kovel and there we became lighter by nearly a whole tonne. My fears gradually evaporated. In broad daylight, sucking out the last litres of fuel, we landed on our airstrip.

The *Sovinformburo* [Soviet Information Bureau, the Soviet news agency during the Second World War – translator's note] newspaper communiqué reported that on the night of 5 September 1942 bomber raids on Budapest and Königsberg conducted in difficult weather conditions caused numerous fires and major explosions. It was also reported that all planes except for one came back home. It was interesting to speculate who didn't come back – maybe Vikhorev from a sister regiment, Loukienok or Doushkin from another division? Was it my fleeting but cordial friend Vanya Doushkin, whose crew had like mine been tragically unfortunate during the encounter with the thunderstorms? And were these three the only ones who had not made it home that day?

Doushkin came home a month later. Having spent too much time on a detour, he had continued to fly headlong towards Budapest but had not had enough fuel even to reach the front line. There was no way out and he crash-landed in the Belorussian forest. He lost his plane but led his crew back to the regiment in one piece. Vikhorev was a long time coming back and Loukienok was only liberated from captivity at the end of the war.

Extremely difficult though the raids on Budapest were, they were not what excited the minds of the Soviet people in those days. The *Sovinformburo* had already twice reported raids on Berlin. This overwhelming news enthralled information agencies across the world. Germany was squirming, trying to belittle the bombing of its capital city and to give events a rather different spin, having recently issued public assurances that the Soviet Air Force had been completely destroyed. But the situation was serious.

On the night of 27 August 1942 the ADD simultaneously struck at military-industrial targets in Berlin, Danzig and Königsberg. Our newspapers reported that all our planes had returned home. But what about Evgeniy Fedorov, our headline Hero of the Soviet Union, a man who would get that title a second time: didn't he count?

The weather on the night of the 27th was terrible. The Baltic seemed to be on fire from the waves right up to the sky. Crews who deviated to the left of the planned route managed to break through with great difficulty, some making it further than others. Some exhausted their potential over Königsberg, others over Danzig, and only those who found the occasional gap in the storms went on to bomb Berlin. Fedorov was not short of experience but even he was caught by the storm. His plane broke apart and the crew barely survived to make it home on foot.

The night before 10 September a new strike on Berlin and Budapest was being prepared. The weather en route to both capitals was expected to be difficult and senior commanders rushed around their planning tables shifting crews from objective to objective. I was assigned Budapest again. Berlin promised to be impassable. As before, at the crack of dawn, having hung bombs in the bays and taken technicians on board, we headed towards a front-line aerodrome, Louga, near Toropets. We went by a zigzag route, avoiding towns and villages, hugging the ground. Immediately after landing we taxied to the woods, turned the machines' tails to the thickets and pushed them by hand under the green tree tops, camouflaging them with nets and branches. The technicians refuelled the aircraft and screwed detonators into the bombs. We fell into a light sleep, waking for the endless briefings and updates. German reconnaissance planes came over the aerodrome and our fighter planes rushed after them. Machine guns rapped in the air. Then the Luftwaffe disappeared. We sat quietly, not sticking our noses out.

The heat was unseasonably steamy. At last it was time. Sweating all over and swearing, we pulled on our fur overalls and fur-lined jackboots. The take-off went according to schedule. One after another the bombers, loaded up to the limit, taxied out of their forest shelters, their engines roaring. They took off with difficulty from the short and bumpy dirt airstrip into the white-hot air. Thick dust lengthened the intervals between take-offs but the crews hurried into the air as quickly as possible because German reconnaissance planes were making circles above us again. Their bombers would come around too but they would be too late – the aerodrome would be empty. At the starting line they poked a red signal flag in my face. Then someone from headquarters rushed along a wing to the cockpit, yelled in my ear, 'You've got Berlin!' and jumped off.

At the same moment a white signal flag appeared along the take-off line. I burned up the runway and released the brakes. We ran for quite a while, jolting and swaying over humps. Speed increased slowly. We hung in the air after the last hump and kept crawling above the scrub and tree tops for a long while after that, trying to climb away from the ground.

'Petya,' I said to the navigator at last, 'we're off to Berlin.' Arkhipov let off a complicated phrase in reply and began unfolding different maps – we always carried them to cover every eventuality. The course layout had survived from previous sorties. It gave us a preliminary bearing which was adjusted later. Machine-gunner/radio-operators Mitrofanov and Shtefourko also understood the meaning of the change and stood by their weapons, concentrating.

The flight was tense. The northern sky was bright and clear, the front line a stone's throw away. The plane clawed its way up with difficulty. We were supposed to be escorted by fighters in this area but they were nowhere to be seen. Perhaps that was for the best, lest we be taken for Germans. We gradually flew into the night, already over enemy-occupied territory. Flak guns shot up here and there. It was good to pinpoint them from afar because that way you got a chance to avoid the zones of ground fire. Our route lay across Lithuania towards the coast line, then, with a minor bend, turned leftwards above the Baltic Sea to a point south of Bornholm Island and past Stettin towards Berlin.

According to our commander's assessment, this raid was later considered the hardest, in terms of weather conditions, of all the Berlin operations. Most likely it was too. The Baltic coast was enveloped by thunder clouds and there was a storm front across the Baltic Sea. The plane was flying in heavy turbulence. Lightning flashed ahead and to the right. We turned left a bit, then realigned more and more frequently and tried to get higher. Against my will visions of my recent disaster kept appearing to me in this new turbulence. God forbid it should happen again. We couldn't tune in to the German radio stations because they were still far away, possibly not operating at all.

The elements gradually quietened down and we shifted back on course, returning to our assigned heading. According to calculations we should have been above the coastline. It would have been good to get a look at a reliable reference point that I might recognise from the previous time I'd travelled this way but there was no chance and we had to feel our way. We pulled up a bit higher and sat in our oxygen masks. Soon stars begin to gleam: Petr adjusted his sextant and caught the star Altair through the astro hatch. Stellar reckoning is not very precise but we were on the right bearing within the acceptable limits of deviation. I didn't give the radio-operators anything to do; we couldn't go on air. They listened to the ground and kept watch.

Over the sea, because of lack of practice, I got the impression that the timbre of the engines had changed. I listened to them, peered into the instrument dials, but the pointers stood motionless, the engines working smoothly. The altitude was about 6,500 metres, and I didn't climb any higher, not even a metre. I didn't want to have to enable the second gear of the pump gun and subject the engines to unnecessary load and fuel consumption.

More sheet lightning on the right. We gradually entered broken and then dense, bumpy clouds. I turned on the landing light in order to have a good look around: an oblique stream of snow crossed the light. Icing over would be the last straw! We watched the wing edges and the tail unit. The plane lurched roughly along its course; it tossed and then leant on a wing. But all these problems passed. The sky opened up and the horizon peeped out. Bornholm had drifted aside somewhere in the gloom. Stettin was visible ahead of us on the left. There was fire from large-calibre guns and we detoured around it. This was the final stretch. Berlin was still far away but there ahead was a solid wall of glittering points of gunfire. White bristles of searchlight beams rose like ghosts in the night mist. There were more than 200 of them. Shells burst at our flight altitude. How could we get in there? Someone was already tangled in the searchlight beams – he seemed to fall and then to straighten up. He twisted in the lights and glittered like a little star. And heavy high-explosive shells came at him over and over again. This fellow seemed to have escaped but then two more latched on ... Losing altitude we flew under the shell bursts – this tactic had saved us more than once. The likelihood of a direct hit was less than that of destruction by an explosion. At 5,000 metres we lined up with the horizon. It was not possible to go lower – we might bump into a barrage balloon.

Berlin itself gradually began to show up. Bursts flashed down on the ground, fires showed crimson here and there. Petya Arkhipov was at his bombsight. Somehow he could see the paths along which we could approach the target. I only heard his commands: 'Five to the left ... Three to the right ...' At the last command I froze. The plane was inside a solid maelstrom of fire. Drop! The bombs exploded along the railway station installations. There was a sharp flash and then a bright blaze of fire. What was that? No chance to find out now. The searchlight beams were stretching towards us, reconnoitring the sky. Shell bursts came closer, following the lights. Fortunately a small clump of clouds had appeared. We flew above it and escaped, pursued by chaotic firing. But it was not over yet. A pair of night-fighters had latched onto our tail outside the ring of anti-aircraft fire. Four long exhaust flames guided them towards us. We flew a broken course, changed altitude, but they followed us, never falling behind, and winked at each other with yellow lights. When they got dangerously close I abruptly turned around towards them. The Messerschmitt 110s dashed past, lost us and disappeared in the dark. We returned to our previous course.

The weather had improved and the ground was visible more and more frequently, its landmarks coming into focus. Some cities took shots at us, but we stayed away from them and looked towards the blazing east with alarm. The dawn would catch us well before the front line and an encounter between a single bomber and a fascist fighter plane would bode no good. We switched to contour flight: it would be hard to pinpoint us from above against the green carpet of the ground and the flak gunners would have no time to catch us in their sights. Only when the front line had flashed underneath did we climb again. Mitrofanov tapped with the radio key, demanding to know which aerodrome we should go to. Ours was closed by fog. They gave us Kalinin and that's where we landed.

There were quite a few aircraft on the parking area – not only was Serpukhov closed but everyone had run short of fuel as well. The engines grew silent. Calm. We got out of our cockpits and, in no rush, wearily stretched our muscles and fell on the grass. Arms spread, I looked into the clear sky – quiet, endlessly deep and eternal – in a state of bliss. Nearby, flyers and navigators, greeting each other as if after a long separation, were gathered awaiting a lift to the canteen. Puffing tobacco smoke and furiously gesticulating, they were discussing the Berlin adventure. But not all of them had arrived yet – the landings continued. I jumped to my feet and walked towards the other flyers. I edged my way into the conversation: 'Well, admit it, who was under fire at point-blank range at about 7,000 metres? They were shooting at one of our guys!'

'Yes, who were they after?' Other witnesses of that joyless scene joined in. After a short pause a squadron commander standing next to me, Alexander Vavilov from a sister regiment, suddenly hugged my shoulders and with an embarrassed half-smile he said, 'It was me, Vasya.' That was really something, taking such a torrent of fire and getting away unscathed – it was like a resurrection from the dead! He hadn't let them shoot him to pieces but had wriggled out of the situation, carried out his mission and driven home a plane slashed up by the splinters of heavy shells. Can you believe the Il-4? It had been heavily damaged but it was still all right, like a battle stallion, and had never wavered over the target. It had been loyal to its commander all the way to landing.

Evgeniy Fedorov had made it home too. Approaching Berlin, he had been attacked by fighter planes who intercepted him, but he managed to beat them off by manoeuvring and machine-gun fire. Then he headed for the attack, hit the target and returned. But Major Lomov – a sturdy and hot-tempered pilot, a veteran of the Finnish War from the leading cohort of Tikhonov's hand-picked men – hadn't come back. He didn't make it to the main target but struck Stettin where the Germans damaged both of his engines with flak fire. The plane flew back losing altitude. Barely dragging himself to Lithuania, Lomov landed on the large Lake Rubikiai. The landing was hard and only he and the machine-gunner, Mikhail Belousov, survived. They were captured by Lithuanian *politzei* and ahead of them lay torture and a long captivity, right up until the very end of the war.

CHAPTER EIGHT

Russian Lessons

The aerial operation targeting deep into the enemy rear was coming to an end. Bucharest was next on the schedule but some of the crews had already been switched from remote targets onto Stalingrad missions. The regiment was preparing to transfer to Rasskazovo, an operational aerodrome closer to the fighting zone, for we had been able to make only one sortie per night from Serpukhov and Rasskazovo would allow us to make two. The commander ordered me to head to the Moscow aircraft works to pick up a new machine and fly it back to the regiment as fast as possible. 'And it will be yours,' he said. My previous aircraft, the Berlin one, was being taken over by a young crew.

Back then working-class men didn't live in luxury, to put it mildly, and it would have been impolite to go to the works empty handed. Responding to my call, the flying personnel shook out all their stored provisions, I managed to buy some bits and pieces, and the canteen people weren't stingy either. Now I could take off. At dawn Gleb Bazhenov delivered us to the works' aerodrome and then headed back without even turning off his engines.

We dropped into the assembly shop and were met by a deafening rumble and squeal of metal. Old men and women of various ages were deep in concentration around aircraft which were being brought to life. Such a scene would have been common at any plant even in peacetime, but here boys of between ten and fifteen were busily engaged in riveting, metalwork and ancillary jobs: that was a bit scary. Noticing the flyers they forgot about their work and kind of swaggered up to us, smiling shyly. With the slightly forced formality of the working class, they put out their still-delicate palms, which were all covered with grazes and cuts, to greet us with manly handshakes. They all smoked, the little rascals, and only a fool would have tried to talk them out of the habit.

Our tobacco moved into their pockets and everyone began to smoke heavily. The tobacco was strong. The smaller boys began to cough and their eyes watered, but they quickly recovered and started to praise the 'good baccy' with the air of connoisseurs. Gradually a friendly chat on equal terms got going. We shared out chocolate, sugar, bread and sausages; everybody got just a little bit but even this was a great joy for them. Now they turned into real kids – so small, defenceless, no longer representing the working class. Their fathers were at the front but many hadn't been heard from for a long time. Some of the boys had already lost their fathers. And nearly all their mothers worked here in the plant workshops. The boys asked us to take them to the front, assuring us they could shoot and do reconnaissance just as well as real soldiers.

Our brand new Il-4 was ready and, having taken charge of it in accordance with all the rules, we took off. After making a couple of test circles over the plant to make sure the plane was behaving itself and its systems were in working order we set out for Serpukhov. The aerodrome was empty. Wasting no time, we picked up the technicians and staff servicemen who had stayed behind and then flew on to Rasskazovo. Life there had quickly settled into a routine. The regiment had already managed to occupy the location and secure a mission; it was finishing off preparations for a combat sortie. We had to catch up. On the night after our arrival we managed to carry out two strikes on pivotal centres of the enemy's defence. From now on it would be like this all the time: two sorties every night, bombing from a height of 2,000 metres – sometimes hitting German fortified sectors, sometimes targeting troops on the outskirts of Stalingrad. It was intricate work. The bombs inevitably exploded in the immediate vicinity of our troops, but we never plugged any of our own men (nor, by the way, did any of the ADD during the whole war).

The front line and target pointers were usually marked with fires and flares, by agreement with the land commanders. Sometimes targets were highlighted by artillery fire. But this time we came across something new: on approach to the combat area every wave of bombers was met by two vertical searchlight beams piercing the sky like bayonets as if forming a gate through which the stream of aircraft could head. This immediately instilled confidence in the accuracy of our route to the target and assuaged our fears for the safety of our troops.

The first pair of searchlight beams was stationary. When we approached the second its bayonets slowly tilted towards the enemy lines, pressing close to the ground and criss-crossing right over the target. The bombs were dropped right onto the crosshair of light. Then the light bayonets soared into the sky to meet another bomber formation before laying over the target again. The targets were situated so close to the front line that the actual drop occurred over our troops and the bombs flew forward, following their trajectory to explode on the enemy's position. The enemy ground defence consisted of *Oerlikons* and other ack-ack equipment. It was shelled by front-line artillery before we arrived and then stayed silent for some time, but when it came back to life everything began again. German fighter planes prowled the area close to the front line. Sometimes oncoming machine-gun traces crossed the sky but mostly from long range and with no result.

A full moon lit the ground so well at that time that it was hard to resist the temptation to descend close to the earth, flying along the route home at an altitude of only two or three dozen metres above the quiet steppes, rivers, villages and groves. There was something fabulous, mysterious and unreal about this landscape. More than once I got right down to the ground and felt the excitement of making such an impetuous slide across it. But on one occasion Mitrofanov said, 'There's a fighter plane following us,' and all those lovely visions instantly disappeared. Calm gave way to a splutter of orders. The guys grabbed their machine guns and my fingers clenched the control wheel. I turned left a bit.

'Where is he?'

'He's gone a bit off to the side.'

I turned a bit more. 'And now?'

'He's turned as well. Looks like he's cutting across.' Oh, the bastard! I returned to the previous course.

'He's tailing us again,' Mitrofanov said.

'Looks like he's closing in!' Shtefourko added. What the hell was going on? Where was he? I turned my head back, trying to see out this jackal for myself. Yes, it looked as though he was following us with one or other of his lights on. I moved left a bit – he did the same. I headed right – so did he.

'That's a star!' I yelled angrily and added something unrepeatable. There was a large, bright star over the southern horizon sitting among a few dim ones; at the least movement of the plane this star seemed to be alive and moving, deceiving us. We might have done something dangerously silly in attempting to evade this 'pursuit'. The moonlit landscape had lost all its attractiveness now and we began to climb.

September was coming to an end. We had a full schedule of work and day blended into night. They were tearing us apart, demanding advances now on one sector of the front, now on another. Strictly speaking that was a job for the ground-attack planes and close-range bombers but they were still in short supply and strained to breaking point. In addition, there were no night flyers among them.

But our main task was stagnating. Troop and armaments trains were coming in via the railway junctions and stations day and night. The

Germans were pushing them over from the Fatherland, withdrawing them from other fronts and pouring this countless force towards Stalingrad. No one but us could reach them. At last we left Rasskazovo and returned to Serpukhov. From there we fanned out on missions to both remote and close targets, pouncing on those herds of railway carriages, making two sorties a night.

The scenery here was hotter and harsher. From just one point in the clear air of a dark night I could see fires and white splashes of explosions in Minsk, Smolensk, Orsha and even Mogilev and Vitebsk. The Germans suffered significant losses in our attacks but their ground defence was becoming more and more dangerous. Bryansk and Smolensk stood like fortresses – the skies above them boiled, not promising anyone easy success. Our losses began to mount. October was far too greedy – Pankratov, Lakomkin, Lysenko and their crews, three men each, didn't make it home. Medvedev's crew, the most experienced, vanished without a trace. Slovesnik came away from his target in flames. He kept control of the aircraft while his crewmen bailed out but ran out of altitude for himself and burned up during landing. The ones shot up over Bryansk dragged themselves to the partisans' domains which covered huge areas around the city, and in a day or two they were brought back to their aerodromes. Smolensk province wasn't the same – it was mostly open terrain, densely settled by the Germans and crowded with *polizei* forces. Few of our men had any luck there. Very rarely someone would become a POW; more often people died; only a handful managed to get away.

No matter how important these missions were for hitting the enemy's reserves and logistics, another and perhaps the most important aim had now come to the fore – to win mastery of the air. The Germans had begun the war in control of the skies and had been trying with all their might to hold on to their advantage. Our superiors preferred to see our Air Force hanging overhead and directly supporting land attacks. As a result our aircraft sometimes spent their time not so much supporting land troops as desperately beating off the numerically superior enemy forces. This prevented Russian land troops from raising their heads and making an attack. Stalin had already noticed, and on the eve of the Stalingrad counteroffensive he reminded Zhukov in a telegram: 'The experience of war against the Germans has shown that an operation against them can be won only in the event of us having superiority in the air.' But the Soviet Air Force wasn't strong enough in numbers to overwhelm the Luftwaffe.

Aerial combat was not quietening down. In fact it was raging with new ferocity on the fronts around Stalingrad. The bombers and ground-attack planes pounced on the German airfields from dawn to dusk.

Given the almost equal numbers of forces and the continuing qualitative superiority of the fascist aircraft, mastery of the air could be snatched from the enemy only by superhuman exertion, but it had to be achieved at any cost. In this campaign the long-range bombers were charged with carrying out the kind of tasks at which they were strongest – raids on enemy bomber groups based in the deep rear. Some airfields, especially permanent ones crammed with aircraft of various types, were defended no more lightly than large railway junctions.

Not everyone was lucky enough to force his way to a destination and remain unscathed. These targets were more complicated to attack than large, spread-out ones. The accuracy of a strike had to be higher in order to hit aircraft parking areas, which provided fairly narrow, small targets. Fuel and ammo dumps were no simpler. Because of the special features of these targets strike altitudes had to be lower and therefore closer to the barrels of the ack-ack guns. It was good when the planes stood wing to wing on the ground: if you set one on fire others would catch too. But often planes were scattered all over an aerodrome, standing in caponiers, and we had to reach them with rotary cluster bombs. Fires would break out in different corners of an airfield but not as densely as we wanted and we wouldn't know how many of the aircraft that didn't catch fire were damaged. We had to make repeat strikes because it didn't take the Germans long to return airstrips and parking areas to service.

The intensity of aerial operations grew. The regiment raided enemy airfields night after night – even the twenty-fifth anniversary of the October Revolution wasn't an exception. All that evening – 7th November – and the following morning Commissar Alexey Choulkov didn't make it home. He was listed as the commissar of Uroutin's squadron but the whole regiment considered him its own, stirring un-intentional jealousy among other political officers at the regimental level who didn't belong to the flying personnel.

Authority – especially of the commissar's kind – is a tricky thing to maintain. The criteria for a command position don't work in this area at all, even if all the external signs of respect for rank are observed. In war the fixed price of respect is usually deeds; if words are to carry weight, they have to be lively, not dead or formal ones. Alexey Petrovich was far from being a conventional commissar. Outwardly he was quite low key, not at all given to rhetoric. He didn't try to beguile anyone with lectures or edifications but was renowned as an excellent combat flyer with a robust natural wit and a kind heart. He was steadfast in combat. Being a loyal soldier of his country he had been through the Finnish War and had fought in the Great Patriotic War from its first day. Now the number of his sorties was into its second century. He'd flown along with the rest of us as an ordinary plane commander but he liked to be the first to take off. Or maybe he didn't actually like it that much, seeing no tactical advantage in it, but considered the place at the head of the squadron his own.

After a raid on Orsha aerodrome Choulkov was within 30 minutes of home when his right engine began to stall: it thudded and coughed and he had to turn it off. Unfortunately the propeller kept rotating, a slide became inevitable and the plane began to descend slowly. They nearly ran out of altitude over the front line but Alexey and his faithful navigator Grigoriy Choumash found a fighter airstrip near Kalouga and decided to land straight away. At night such aerodromes were closed – they didn't even have facilities for night landings – but a T of after-hours oil lamps was burning and Alexey successfully closed in along the landing strip. However, the aerodrome was tiny and had been disguised with haystacks and dummy animals. When the plane reached the very end of the base the machine-gunners saw this 'rural landscape' and all yelled 'A dummy airstrip!' Alexey responded to their cry and although the next moment Choumash yelled 'Land!', it was too late. The left engine kept dragging the plane onward at full throttle but it was unable to restore the lost speed and altitude, especially as one section of the landing gear remained unretracted. During the turn beyond the airstrip the plane touched the pine trees with a wing, dropped to the ground and caught fire. The flames crept towards the pilot's cockpit. Choulkov was wounded and couldn't get up by himself; he burned. Radio-operator Dyakov died in the fire too. Machine-gunner Glazounov got out through the gun slot in the turret, overcoming pain from his injuries and grazes, but he couldn't reach his commander through the fire. Choumash had been thrown out of his navigator's shell and broke his hip in two places in the fall. He crawled away from the fire, bandaged his bleeding wounds with shreds of underwear and waited for help. It came from the aerodrome. After many operations his leg became noticeably shorter and he had to bid farewell to flying. Alexey Choulkov was posthumously awarded the title of Hero of the Soviet Union.

At that time I was flying tirelessly. My spirit was challenged, my nerves stretched, but my internal discipline and good sense seemed to stay with me. The crew had done some good flying together. Petya Arkhipov carried out his bombing quietly and without missing: we rarely came home without leaving visible signs of damage on our targets.

On the way back on a good night, when the plane was flying to schedule and nothing and no one threatened us, a song would drift through the headphones, quietly and cautiously at high notes – a gentle, peaceful song, apparently born in the very heart of Russia. Our necklace microphones were switched into the onboard intercom direct. There were no intermediate buttons and Petr's voice was heard by everyone.

Initially the song was unfamiliar to me but it was easy to pick up the lyrics and the tune and I began to sing along as second voice. Petr's romantic mood didn't raise any particular questions: that was the time when he got acquainted with the very cute and diminutive Nadenka in Serpukhov and she later became his wife for the rest of his life. It was good to have singing during a flight; it made the time go faster and by morning those of us who sang weren't too sleepy from the monotonous buzz of engines.

It turned out that during the last several dozen sorties we hadn't been hit by a single shell splinter or bullet, despite the fact that every night the German ground defence had been desperately hammering us, not to mention the danger posed by flak and occasional swoops by fighters. There was no guarantee of a favourable outcome, but so far fate had been gracious. Someone coined the somewhat slippery word 'invulnerables' for our crew and the divisional newspaper wrote about us. But we were vulnerable – and how!

One stormy night at the end of autumn 1942 I got into powerful turbulence on the approach to the aerodrome. A cold front was driving torn, whirling clouds from the north and a dull moon aggravated the gloomy and forbidding scene. The plane tumbled from one wing to the other. Regardless of my efforts it sometimes soared upwards and then ducked down. The instrument arrows swung madly across the scales. It was better not to chase them but to rely instead on the steadier gyroscopic horizon indicator. Watching it closely I confidently flew through the clouds, gradually climbing. The indicator bar had frozen as expected but then it slowly began to move up, showing that the plane was switching to a descent that was too steep. The natural reaction in these circumstances was to pull the control wheel; the bar continued to move and, trying to end this near-dive, I pulled forcefully, even excessively. The bar didn't react. At the same instant I was gripped by a premonition of imminent disaster – the speed gauge was creeping towards zero and the altitude wasn't changing. But it was too late. The engines stalled and I felt the plane duck down and sway to the right. A spin! What have I done? Science came to my aid: I pedalled against the spin, gassed forward as far as I could, pushed the control wheel away and began to wait. The plane should go into rotation mode, and only after two or three turns, or even more than that (after all it was a bomber, not a fighter), it would be capable of getting out of the manoeuvre. But did we have enough altitude?

There was eerie silence, nothing but the hissing of air. The guys panicked and, not knowing what was going on, began hailing, talking over each other: 'Commander, commander!' I, clenching my teeth, held the controls tightly and waited till the very last moment to move them, hoping to avoid a smack into the ground. Still spinning, we left the clouds. A black overgrown gully in a dark-grey plateau flashed straight in front of my eyes. I was running out of altitude and couldn't take any more chances. I carefully turned the wheel and pulled it to me: the nose lifted up. I pulled with more confidence. The plane obeyed the controls and stopped spinning, and when it levelled at about 100 metres or maybe even 50 the engines began to pull as one, dragging the machine forward. The horizon bar was dead. It had stuck at the very top, tilted and frozen. It had stopped working, the bloody thing, but so treacherously, so smoothly and gradually, as if nothing was happening to it. 'What's wrong with you chaps? Everything's fine.' That was all I could manage to say. I was greeted by complete silence.

I entered the landing circle. Someone was on fire on the bank across the Oka. Later we found out it was Ivan Shoubin, a young, handsome, blue-eyed, blond chap who had not been with us long but was a robust flyer. They said he'd been hit. He had come out of the clouds with a burning engine and hit the ground on his third turn. It was the turbulence that finished him off of course.

Our landing was ordinary. I taxied to the parking area but after getting out of the plane I suddenly felt an unfamiliar weakness in my body, an apathy, almost a drowsiness. My legs went floppy. I walked under a wing, stretched out on the withered grass and breathed heavily. Damn it all! At that moment I wouldn't have been able to take off again. The guys were smoking a little way off. Then the feeling passed and, after vodka at breakfast, the incident was almost forgotten. But during the day, when it was time to rest, my bed sheets kept twisting into braids, tangling my feet and making it hard to sleep.

By evening our crew had been assigned to a new mission but the same heavy clouds were rushing across the sky and the cold wind showed no signs of easing. All this brought back memories of the previous day's breakdown and gave rise to an unpleasant feeling, not really uncertainty or fear but a kind of uneasiness of the heart. I had to overcome it.

I left early for the aerodrome with my crew. The plane had been fuelled and was ready to fly. A new horizon indicator had been installed and the bomb hanging was almost complete. 'Take the bombs off,' I ordered. The armourers exchanged perplexed glances. 'Take them off, I need you to take them off.' I got into the plane in wild excitement, took off easily and went into the clouds straight away. It was as bumpy as the day before. I pulled towards the front line a bit, turned and after making several steep turns throttled back and closed in for landing. My spirits returned, my mood soared, the chaps became more talkative, responded to my jokes, added their own. 'Put the bombs in, we're off to the war!' Nobody apart from the crew ever knew about my spinning out.

One blizzard-filled December day a machine-gunner from my previous crew, Alexey Nezhentsev, suddenly appeared in the regiment. For nearly half a year he had been completely lost from sight; my navigator Alexey Vasiliev and radio-operator Nikolay Chernov still were. Nezhentsev remembered well how difficult it had been to resist the stormy turbulence during our ill-fated flight, to stay in his place, grasping the gun-turret frame with both hands, but the last bump was not fixed in his memory. Buffeted by the oncoming airstream, he had come to his senses in free fall. Quickly pulling himself together he opened his parachute. Probably at the last moment Alexey had hit the edge of the cockpit with his head and, letting go, had been thrown out of the plane through the hatch or most likely through a breach in the fuselage.

He landed in dense forest. He waited all night in thunder and heavy rain and in the morning took off to look for a way out of the thickets. On his way he came across a smashed, still smoking Il-4 but it wasn't ours. By the end of the day, having roamed all over the forest, he came to a village and seeing some of the local men, he calmly and trustingly headed towards them to ask the way to the front line. By all accounts this was Broutovo – the village I taken a dislike to for some reason while staring at it from the old man's garret. It seemed dangerous to me and fortunately I rejected it in favour of Rassvet. Having disarmed and searched Nezhentsev the men in Broutovo tied his hands and walked him to the German commandant's office. The same day he was transported to a large headquarters. He was interrogated. Alexey put up a good show and, pleading his rank of private, regaled the Germans with information they weren't interested in. They pressed him. To prove they had a broad spectrum of information at their disposal even without him, and to provoke him into more open conversation, they showed him their handbooks which contained quite comprehensive details about a whole range of ADD commanders and airmen. They presented him with photographs of some of the men, especially of the ones from high command. Nezhentsev certainly didn't know all of them by sight and was able to recognise only the regiment and division commander out of the mostly highly ranked officers. He saw his highest superiors for the first time in those photographs, there in the fascist headquarters.

Captivity followed – POW camps near the Baltic Sea not far from Riga. In the middle of September when POWs were being transferred to do some work in Belorussia he and his comrades knocked out the lower side planks of their railway truck one night before dawn and while it was moving they leaped out through this slot into the dark. The escapees were in a small wood and initially lost each other but five of the men managed to get together again. Now Nezhentsev and his friends were extremely careful. They managed to find the partisans and with their assistance crossed the front line in October. The NKVD machine began to do its job: initially they were checked out by the *Osobyi Otdel* of the 4th Shock Army. Then Nezhentsev was 'x-rayed' in a camp near Toropets and at last he was released to the regiment from a transit point in Souzdal just before New Year's Eve. Alexey flew again as a machine-gunner/radio-operator and fought right up until the end of the war.

Twenty-two years after that memorable disaster near Chernoushka, during an unusually dry summer, a local forester found our crashed plane and the remains of a man in the woods. In a preserved plastic cartridge there was a note with his name and his family's address. It was the navigator Alexey Vasiliev. No remains of Nikolay Chernov were found among the debris. And they would never be located. Chernov responded to my order to bail out and even if he hadn't he would have fallen from the plane. But what happened to him afterwards is a matter of speculation: he may have died during his parachute jump or met his death in a skirmish with pursuers. Captivity? Unlikely. There would have been rumours.

With the arrival of Nezhentsev the fate of all my crew, scattered across the flooded woodland that stormy July night, began to become clear, though the process of discovery would take years. No one had reached the targets back then and those who had tried to break through paid for their conceit – some with their plane, some with the bitter fate of a POW, some with their lives. Wasn't it then that Stalin asked Golovanov who was sending the ADD flyers to remote targets on stormy nights? The question was menacing but the chief commander took full responsibility, reporting that it was his decision. The weather beyond the front line was always unknown, he said, and he had no choice but to estimate meteor-ological conditions, allowing each crew to drop their bombs on an alternative target or to return to their aerodrome if they encountered storms. Stalin replied vaguely, 'Well, if that's the case ...' He never raised the question again.

On 23 November 1942 330,000 fascist troops were encircled before Stalingrad by a double ring. The inner one kept contracting and splitting the pocket into pieces; the outer one held against the pressure of the German armies attempting to ram through from outside. Those who were in the pocket were not going to surrender and threw themselves into counterattacks, looking for gaps. It was necessary to complete the destruction of the enemy in the shortest possible time so as to release front-line troops for new operations. The ADD participated in this effort, pressing on the German operational transports supplying the front with reserves. Then a week after the New Year of 1943 part of our force was shifted closer to Stalingrad.

Our regiment occupied a field airstrip near Kamyshin. The flying personnel were billeted in the tiny school of the village of Unterdorf, which was previously populated by Volga Germans who had now been deported. The village still bore signs of the recent order amidst the morbid desolation and destruction. It was about 5 or 6 kilometres from the aerodrome. We made our way there down a snow-drifted road, standing, holding onto each other, on wide wooden platforms which slid under the tow of tractors that would slip every now and then on the steep snow ridges.

The wind chill penetrated our fur outfits and burned our faces blue. Heated dugouts were the only place on the aerodrome to escape from the frost. Between sorties we would sit around red-hot stoves, storing warmth for another flight. Sometimes at a height of 1,000 or 2,000 metres we would come across an inversion layer where the temperature was noticeably higher than on the ground. But it was hard to understand how our technicians and armourers could endure the severe cold in their much lighter clothing, which was certainly not made of fur. They fitted out firearms, refuelled tanks, replaced cylinders and spark-plugs almost with their bare hands. It was impossible to look without shuddering at the purple, red-blotched, frost-bitten face of my aircraft armourer Arzali Alkhazov, a guy from the south, a mountain man from the Caucasus who would get chilled through to the last cell of his body but still be able to perform accurate movements when screwing in detonators, lifting bombs and hanging them on clamps. His ruddy appearance, with its hoary ginger eyebrows and big runny nose, gave his friends and comrades a reason to nickname him 'Rose of Stamboul', echoing the title of a pre-war movie. Arzali never took offence: he had a kind soul and a healthy sense of humour.

Even after they let the planes go the technicians and armourers wouldn't rush to the hot stoves. They would set about preparing new sets of bombs, moving fuel trucks around, bringing up bombs of compressed air and carrying out God knew how many duties so that when the planes returned from a combat mission they could immediately be made ready for the next sortie. These men wouldn't leave the aerodrome – they ate and slept there. Their ingenuity was extraordinary, not only in the way they carried out their routine technical duties with no facilities, but also in the methods they found to cope in extreme situations. For example, more than once they had to lift and put to rights a badly damaged plane that had force-landed on open ground far away from quarters and with its gear retracted.

Among our specialists in this area there was none more skilled and inventive than Ivan Vasiliev – a flight technician, later a squadron engineer. He returned to service with the regiment no fewer than half a dozen (if not a whole squadron) of planes that seemed to be beyond repair. And his tools mostly consisted of logs and ropes scrounged from who knew where. You can't put a price on the greatness of the front-line feats of that remarkable and excellent breed, the technical personnel of combat aviation.

We began to make two sorties a night from near Kamyshin but after two or three days we switched to three a day – both by day and by night. The Soviet Air Force seized the mastery of the air. The skies were now controlled by our fighter planes although in the daytime when our fighters were not nearby we couldn't avoid skirmishes with the Germans. And this was not without consequences, often grievous for us. Clouds, when there were any, offered substantially more reliable protection than fighters.

The low altitude of our strikes, while presupposing a higher accuracy of bombing, led us into the heaviest ack-ack fire from all calibres of weapon. No forces were assigned to neutralise these ground-based defenders for they were being saved for the destruction of primary targets – aircraft on the ground, fortified districts, assault formations. And for this reason, even given our superiority in the air, some of us would come back with shell holes. But we weren't worried about it: the resistance of the fascist ground defence was growing weaker day by day.

We slept little, in snatches, in stuffy rooms with icy draughts on two-storey plank beds with straw mattresses, sometimes still dressed. So when I noticed an unusual heaviness in my body and a white spot flickering in front of my eyes I ascribed it to a bit of fatigue. But on the evening of 20 January, having returned from my second sortie of that day, I was approached by Dr Matsevich as I reported to the commander about the completion of the mission and my readiness to fly again. Matsevich turned to Tikhonov and said heatedly, 'You can't let him go anywhere. He's sick!'

I began to protest. 'What are you talking about, doctor, I'm fine!' But he was already poking a thermometer into my armpit and when it was pulled out I was surprised myself: it read almost 39. My nervous tension vanished straight away. Now I felt an incredible weakness, a splitting headache and pain in my joints and muscles. I had to give in. Matsevich dragged me to sick bay straight from the command post.

It was divinely warm and cosy in the small house. I couldn't wait to dive into the bed sheets white as summer clouds and at least for a short while into a world of silence and calm. Having put on fresh underwear and obediently swallowed powders and pills, I finally reached this paradise and fell asleep in perfect bliss. I slept for a very long time. I remember leaning over towards the washstand in the morning and then waking up in bed, bewildered. A female doctor and a nurse stood over me in silence. 'How did I get here?'

'You fell like a log,' the doctor said. 'It's just as well you didn't smash your head. Stay in bed and don't dare get up.'

The illness wasn't too serious and after a week it had all passed. Matsevich insisted on giving me a couple of weeks' rest and I flew off to Moscow on a passing plane to see Fedya: he was at home at the time. There I found out about the surrender of the Stalingrad German army group and the capture of its chief commander, Paulus. People were rejoicing, apparently sensing the dawn of victory. But as it turned out the battle wasn't even half done. The Germans were hastily concentrating huge and powerful forces for a decisive clash near Orel and Kursk. The ADD again rained down all its striking force to break up the enemy's supply lines. It later emerged that the fires in railway junctions and stations had not been set in vain: our strikes had forced Hitler to postpone the advance for nearly a month.

Having had an unplanned but welcome rest at the same time as me, my crew were fully prepared for action. Not that they were bursting for a fight, but rather they quietly resumed their interrupted duties and didn't miss a single sortie. At the end of March an unusual, unexpected, even perplexing task appeared among the ordinary, routine ones the commander had been setting us day after day: photographic surveillance. Usually it was assigned to specially trained crews but this time it was up to us. I knew how to do it but I had never flown with cameras to check the results of a bomb strike and had never felt any kind of affinity for this variety of aerial warfare. I saw no attraction in a sortie that caused no material or personnel losses to the enemy, preferring to deal with bombing. I only understood when I was over the target (it was Konotop railway junction) how special a night photo-reconnaissance pilot's self-mastery, iron nerve and valour had to be, so as not to miss the chance of securing an aerial image which was awaited in high-level headquarters. The pictures had to be taken after a very long attack approach, from which you were not allowed to deviate no matter how heavily you were shot at – especially after the moment when all the PhOTABs [photographic aerial bombs – translator's note] had been dropped and the last one was still to explode after an unbearably long and agonising period of suspense. The most awful thing was that we were supposed to begin the photographic surveillance only after a bombing strike had ended, when literally everyone else had already left the target. We, being the only ones left in the air and faithfully following the horizon right over the centre of the target as if we were on a rope, were captured by the searchlights and shot at by all available artillery, which now had time to aim and zero in.

During the bombing run Petr Arkhipov and I spent a lot of time trying to guess which side it would be better to start our strike run from and when at long last our moment had come we decided. All but crossing ourselves we headed across the very middle of the railway junction. I wouldn't have endured such flak during ordinary bombing and would have turned away and started from scratch, but now it was just best not to look outside!

Slowly, sticking to the prescribed intervals, the photographic bombs came out of the hatches. The last one had gone but the first one hadn't exploded yet. When the hell was it going to happen? Then the whole sky was lit up by a dazzling flash, then another one, a third ... I counted them, impatiently waiting for the last. Finally it went off. The firing had become more scattered (apparently the flashes had dazzled the gunners). I turned steeply to one side, then to the other, changed altitude, slid down on one of the wings – I didn't give them a chance to aim but the shell bursts still followed us like a swarm of mosquitoes. However, we survived. The photomontage showed not only the smashed and still burning Konotop railway junction but also traces of flak bursts, imprinted as motley speckles all over the sheet.

I wasn't assigned to photo-reconnaissance again. And I never asked to fly another of those missions.

CHAPTER NINE

The East Prussian Session

The second spring of the war took us on another long road – Danzig, Königsberg, Tilsit, Insterburg ... Although we hadn't visited them for quite a while, since the previous summer, Königsberg and Danzig looked like they had been waiting for us every day. Their powerful and well-organised defence met us boldly and it strongly resisted the bombers' pressure. The two cities' firing regimes were somewhat similar: they would start from afar, shoot at us both from the coast and from ships, and would then track us with both barrels.

We attacked Königsberg first. When we approached this monster there were already six fires blazing. Not many, but it was only the beginning. Our target – the *Maschinenwerk* – was already ablaze. We approached it for quite a while through a barrage of explosions but the searchlights didn't catch us. There was a full moon and candle-bombs lit up everything: the city was in full view. Petya Arkhipov aimed meticulously and sank the bombs into the fires. Two days before the weather over the city had been difficult and a raid had basically failed. But this time Königsberg was rocked for about two hours and continued burning long after that.

Reaching the final destination and getting back stretched the crews to the limit of flying range unless their aircraft had been fitted with additional fuel tanks. That night, 16 April, a powerful and constant head wind had eaten up more than half our stock of fuel long before we approached Danzig. Arkhipov and I began to worry in earnest: should we keep going or turn back towards Königsberg before it was too late? There was a chance of a stronger wind on the return bearing, just under the ceiling for this plane; on the journey back, of course, it would be in our favour. But what if the wind direction up there was different or the wind was not very strong? We decided we had to go for it anyway.

When Danzig was behind us after the bombing we had so little fuel left that if there'd been no following wind we wouldn't have dragged ourselves even to the front line. But our mighty 'fellow traveller' exceeded all expectations and we barely managed to note the landmarks as they flashed by incredibly quickly beneath us. We landed at home just like all the rest who had been through the same frightening experience.

But the wind had played a bad joke on some. In the neighbouring regiment the well-seasoned and venerable crew of my good friend Alexey Sviridovich, not wanting to tempt fate, had bombed Königsberg (and there was nothing wrong with that course of action). On the way back, without bothering about detailed positioning or time-based calculations, Sviridovich's crew whizzed over the front line like a bullet, driven by a tail wind. The plane raced past its aerodrome and, not suspecting that he was already near Kazan, at dawn Sviridovich reported full depletion of fuel. His crew reported that they were 'forced to land on a casual strip near the front line'. Well, funny things used to happen sometimes – and this one wasn't the most tragic and pitiful.

As for Tilsit and Insterburg, these were very important road junctions and major supply bases crammed with trains, commissariat and ammunition. They were excellently illuminated and, having weaker anti-aircraft defence than their bigger brothers, were bombed especially fiercely. The fires, initially burning and exploding from separate locations, would merge into continuous fields of conflagration.

But that East Prussian campaign of the spring of 1943 didn't go easily for us. All the newspapers reported it in brief accounts; the military press added laconic stories that our aircraft had been attacked by fascist fighter planes far away from their bases but that the attacks had met with no success. At the same time, as mentioned in dispatches, on some days one or two planes hadn't returned home, and three had failed to come back from one raid on Danzig. No one knew how they had disappeared.

It was hard to say whether all the losses were accurately reported by the media, even if on the last occasion two out of the three were from our regiment. I don't think we were the most unlucky of the dozens of ADD regiments. However, Major Uroutin was one of those who didn't come back. Being left without his faithful navigator Matsepras after the Korotoyak disaster, he was flying with various others, frequently the senior regimental navigator Major Heveshi. The latter was a remarkably self-disciplined and bold man. The revolutionary life of his father – a Hungarian communist – had given Akosh Heveshi a new motherland, the Soviet Union. During the Spanish Civil War he, already a seasoned navigator, had gallantly fought against the fascists in the Soviet volunteer bomber units. He came back from that conflict with several decorations and was appointed a navigator in the Odessa Military District Air

Force. This high position wasn't to be the last step up in his military career. At the beginning of the Second World War he was initially appointed a navigator in the Army and then in the Front-line Air Force. But he disdained dizzy career heights and insisted on going his own way: he joined a combat regiment. The commander worshipped him; he protected him, flew only with him and rarely entrusted him to other flyers. But it wasn't that easy to hold Heveshi back and he would take part in combat sorties much more often than the regiment commander could. The flying personnel felt an affinity with him, listened to his advice and demands, and the flyers deemed it a special privilege to find themselves in a crew with him. He flew with me more than once. Only recently I had headed out with him to bomb gatherings of railway trucks at Unecha. It was a sortie like any other: what could be special about it? The route was an easy one and the target was nothing to rave about. But nevertheless I felt a sense of pride not only because of my confidence as a flyer but also because of my association (inasmuch as we were carrying out the same mission) with the high professional authority of this most experienced navigator. We remained unscathed in the face of quite powerful flak and the bombs dropped on our two approaches exploded all along the trains. We were coming home in good spirits when I heard Akosh begin to hum the song 'Fare thee well, my beloved town' [a popular Navy song during the Second World War – translator's note], which had just become popular. We were soon singing in perfect tempo. A sense of light-heartedness sometimes came over us during sorties when everything was going well. It was certainly the case this time; it hadn't been a tiring mission. In fact it was a pleasant one, if you can speak about a bombing raid in those terms.

But then came 16 April. The crew of three headed towards Danzig: Uroutin, Heveshi and radio-operator Sasha Garankin. There was no machine-gunner with them – Sharikov had fallen ill and they had not found a replacement. On the way back after completion of the mission, and having already crossed the Lithuanian border, the plane was shot down by an accurate attack from a fighter plane no one had noticed. The attacker, striking from behind and to the left judging by the glow of the tracers, should have been seen by Sasha, nobody else but him. But he let his attention wander and didn't see the German or return fire. The aircraft lost control and tumbled. The left engine caught fire. Garankin received the commander's order to bail out and didn't hesitate. The navigator had lost communications and the handle of the elevator lever had gone slack. He wasn't getting any orders and the plane was being drawn into an ever-steeper dive. Was the commander at the controls? Not likely. When G-force had multiplied many times Akosh Heveshi reached for the hatch (only his well-trained iron muscles could overcome the wild force of inertia) and left his cockpit. The plane whizzed past and exploded right under him.

The terrain was woody and alien, with nothing of the Russian landscape about it. Gathering the crew was out of the question. Heveshi would have set out on his journey home but he couldn't move very far because he had broken a rib in the jump. A kind Lithuanian family picked him up near Vilkaviskis, hid him and treated him. Having recovered Heveshi chose an almost dead-east bearing – the shortest route to the front line – but on reaching Polotsk he was captured by the *politzei* and became a POW. The Germans unearthed his background, found out some details of his combat record and spent a fair bit of effort trying to persuade him to commit treason, tempting him with a general's rank in the Hungarian Army, but all in vain. Coming to know the ordeals of POW camp life in all its unbearable fullness, he was to be freed only at the very end of the war.

Uroutin landed safely and, wasting no time, headed towards Minsk, apparently hoping to reach areas of partisan activity. He managed to cross Lithuania but in the Belorussian woodland he suddenly came across armed people who were not in uniform. They hailed him but not in Russian. Who were they? Uroutin began to retreat. They began to chase him. His pursuers approached and opened fire. Mikhail Nikolaevich shot back and kept firing for quite a while, but he was killed. The partisans could not work out who he was but they guessed that he was probably on their side. Right there in a small glade they dug a grave for the stranger and quietly buried him.

Garankin was marching in the same randomly chosen direction. His fur jackboots had flown off during the parachute jump and after several days of walking across boggy hummocks and through forest thickets his legs could barely support him. He was dizzy and faint with hunger. He was no longer walking but crawling. He stopped at villages, sometimes finding food and help. Emaciated, weak and ill, this shadow of a man aroused neither suspicion nor curiosity, but rather compassion. Sasha lay down a lot, sometimes in the forest, sometimes in haylofts, to give his feet rest. Not till the end of summer did he reach the Belorussian forests. An old man who grazed livestock and brewed *samogon* [moonshine – translator's note], whom Garankin was lucky enough to meet on an empty byroad, apparently gathered something from Sasha's incoherent speech and led him to the partisans. They greeted him harshly; initially they put him up against the wall and kept the barrels of machine guns trained on him, even letting off a few bursts, sending bullets past his ears, but eventually they walked him to their detachment commander.

At the end of the interrogation Garankin asked, pointing with his eyes at a Finnish knife lying on the table, 'Where did you get it?'

Refuelling an Il-4. It took up to 45 minutes to fill the tanks.

Operational control at a temporary airfield. Note the Il-4 in the background and the Lend-Lease V-100 radio set, produced by Pilot Radio Corp, with its crank generator.

Vladimir Petrov, the pilot with his own personal bomber.

Pavel P. Radchuk's funeral.

Heroes of the Soviet Union
Vladimir F. Roshenko, Pavel
P. Radchuk and Pavel P.
Khroustalev before they
received their decorations.

Mark I. Shevelev, 1942. He
was later ADD chief-of-staff.

Vladimir Samosudov,
navigator, 1941.

Captain Valentin G. Chernichenko, 1942.

Petr S. Arkhipov, navigator, 1945.

Nikolay S. Skripko, 1942. He became Chief Marshal of the Air Force.

Viktor Kuzin and Alexander Lomov, May 1942.

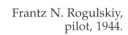

Frantz N. Rogulskiy, pilot, 1944.

Ivan E. Doushkin, pilot. He was posthumously awarded the Gold Star of a Hero of the Soviet Union. His plane was shot up over Mga.

Maxim N. Alekseev, navigator.

Mikhail P. Smitienko.

Squadron commissar Alexey D. Tsykin.

Captain Serguey Pavlovich Kazmin,
March 1942.

Gleb F. Bazhenov, pilot.

Ivan I. Vasiliev, flight technician
and later a squadron engineer.

Vasiliy Reshetnikov, 1960s.

Vasiliy Reshetnikov, 1980s.

The commander, to whom much had apparently become clear, asked in turn, 'Do you know whose it is?'

'It's my commander's – Major Uroutin's.'

Next morning the whole camp marched towards the grave. They carefully dug it up and when Garankin recognised the familiar face, not yet ravaged by the forces of death, the detachment was lined up, the commanders made military speeches, and Mikhail Nikolaevich Uroutin was buried again. Then a thunderous salute was fired. Garankin returned to the regiment in November 1943. After rest and treatment he resumed his flying career, which continued till the end of the war.

Back on that same April night, just crossing Königsberg, yet another crew was shot down by an unreciprocated attack in nearly the same way as Uroutin's. It was the crew of a young but tough and gallant combat flyer, Gavriil Lepekhin. He had no machine-gunner either. Any radio-operator who has to divide his attention between his machine gun and radio station, even a skilled and careful one, is always in peril of letting through a sudden strike by an aerial foe.

East Prussia was under Lepekhin's plane. His left engine was on fire; he had no communications. Gliding failed to put out the flames and the aircraft rapidly lost altitude. The commander gave the order to bail out with a light signal, pressing all three coloured buttons at once. He waited a while, then opened the canopy and, sharply pushing the control wheel away, he flew out. His fur jackboots were unfastened just like Garankin's and flew off when his parachute opened. The plane quickly hit the ground and flared up in bright flames. To avoid a possible encounter with the Germans Lepekhin began to glide energetically sideways, but in the darkness he didn't realise how close he was to the ground; he had no time to release the straps and landed at very high speed.

He came to his senses in bed, smashed up and torn apart, in unbearable pain. There were Germans in uniform in the room. A lorry came towards evening and the soldiers, having shoved his inert body in the back, jolted him along to Moritzfeld camp. He suffered with every bump in the road. Then he was dragged to the interrogation point, for he couldn't stand upright. Lepekhin tried to pretend to be an aerial machine-gunner but his radio-operator/machine-gunner, Mikhail Bourenok, was already in the camp and the Germans had Lepekhin's identity papers in their hands. His story didn't hold up.

A month later Lepekhin was able to stand but could walk only with two sticks. In the camp there were faces familiar to him. He had a short encounter with Heveshi, who had been transported there from a neighbouring prison. Long months of concentration camps and failed attempts at escape lay ahead of him. In April 1945 Lepekhin found himself in Buchenwald where on 11 April a crowd of many thousands of POWs, anticipating mass executions, broke through the barbed wire fence in a surge, destroyed the SS depots and went out to meet the 3rd US Armored Division. Lepekhin and his comrades captured a German vehicle and rushed towards Torgau and the Elbe, following the Americans. There at last they met our troops. Then they reached Warsaw and everything went by the book. The friends were issued with travel documents and directions for checking into an NKVD camp at Alkino station near Ufa. Lepekhin would come across Heveshi once more there. They and dozens of other prisoners were cross-examined. Not a scrap of suspicion stuck to them and by written instruction of Chief Marshal of the Air Force Golovanov both were placed at his disposal. Since the flight-fitness of both turned out to be satisfactory Heveshi was assigned as a regimental navigator in Ivanovo and Lepekhin as a squadron commander in Poltava.

All this happened after the war, but in spring 1943 the conflict was still at its height.

CHAPTER TEN

Everything has its Price

Some people, confusing the DB-3 with the Il-4, lump the latter in with obsolete types of aircraft, thinking that it differed from its already ageing predecessor only in its altered configuration. In reality the Il-4 was designed as a new plane with not only more powerful engines but an upgraded airframe and improved aerodynamics. Born on the eve of the war, in 1940 the Il-4 yielded nothing to the German bombers and was superior to them in many aspects. The Germans had no reason to look down on it. The aircraft was improved and became more robust as the war progressed: the suspended fuel tanks significantly increased its oper ational range, new armaments strengthened its defensive capability and the bomb load grew twofold. Its initial norm was regarded as a tonne, but on the front line flyers immediately added half a tonne more off their own bats and then made it two. The aircraft designer, Ilyushin, was alarmed at this development and began testing the soundness of the plane's joints, but as it turned out the safety margins hadn't been ex-ceeded. Then the most enthusiastic flyers went further.

People said that either Borisov or Opalev, flyers from a sister regiment, were the first to lift 2.5 tonnes into the air. There were other claimants for first place, but our flyer Mikhail Pronin – a superb airman of the older generation, a kind, cordial and surprisingly modest man with a spirit overflowing with energy – did it independently of them, and maybe even before them, without making a fuss. His debut as the first 'heavy-weight' didn't go unnoticed. A large-lettered placard reading 'Guard Honours and Battle Glory to Captain Pronin for Lifting Two and a Half Tonnes of Bombs!' was hung along the wall of the flyers' canteen. The placard was clearly an invocation and it wasn't long before others followed Pronin's lead: Shaposhnikov, Chernichenko, Radchuk, Kour-yatnik, Rogulskiy . . .

There were serious reasons for carrying that extra half-tonne. But in addition, failure do so would have threatened a pilot's self-esteem, as if there might be some damage to his professional standing because he hadn't dared to 'jerk' that maximum load. Our crew carried it too, but I didn't like those weightlifting exercises. With such a load (and even with 2 tonnes) we were ordered to turn on the afterburner during take-off, squeezing the last juices out of the available horsepower, going to a limit beyond which lay destruction. Even without the extra load the engines would sometimes come home with wobbly cylinders, burned-out pistons or cracked piston rings. In fact, I never switched the afterburner on, even with 2.5 tonnes on board, being fully aware that my stallions would pay me back for that couple of minutes of violent treatment, taking brutal revenge somewhere far away from home sweet home. And although a take-off loaded to the limit and without the afterburner was tricky, I encountered no particular difficulties for I knew how to do it. I would set the plane on the very edge of the airstrip, start my run-up at full revolutions and lift the tail as early as possible in order to gain speed more rapidly. The plane would take off just before the edge of the village vegetable gardens and, having retracted the landing gear, I would float above the burdocks for a while, carefully flying over the trusses of the railway bridge across the Oka. Only then, having gathered speed, would I switch to climbing, gradually reducing revolutions.

The weightlifters wouldn't let up, but their numbers began to fall little by little. Noticing the premature wear that the extra weight inflicted on the engines some flyers began to cool down a bit. And Radchuk, having returned to 2-tonne loads, was capable of doing four sorties per night rather than two. I was among the apostates.

The planes, exhausted by lifting heavy loads, began to line up at the edges of the aerodrome because the life of their engines had been truncated and they were low on power; they were almost useless for combat missions. Finding no other way out of this unpleasant situation the regiment commander requested me (indeed requested and not ordered!) to work them into the ground on nearby targets with light – just internal – bomb loads. I estimated it would be too much work for one crew and had to subcontract Gleb Bazhenov and Franz Rogulskiy. Over several nights we wound back the useful life of those feeble, pinking engines to zero. Now they could be removed and replaced by new ones, if we were lucky: most likely they would be overhauled.

But Pronin, who had already become a major, kept dragging the same crazy weight into one sortie after another as if nothing had happened, still inspiring two or three enthusiasts who had yet to go off the idea. The end of the story came on 13 July 1943 at the height of the Battle of Kursk. After take-off and a simple manoeuvre Pronin found himself over the centre of the aerodrome and was already headed for Bolkhov where we were tasked with cracking the German fortifications with heavy bombs. Then the left engine of his overloaded plane, which had scraped together barely 200 or so metres, suddenly banged resonantly, rumbled and flared up. We froze. The take-offs stopped. Pronin was going to meet his death. It was impossible to come in for a landing: he would have lost all his altitude during the turn and wouldn't have made it to the aerodrome anyway. If the crew bailed out their parachutes wouldn't have time to open, and the falling plane would not only wipe them out with the wave of its explosion but if the bombs went off, they would plough up the whole aerodrome. The only option was to land directly ahead. Without changing his course Pronin flew towards Tula. Would he land on the undercarriage? But what would God put under his wheels? Turning over on some small ditch would mean burning up. Would he land the plane on its belly? But there were three half-tonners hanging underneath with their detonators sticking out ...

The roadside turned out to be very rough and bumpy. The bombs, although set on safety, went off because of the direct hit. An orange blaze spread wide across the night sky. The noise – horrifying for its connection to our brothers' last moment of life – burst through the air. The atmosphere shook and breathed in our faces. It took a minute more for the aerodrome to get over its paralysis, but then someone came back to his senses, began blinking his lights, gunned his engines and took off. The rest followed. From the planes passing over the tragic fire came flares and the rattle of machine-gun bursts.

Life on the front line was reorganised on the run more than once. In the thick of combat operations another total reformation occurred: the ADD regiments were each divided into two parts, forming two-regiment divisions. These in turn were converted into corps. Tikhonov became division commander, Loginov, corps commander. I was appointed squadron commander and the previous squadron commander, Alexander Shaposhnikov, became my regiment commander. This indomitably tenacious and strong man, unhurried in his movements, ironic and reasonable, had deservedly overtaken many other quite worthy candidates for the new position. He was notable not so much for his qualities as a commander but for his maturity, intellect and erudition, not to mention his combat experience. He had been through the whole Finnish War, bombed Königsberg on the third day of the Great Patriotic War, distinguished himself in dozens of combat sorties and got his plane burned in the air a few times. Once it had taken him twelve days to make his way back to our lines from the German side. He rejoined his regiment to take up normal duties as if he had not had the sort of shock from which people don't recover straight away. At the beginning of 1942

Shaposhnikov was awarded the Gold Star [Hero of the Soviet Union – translator's note], a rare decoration for that time.

He constructed his regiment as he would have built his own house. There was a core consisting of sound, seasoned crews and a small group of youngsters accustomed to combat operations. Nor were we short of aeroplanes. Fresh forces were due to join up – recent graduates of schools for long-range night bomber crews working in Central Asia [Central Asian republics of the USSR – translator's note]. Having mastered the short-term training programmes, they were not yet ready for action by the strict standards of combat flying although they were eager for battle. There was still a lot of work to do on them. And there was a different atmosphere in the Air Force now – this wasn't 1941, when, after the first doomed wave of the strongest and most experienced crews of pre-war fame, whole bunches of inexperienced and under-trained flyers were thrown into battle just to keep faith with their pre-decessors.

We, all three squadron commanders (Frantz Rogulskiy, Sasha Romanov and I), together with Pavel Radchuk who by now was deputy regiment commander, would come back from a sortie and then get into another plane. Sitting in the front cockpit while it was still dark, we would make circles above the aerodrome on flight after flight with the young airmen whose long wait to join us had finally ended. The regiment commander himself joined in the instruction effort. There were very capable, not to say talented, blokes among the young men who joined the new regiment, some in the first wave and some later. Having become superb combatants they yielded nothing in skill to any of the old guard. They were notable for their diversity. Maybe their main strength was the uniqueness of each of their characters.

Nestor Kroutogouz was a very colourful character – a huge bloke with iron hands and a quick temper. There was something of the ancient warrior in him and his unusual and rather patriarchal first name only emphasised the apparent similarity. This knight flew very well and was bursting to go out on a combat mission. He needed to be restrained and cooled down. Otherwise, completely ignoring even the obvious hazards, he could have got his neck broken in his first encounter with any one of them. Nestor got the combat mission he was thirsting for before the rest, but his pride was deeply wounded when I got into the front cockpit. The night of his debut happened to be excessively black and hazy, and the target (it was still Vyazma), near though it was, was a menacing one, dazzling us with a mass of searchlights and firing pitilessly. When I had lined up for the attack I immediately felt the control wheel tightly lock in his clutches: I wouldn't be able to adjust anything during the flight. I was left to rely on making orders via the intercom rather than physically intervening to change the steering. After that night Kroutogouz wouldn't miss a combat flight, no matter how difficult.

Fedya Alexeev was different. By no means inferior to Kroutogouz in flying or combat qualities, he was more subtle and refined, not only in his appearance and his restrained manners but also in his cultivated piloting technique, his art of combat flying. Where someone else would be smashing through the walls Fedya would find a door.

Somewhat later quite a young flyer, Volodya Petrov, arrived with another group of newcomers. They flew him a brand-new plane direct from the aircraft works. A dedicatory inscription in large script stretched across the whole fuselage in one line (lucky there was enough space): 'To my son the flyer from his father Ernolay Loginovich Petrov'. Volodya's father lived in Bouryatia [an autonomous Soviet republic in eastern Siberia – translator's note] and was the chairman of a wealthy collective farm renowned, apart from all the usual things, for its large-scale bee-keeping. And they'd got together a bit of money, no more and no less than the price of a long-range bomber! In spite of his position as a 'monopolist ship-owner', Volodya, like all his contemporaries, was initially thoroughly examined in his piloting techniques, chaperoned and trained in all possible weather conditions and at all times of day. Only then did he go into combat in his own plane. He was to fly it for the rest of the war and he fought fearlessly and faultlessly. He was gallant, self-disciplined, would go for any target, could take a risk and wouldn't lose his presence of mind in difficult circumstances. He was often held up as an example and didn't go short of decorations. A career as an aviation commander lay before him, but after the war he suddenly and decisively quit the Air Force.

To be honest, by the end of the war we had begun to get all kinds of men, and the candidates were weaker the longer the conflict went on. There were hardly any good finds among them. It was not so much the transience of training that was telling, but rather some deficiency in the selection of human resources. Flying commanders were kept busy not so much wet nursing them as attempting to tame their dissolute tempers and uncontrollable passion for booze. And these guys were rarely allowed to carry out missions: other men fought for them. Only after the end of the war were they successfully kicked out of the Air Force, to our relief.

On 15 May we bombed Dnepropetrovsk, my native city. I was born, grew up and studied there. From there I'd left to join the Air Force. I knew every side-street, every house like I knew my ABC. Of course we were bombing not the city itself but the railway junction. This was the third raid but I was still agitated by the experience: I couldn't bear to think about the German occupiers walking down the city's boulevards –

and on top of that they were shooting at me from behind my native walls, so dear to me. Where were Father and Mother?

Only after the liberation of the city did I find out that my father, being a 'great strategist', had decided the Germans wouldn't be capable of crossing the Dniepr because it would be too wide for them, and that the war wouldn't last too long. That's why, having gathered up the family and only enough gear to live far from home for a short time, he moved to the other side of the river and stopped in a village he'd taken a fancy to. The Germans passed around them. They had to move back to the city but looked for shelter on the opposite side to home, rightly guessing that the Germans wouldn't turn a deaf ear to word of their son the airman from incautious old neighbours. However, something similar was to happen at their new place. Once, the daughter of people we knew brought two young Germans who were courting her right into the apartment, trying to convince them that the Soviet airmen's uniform was much more beautiful than the German one. She said to my mother straight out: 'Show them your Vasya's photo in his flying uniform.'

Poor Mama was stupefied and barely managed to convince the little fool that she had no photographs, that she was confused and that Vasya wasn't in the Air Force at all but had gone missing somewhere. It was hard to say whether the Germans understood what was said, but my family were left with a sense of deep unease – what if the Germans came to their senses and returned, this time without the slut? And now at any moment I might be tearing past carrying bombs over my parents' heads.

The ground defences at Dnepropetrovsk were firing well, not wasting ammunition, and the city had a hell of a lot of searchlights. On the run-up at high altitude the roads became visible. I recognised our main thoroughfare, straight as an arrow, parallel to the Dniepr – it was Karl Marx Avenue – and estimated where our house was in the solid blackness. The searchlights had already locked on to us but my attention was distracted and I didn't notice the heavy shells beginning to come closer and closer.

'Commander, commander, turn in left, stay on course, stay on course.' Petya Arkhipov was by now seriously angry and nervous.

'I'm turning, Petya, I'm turning,' I muttered absentmindedly, unable to bring my thoughts back to the present.

'What are you doing, commander?' Petya yelled.

I came to, turned in left and at the same moment a large shell burst just next to us. The right engine shuddered, choked, threw out a long orange tail of exhaust flame and a fairly large piece of duraluminum peeled off it. The instrument panel registered fluctuating revolutions. I tried slowing the rate down a bit: the flame grew shorter and the banging eased. The right engine was fine after all and still pulling. Now I was holding the course straight and my mind was back on the job: how could I get to the front line? Arkhipov grumbled angrily, made me do some extra minor turns and led us to the target, although the Germans continued to surround us with bursting shells. We managed to drag ourselves to the aiming point and at long last got rid of the bombs.

Just as before, the engine was pouring out tongues of flame and working fitfully. Please don't let it catch fire! It quietened down a bit at lower revolutions and held the temperature and oil levels as if everything was all right. On we flew. Time went by terribly slowly. Don't let us down; hold out a bit longer! It seemed to me that I could see the Donets river flashing on the horizon. Our lines were behind it and there could be nothing scary in that direction. But then no matter where we went shell bursts flashed around us and three or four searchlights raised sleepy beams. It was a pity I had to lose altitude but I slowed the engines down slightly so as not to be easily seen or heard.

At last the front line! Home! We went over the list of aerodromes that lay along our route and decided to land at the nearest. But the altitude held out. The engine didn't play up any more and dragged slowly along like a wounded soldier. Was there any point in landing at the nearest airfield? Maybe it would be better to pass on to the next one? Finally we had crossed all of them and by morning we landed at home in Serpukhov.

A curious scene met us on the ground. A metre-wide piece had been torn out of the engine cowling. The heads were smashed on two cylinders and the filters were full of iron. The engine had to be replaced and the cowling was patched by technicians with a huge piece of duraluminum on which they had engraved in large letters: 'Dnepropetrovsk'.

One hot July evening well before sunset the regiment was sitting under the planes awaiting signal flares from the CP, either green ones for an immediate start or red ones for a stand-down. The weather reconnaissance planes looking for passages to Orel were coming back one after another reporting impassable thunderstorms but the commander wouldn't order stand-down. Obviously his superiors were keeping him wound up too. Right now, that very night, it was of paramount importance to strike the railway junction and the trains crammed there dragging troops, arms and fuel towards the German lines that were crumbling in the raging Battle of Kursk.

We were anxiously smoking, chatting, arguing excitedly about this and that, trying to distract ourselves from the impending ordeal. When a green flare suddenly soared from the CP the aerodrome would freeze in silence but no one would move – we were waiting for the next one. A red one came. One more green one and a red one again. It meant we had to wait. We couldn't stand these delays. We would rather have gone into the air, anywhere, even into thunderstorms. Our nerves were wound to the limit. In other cases in such weather they would call stand-down and an exultant yell would roll across the aerodrome. Everyone realised how important it was to strike again at the fascists' rear and their fortifications, and we were ready to do it with all possible zeal and relish, but when a clash with natural forces was more dangerous than a clash with the foe, the guys, whether they really wanted to or not, would openly show their joy after seeing a series of red flares. It meant that there was a guarantee of remaining alive, at least till the following night. For the whole day we would not be shot at and we would not be breaking our aircrafts' bones in foul weather. But this time they were delaying us for a reason, and it didn't look like an easy decision to make.

Suddenly a UT-2 rattled above the aerodrome and rapidly, with a steep turn, closed in for landing. This was our corps commander, General Loginov, of course. Everyone knew his small, sporty machine in its livery of white with red blotches. Usually after appearing at the aerodrome he would taxi up to the CP and deal with the commanders but this time he demanded a general meeting of all flying personnel. The reason was unexpected: five men from our division had been given the rank of Hero of the Soviet Union – Pavel Radchuk, three navigators (Maxim Alexeev, Pasha Khroustalev and Volodya Roshenko) and me. I was happy of course! Loginov didn't hold us up any longer and we went back to our planes.

Andrey Kholod had gone to do weather reconnaissance but came back early – he had failed to break through. Frantz Rogulskiy was the next to go. If he couldn't get through, no one would. He was sending alarming messages – thunderstorms to left and right. Now they were sure to abort. God forbid they should order us to take off: after this award I couldn't come back without a hit on the main target. And no reserve target would tempt me.

A *polutorka* was rolling through the parking area. Hanging from the running board was a messenger from headquarters who announced to the crews as he passed that only the 'old boys' should be ready. There was no need to clarify who the 'old boys' were: there were no more than a dozen and a half of us in this new regiment.

It was already getting pretty dark. There was no point in waiting: it was now or never. At last a flare soared – a green one. The second one was green too. This was it! 'Start engines!' We all turned our engines on at the same time and taxied to the take-off strip in a crowd.

In the sky before Tula I ran into storms. I didn't climb higher – there were impassable flaming walls. I swirled in the tangle of clouds near their lower edge, which was ragged and not at all solid. Sometimes I found myself in a rainstorm, sometimes in billowing clouds. Then the ground broke through again – black, pitch-dark, revealing its landmarks only during flashes of lightning. There was a full moon behind the clouds but its light barely penetrated here. Petya Arkhipov watched each kilometre of our course and kept his eye on the ground. Although the course swung around we did not get too far away from the railway leading towards Orel.

It seemed we were the first to arrive – there was not one explosion on the target. The station was clearly in sight: how could it not be, such a large area marked out by puffing steam engines? Apparently having put its trust in the thunderstorms the ground defence was a bit late, but it opened fire nevertheless. Later, searchlights flared up. Two anti-aircraft regiments and up to sixty searchlights – a bit too much for one bomber. There was only one consolation: they wouldn't fire at us simultaneously until they had all come to their senses and that might take a little while. Petya laid down all our bombs over the tracks and trains in one salvo and, accompanied by flak bursts, we quickly retired, dashed into the clouds and headed home.

I was so agitated by all that had happened that I didn't even try to find out if anyone else had bombed Orel. There was no time to think about it after landing because I was rushed to the last vehicle (everyone else had already gone) heading for a festive dinner that had been arranged in the airmen's canteen, even though a new dawn was breaking.

The commanders – Loginov, Tikhonov, Smitienko, Shaposhnikov – and the political commissars sat at the main table. The officers of the two regiments sat at long common tables. Our girls, the waitresses, rushed around the hall, dressed up, fragrant, wearing nice shoes. Speeches were made. We said something in reply. It would be silly to try to recall what was said that evening and by whom, but a phrase from an old army paper, with which I started my speech in reply, survives: 'My life belongs to the Motherland ...' I said it with feeling. We all belong to the Motherland: it is as natural as the feeling of love for and everlasting affinity with one's paternal home, love for a mother and father, just like their feeling for their children.

The ceremonial part of the affair didn't last long. The tables were pushed to the walls; the regiment's *bayan* players, eager to show off their skills, stretched out the bellows and the dancing began. Women head-over-heels in love with Tikhonov dragged him to the middle of the hall and he, absolutely indifferent to dancing, upright as a pole, began to paw the ground lazily, tapping with his heelplates in time with *chastooshka* [joyful comic singing – translator's note] rhythms. Our ladies were buzzing around him like bees but, having gradually pushed the others aside, a girl called Masha got personal control of Tikhonov. Diminutive, elegant, light as a ball in her colourful belled-out skirt she whirled around her handsome man like a humming top, tap-dancing and singing one *chastooshka* after another in her sonorous voice. The guys gave her their full support, dancing round and throwing in new verses. Masha responded to them accordingly, making up new lines to follow them.

Our girls – lonely, widowed, deprived of husbands and family – you were so dear to us. Among them were many refugees from the occupied territories, from destroyed cities and villages. Nobody knew when they had leisure time – or even if they had any at all. The canteen was busy day and night: some airmen were always due to fly out on reconnaissance, some for flight calibration; others would be going on a mission or coming back. The girls would always be there, quick and deft with their heavy trays. But when a joyful moment like this came along, however short it might be, they wouldn't miss it. Many had love affairs: some were hopeless, but others quite serious and with prospects. You should have seen how they would rush with anxious questions towards the first airman to come into the hall after a flight: 'Is everyone back? What about mine?' They went through so much worry every night, waiting for us to come back from combat missions. How they suffered when they lost their loved ones, or even just guys they'd known and seen every day, those who had been kind and affectionate towards them. And they weren't the only women who worked side by side with us, knowing no rest, living in anxiety and grief. There were also lab technicians, two-way operators, medics and others. Saintly feminine souls, our unforgettable madonnas of those hard times.

... The morning was lit by the rays of the sun. Time for a rest. A new combat mission already awaited us.

Night after night, as part of a large ADD force, we rained heavy bombs on the troops of a powerful German formation which was trying to break through to Lake Ladoga from the Mga area to close the blockade ring around Leningrad again. But at that time, which was still full of danger for our northern capital, some of our forces had been switched to other sectors of the front.

The railway junction of Unecha was not the most difficult of targets. The flight path was full of clear and characteristic landmarks. It used to take me just three and a bit hours to fly there and back, and the regiment commander, foreseeing clear skies, decided to send the newer crews. However, over the previous few days (it was now 8 August) the front within the Bryansk sector had become noticeably more active. Quite a few sources of flak had been located in the operational area and even on dark nights fighter planes had begun to take off from Zhukovka aerodrome, past which we were to fly. In addition, Unecha itself had acquired more searchlights and flak batteries, altering the defence system and making it no simple matter for anyone to get near. But generally speaking it was an ordinary target: a hard nut with the proverbial full set – a bit of everything.

My plane was in for maintenance and I was not going to fly that night but I had come to the aerodrome with the squadron navigator, Ivan Plaksitskiy, and signals chief Nikolay Mitrofanov to check on preparations and see our young team off on their mission. I'd left the aerial gunner, Vasya Shtefourko, in town so he could have some fun, and we intended to get back there after take-off to pop into the theatre or to catch a movie of some sort. We were all in fresh blouses which were ironed and sparkling with our awards. Ivan had screwed his medals on his chest, Mitrofanov was in his decorations and I was wearing my Gold Star.

The crews were just about to disperse to their aircraft when it became known that a small part of the route around Kalouga was covered by a barrier of solid and bumpy clouds and around Zhukovka German fighter planes were targeting our bombers using radar. They would attack, closing in to firing distance, even in conditions of poor visibility and for this reason the regiment commander ordered that the reverse course be set with a detour to the east of Zhukovka.

We were not great believers in radar back then and considered attacks led by the equipment to be governed by complete chance, but the clouds were a serious issue for a flyer called Syrykh. Only days before, during a training flight, I was surprised to discover that he couldn't handle clouds very well. He was a good pilot but had managed to lose the skill of flying blind. We should have taken him out to fly in the milk once or twice more to teach him how to use the instruments efficiently. How could we let someone like him go on a mission? I'd have to stop him flying this time, but there was no one else to do it and no time to think about it – the command to start engines had already rung out. The decision was made instantly. I rushed to the plane with Plaksitskiy and Mitrofanov, got Syrykh's crew out of it, took their helmets and their maps away from them, and made the take-off ourselves. There was no gunner in Syrykh's crew and his radio-operator was no good for the job either. 'No drama, I'll be all right without a gunner. I'll feel more comfortable that way,' Mitrofanov decided. I don't know why but radio-operators didn't like having unfamiliar aerial gunners in their cockpit.

Syrykh was offended by the decision but time would tell I was right. Later on we went into the flying zone together to polish his blind flying techniques and he became noticeably more comfortable. He seemed to have mastered the necessary skills, but apparently not completely. One day in the spring of 1944, coming home at dawn from a combat mission and searching for a safe aerodrome, he entered dense clouds of lifted fog that appeared out of nowhere, lost control and crashed. Syrykh was apparently one of those whose body's balance system is not well tuned, and he had a tendency quickly to lose the skill of flying by instruments which he had acquired by hard work. It wasn't easy to keep your eye on flyers like this and give them a hand at the right time. Sooner or later they came apart. Maybe his plane had been damaged en route or over the target. Who knows. Syrykh would have landed without a problem in cloudless weather.

Back on 8 August 1943, having replaced Syrykh's crew we took off without even thinking to throw other clothes on top of our summer blouses, and very soon we regretted it. It wasn't because we were cavalier: we had merely seen the whole situation as routine and ordinary. Indeed, what could be a threat to us? It wouldn't be too hard to bypass the ground defence centres on our way. I knew how to break away from two or three searchlight beams by gliding, unless I was on the target run. We wouldn't make much noise over the target and would get there almost unnoticed in the general rumble. That left only mistakes and accidents to get in our way, and no one was insured against them. Actually, there was the danger of being intercepted by fighter planes led by radar, but that would only happen if we completely failed to concentrate: after all, a Messer needed to close in to see the target. If you got in front of one it would dash out from under your tail. The Germans wouldn't go on the attack against machine guns shooting point blank.

Having climbed to an altitude of 3,000 metres we were pretty relaxed. An artillery duel was raging to the left of us along the front line in the darkness of the night. Flak gunners had sent a good stream of fire towards us but they were working blind, apparently guided by sound, and they didn't cause us any trouble. Somebody was bombing Bryansk. As always the sky above it flashed with dozens of powerful searchlights and glittered with bursts of heavy shells. Zhukovka, which had intrigued us most of all, showed no signs of life. But Unecha seriously bristled. Although we thought we had squashed it with ruthless bombing, almost drowning it in fire, it hadn't fallen, and was vigorously defending itself, tenaciously grabbing planes with its searchlights and firing at them from all directions. A spot for our bombs was pinpointed. Plaksitskiy was a seasoned navigator and an excellent bomb-aimer and it wasn't the hardest task for him to hit a brightly lit target.

By now the chill of the night had frozen us completely. Mitrofanov was lucky because there were aircraft covers in his cockpit as usual. He had managed to warm himself up by throwing one of them over his shoulders and he didn't hesitate to brag about it. His teeth almost chattering, Plaksitskiy gave me a return course bypassing Zhukovka and Bryansk, but it would make the route much longer, and after discussing it a bit we decided to take the direct one. We passed abeam of Zhukovka quite safely, keeping our eyes on the surrounding area. And there ahead was the front line. Skirmishing fire continued but the air wasn't under attack and even the batteries that had seen us off to Unecha were silent. The night was quiet and clear at this altitude. The stars were densely sprinkled all over the sky and I saw the Great Bear just in front of me. That was our course: towards the middle of its ladle. As soon as the front was outlined below us Plaksitskiy announced the time of intersection. At the same instant shell traces pierced the fuselage, bursting along the port side. The attack had come from behind and underneath.

'Mitrofanov,' I yelled furiously, at the same time trying to turn aside and downward, but the plane was already uncontrollable. Mitrofanov replied with a monosyllabic sound. The machine gun was silent. 'Hell, he's missed it,' flashed through my mind. Fire blazed up from the left engine. The plane lowered her nose and went into a left turn. I couldn't do anything for her, and with no hesitation gave the order to get out. A stiff stream of air issued from the navigator's cockpit. Plaksitskiy was an experienced parachute jumper and had bailed out instantly. I thought Mitrofanov had also been in time – it would have been easier for him to get out. But maybe Nikolay was wounded? He had made only a single strange sound – 'oh', 'what' or something – and nothing more. I leapt out to starboard. Opening my parachute without delay I could now see and hear the artillery fire. Where were our lines? Where was the enemy? Was I really going to land on the German side? While I was falling, although it didn't take long, everything got mixed up. I quickly found the Great Bear and, winding the strings of my parachute shroud from that direction, I began to slide northwards. Glancing at the ground I felt the parachute was moving towards our lines, but slowly. Would this slight drift be enough to save me? All my attention was concentrated on just one thing – to get as far north as possible.

The ground was approaching me quickly as just a thick mass of blackness. I managed to release the straps and a few seconds later landed hard amidst scrub and broken ground. There was not a soul around, but multitudes of flares soared in my direction and intense shooting rang out. Whose flares were they? Who was shooting? There was no certainty of salvation. I couldn't see where the plane had crashed and didn't know where or how the guys had landed. Feeling that the front line was behind me after all, I instinctively ran northwards. The chaotic landscape was covered with bushes, humps and deep furrows. I walked just a little way and came across a barbed-wire fence. Here I pressed myself against the ground to have a better look at the fenced area against the background of the sky – an empty field lay behind it. Without thinking too long I spread the wires, crawled through the fence and, bending over, began to stride forward, looking around me. The ploughed up plain all around me was still as deserted as before. Holding my loaded pistol in my hand, I now walked fully upright, pondering how my march would end. I didn't have my helmet on – it had come off during my jump. A stream of blood that would not abate kept running down my left cheek from a wound on my forehead (apparently I'd split it when I hit the cockpit sidescreen) and I kept wiping it off – now with my hand, now with my handkerchief. My right foot and ankle bone were aching a bit – most of my weight had fallen on that side when I landed on the overgrown hummocks. But none of this distracted me from the main question: where was my crew and who would I come across first?

At last another barbed-wire fence came into view ahead of me. Beyond it in a wide and shallow hollow was a road along which tractors with trailers and trucks were rumbling in complete darkness, no lights on. Carts moved past too. I hid, listening to the voices of the drivers. Suddenly I heard the unique sound of Russian cursing, so dear and sweet to my ear and heart at that moment. My people! But I couldn't relax yet: for a first contact I needed to catch someone on his own.

A man was walking down a footpath beyond the road, along the side of a timber plantation. I went to meet him. He was a *starshina* [sergeant-major – translator's note] with a submachine gun on a strap. He swept the beam of his torch towards me but I asked him to put it down. Next minute the tension eased. The *starshina* knew about the crashed plane and he walked me to the battalion's CP.

At the doorstep I was met with a question: 'Where have you been? They found your parachute 100 metres from our lines and they're still looking for you.' When I mentioned the barbed wire and torn-up ground everyone froze, opened their mouths and began to bat their eyelids. I was taken aback too: what was wrong with them? 'That's a minefield!' a battalion commander drawled. 'How did you manage not to notice?'

I wasn't at all upset by the news for I was still alive. 'And what do you know about the navigator and the radio-operator?'

'The news is not good. We've had reports from the front line that a plane crashed beyond the lines near the village of Boukan, and two men on parachutes landed on the German side.'

How could this have happened? Apparently we were still a little bit short of the front line when Plaksitskiy gave the time of crossing. Two or three kilometres didn't mean much in terms of timing because the navigation time was not calculated in seconds. Perhaps having decided to tap a message to the aerodrome Mitrofanov had moved away from the machine gun to the radio set. By showing this customary punctuality he was expressing his craftsmanship and class according to the unwritten code of honour for signalmen: his professional style, if you like. If only there had been a gunner at the ring mount watching the air at that moment. But we hadn't taken him with us. Well, we understand others' mistakes best through our own. I guess my overconfidence had so surpassed the level of my common sense that it had become more dangerous than a novice's inexperience. Everything has its price.

One can get used to anything. People get used to danger just as they get used to where they live and their daily routine. When you lose touch with the dangers inherent in a particular situation, the thresholds of risk perception are eroded; when you are seized by overconfidence, fervour and sometimes even bravado, serious consequences are inevitable. What had happened to my crew cannot be compared with the reverses that come with fluctuations in the fortunes of war. It seems that trouble comes suddenly and unexpectedly.

The fate of Ivan Plaksitskiy and Nikolay Mitrofanov passed into eternal obscurity that night. Around Boukan, which was in a zone of deeply dispersed defences, there was a high concentration of enemy troops. The local population had been expelled by the Germans from the war zone and not a single witness to the tragedy was found after the liberation of Boukan. No news about two parachutists ever reached the area, not even rumours. One can only assume that the Germans, furious after the failure of the summer offensive and their brutal defeat in the Battle of Kursk, made short work of them, rejecting the idea of taking Soviet airmen prisoner. I'd known both of them pretty well and was confident that they met their death in a shoot-out. They wouldn't have let themselves be taken alive by the enemy.

Next morning a U-2 flew over to the infantry position to pick me up.

*   *   *

The appearance of radar in the enemy's hands didn't put us off our stride, but it did arouse some uneasy curiosity. Initial intelligence about the equipment was little more than rumour. Now it seemed to be a matter of fact and we knew this technology presented a problem. Reports that came in of crews suddenly disappearing over Prussia, Germany and Lithuania were now seen in a new light: it was in these very areas that the Germans had been equipping their air force with monitoring and director stations. Corps commander Evgeniy Loginov understood the implications of this innovation and the unpleasant threat it posed to us earlier than to others. He suggested the first countermeasures: circuitous and erratic routes, changes of altitude. Radio-counteraction was out of the question back then unless one took into account the invention of a young engineer called Delnov – a pipe with levers and shutters through which foil bands would be scattered and which would reflect radio waves and stuff the radar screens with a multitude of false target signals. It was thought that a bomber's indicator would be lost among the other signals but no one really knew if it worked. Many crews suffered attacks by night fighters but they were victims not so much of radar as of their own rashness. Nevertheless, our bombers managed more than once to shoot down Messers that ran into the forestalling fire of the aerial gunners. So the score was not one sided.

Astounding coincidences happen in combat life. The very night of my ill-fated flight – 8 August – Ivan Doushkin's plane was shot up over Mga. His right engine had been hit, although not too badly, but on his way back towards Kalinin where he was planning to land he came across a storm front that had flared up towards nightfall. Ivan entered its cloudy whirlwinds hoping to make his way through by following the horizon reading, but his battle with the elements was unequally matched: the damaged engine stalled, the plane began to lose altitude rapidly and with another jerk, falling sharply onto one wing, it went headlong into the ground. Only the radio-operator managed to bail out. He told the story of the crew's last minutes. Local peasants buried the three dead airmen not far from the place of the disaster. A month later Ivan Doushkin was awarded the Gold Star of a Hero of the Soviet Union. He had been put forward for the award while he was alive but got it posthumously. A little more than a year before, on the same night in July, Vanya and I had abandoned planes destroyed in thundery clouds. And here was another tragic night for the two of us. This time he wasn't spared.

The Battle of Kursk, which crushed a major German formation without mercy, was still going on, but the Battle for Dniepr had started too. The war had shifted westwards and the Germans went on the defensive. The fronts occupied a huge area and required us to strike not only at enemy reserves and aviation groups but also at fortified districts and defensive installations on the front line – the hardest, sometimes insurmountable, obstacles for advancing troops. The ADD had started using 1-tonne bombs. Our targets were mostly in the direction of Belorussia but there were also some in the south and near Leningrad. We went where the difficulties were most acute. Our Air Force was justly nicknamed the 'fire-brigade' at the Stavka.

Towards the end of September 1943 autumn weather began to make its presence felt – winds started to blow, rain became frequent and low clouds arrived. The strain of battle didn't lessen because of the conditions, but puppy-walking the youngest flyers – the recent graduates – came almost to a halt. Some of them still needed easy weather conditions but these were available less and less often and it was becoming harder to snatch a few hours of flying time for training in between combat flights. The muster-rolls of flying personnel yawned with gaps awaiting the names of new crew commanders.

After a sortie on 5 October Radchuk and I were getting ready for another flight with the novices. That night the regiment had been bombing fortified districts in the German defence lines along the Dniepr. We came back by morning after a seven-hour flight. Clumps of low-level cloud were dragging above the aerodrome and the air was full of damp haze. None of this was conducive to training flights, and we left for Serpukhov, our canteen and barracks. But after breakfast we were surprised by a change in the weather – clear sky, sunshine, calm. Radchuk was walking beside me. He raised his head and said, 'You know what? Let's go back to the aerodrome and do some flying with the youngsters.' I began to try to talk him out of it. I said it wasn't worth doing now. We'd be better off flying in the evening before the sortie, after a nap.

'No,' Pavel Petrovich insisted, 'the weather may spoil by evening. And the guys are waiting for us.' I failed to persuade him out of it, but I didn't agree with him either and went to bed. After midday I was woken by noise, agitated voices, the tramping of feet. Somebody appeared next to me. 'What's happened? What's all this noise about?'

'Radchuk's dead!'

'That's crazy!'

No one managed to uncover the cause of his death. There were no witnesses and the debris told us nothing. In the midst of the mess were Pavel Petrovich and the crew of the very young Lieutenant Chebotarev. Somebody maintained they'd flown into an enormous cumulus cloud and tumbled out of it in a chaotic fall. There were a lot of theories – maybe it was the result of mechanical failure, error, fatigue. Some talked of a visiting Messer.

Before sunset I managed to fly with a young crew and that night I went on a bombing run against Minsk railway junction. The next day we buried Pavel Petrovich and his young comrades. In the evening we flew off again to the front line near the Dniepr. There was no time for a wake.

CHAPTER ELEVEN

Time to Sort Things Out

By the end of 1943 the ADD Commander, Alexander Evgenievich Golovanov, had begun to muster his regiments on aerodromes south-east of Leningrad. We had to sort things out with Finland. She was still fighting on the side of fascist Germany and was not ready to lay down her arms. But it was time to make her do so. Leningrad was still not completely rid of the blockade and couldn't put up with a neighbour like this any longer.

Vasiliy Gavrilovich Tikhonov had moved both his regiments to Bataly aerodrome west of Andreapol. This remote village lost in the forests and far from roads was hard to locate either from the air or on a map. A whole division of long-range bombers squeezed into the wretched, squat huts in which old people and children vegetated, where there had never been electricity or radio. Quite a few of the old people passing their lives in this cocoon had never even heard the whistle of a steam train.

The overcrowding was horrendous but room was found for me. In a crooked hut (not the worst in the village), having delicately pushed the hostess to the oven in her kitchen and thus taken over a portion of a tiny room with a window you couldn't see much out of, Gleb Bazhenov, the regimental surgeon Fedya Gorbov and I knocked up three plank-and-trestle beds. Set up at right angles to each other, they formed an open square and the fourth side near the door was allocated to the deputy chief-of-staff, Zhenya Larin, who slept on a movable bench. In the centre of the square we built ourselves a solid table and mounted a lamp on it – a shell case filled with petrol and lit by a wick which was clamped into it. Compared to other lairs it was almost luxurious.

The second, smaller, part of the room was separated from us by a dark-blue soldier's blanket which hung from the ceiling to the floor. Either three or four young women who worked in the aerodrome catering battalion were accommodated on two-storey bunks behind the blanket. They would sneak around quietly like shadows and go off to work before we woke. None of us, it seemed, displayed any kind of lecherous interest in the residents of the area behind the blanket, observing an unwritten rule: no affairs in-house. We chased all other suitors from the doorstep.

We were a long time getting around to the main targets. The winter was surprisingly snowy – blizzards interspersed with sudden thaws and night fogs. But for such a major aerial operation with mass application of the main ADD forces it was essential to have stable flying weather over the vast area that encompassed not only the new base zone for the long-range bombers but also our targets. For the time being we had to make raids on logistics lines in areas relatively nearby – Poustoshka, Vitebsk, Idritsa. Some regiments flew while others sat waiting, grounded by foul weather.

Sometimes on inclement days fierce snowball fights between regiments raged in the village square. Heated skirmish lines rushed in for the attack with belligerent shouts, pressing the foe, then retreating under his onslaught. Solid lumps of snow whizzed through the air from opposing directions and cost some imprudent warriors many bruises. The division commander would come out onto the front steps of the headquarters house at the high point of a battle. He watched the battlefield and if he detected excessive ferocity in the action would let off a red flare to stop it. The warriors then picked up their hats, jackets and gloves and dragged themselves home.

After dinner the long routine of night life began to unfold in the huts – dominoes rattled, songs were sung. In some places card games started up, spectators closely gathered round. The flyers made visits to other huts and played practical jokes on each other. Quite a few of us read books by the light of wick-lamps. We didn't have many books in our trunks, but it is true to say that there's no substitute for reading: people grow dull without it and stop thinking. My books were passed from hand to hand and a thick pre-war volume of Mayakovskiy [a famous Soviet poet, 1893–1930 – translator's note] became very popular, apparently after my loud readings, sometimes given from the page, sometimes from memory. Our hut was no exception to the general pattern of merry assemblies. What didn't go on there!

Fedya Gorbov always returned from his outpatients' surgery late and very tired. You might wonder what kind of worries a regimental surgeon could have during non-flying time, but there wasn't a single doctor or even a medical orderly in either Bataly or the neighbouring villages. The news of a military surgeon helping village people quickly spread all over the neighbourhood. Queues to see Fedor began to build – children, old men and women. From morning till night he examined those unfortunate people who were suffering with undiagnosed diseases, treating them as well as he could and with what he could. They were terribly downcast by his resolute refusal to accept a hen, eggs or anything else in return. But he was helping them not only because of his kind-heartedness and devotion to duty (that went without saying) – he simply couldn't live without medical practice and the people who recovered due to his efforts brought joy to his soul.

Once I happened to find myself in his hands. One autumn day I came off an unfamiliar motorcycle whose brakes had locked at a full speed: ploughing into the cobbled pavement, I punctured my stomach. I nearly ended up with peritonitis. Applying streptomycin, which had just become known, Fedya Gorbov fixed me up in a week, although back then the usual medical approach would have required a lot more time. He was openly oppressed by his role as a regimental surgeon, whose functions were limited to pre-flight medical checks and being on watch during take-offs. His requests to be reassigned to a land unit closer to the front, its hospitals and its medical battalions had not been successful so far, but he kept pestering the commanders and eventually they gave in to him.

New Year 1944 rolled up. Snowfalls and thick fog grounded us for a while but after a drawn-out period of bad weather the conditions improved a little and we managed to raid the targets closest to us, bombing a couple of railway stations and some aerodromes. We carried out these missions without incurring any damage, but we inflicted a lot of destruction, burned out plenty of matériel and blew several things up. Then the skies came down again and the wind began to blow. The planes were pushed closer to the woods, their covers tied down even tighter, and we knew straight away that this would be the situation for a long time. Only at the beginning of February did an anticyclone begin to make itself felt. Corps commander General Loginov gathered the regiment and squadron commanders and their navigators in his CP at Andreapol to rehearse the forthcoming sortie meticulously. The task was worked up in the regiments in even greater detail – after all, this was going to be a strike by a major force on an enemy capital.

We took off on 6 February. It was quite frosty on the ground and down to −50°C at flying altitude. The engines, under tightly closed skirts, could barely maintain minimum temperature. At times we had to play with the propeller pitch and the angle of attack so as not to chill the cylinder heads completely.

Helsinki greeted us even before we crossed the shore line. The bombing had already started. Illuminating explosions hung thickly over the port and city; bombs were going off under them with incredible density, as if tipped from a sack. There were so many aircraft around that I was afraid of colliding with my neighbours. We had plenty of targets to go for – plants, barracks, depots ... Each regiment had its points to aim at. Plumes of smoke entwined a huge area covering the city; fires burned crimson beneath them; explosions flashed. Searchlights broke through towards us from below, but the smoke and fires seemed to dazzle the operators because the beams rolled around the skies as if blind. The ack-ack was inaccurate but it was still firing with all possible ferocity, peppering the routes to our targets with shell bursts. There were so many aircraft that the shells sometimes found them just by chance. And when the searchlights managed to grab hold of someone a proper execution would commence. We couldn't avoid losses: apparently they'd been expecting our strike on Helsinki and had prepared a strong rebuff. Petya Arkhipov led our plane over a wharf, dropped his bombs after aiming at the fires, and then we broke free, surrounded but untouched by bursting shells.

At that time one of the men got his feet well and truly frostbitten. And it was no wonder: we hardly ever removed our fur-lined jackboots – people would walk in them and fly in them. There was nowhere to dry out the moisture they accumulated and insoles saturated with sweat were no help in a −50° frost. But the intense cold didn't do me any harm because I wore my old, worn-out, fur-lined boots on the ground and travelled to the aerodrome with the new ones hanging over my shoulder, putting them on before I got in the plane.

Petya's feet were nipped during the first flight. He wanted to turn a blind eye to the situation and head off for another sortie but the surgeon stopped him. We had to look for another navigator. We found Kirill Doubovoy from Nikolay Strelchenko's crew. Nikolay also had swollen heels and toes. He couldn't fly and, letting me have his navigator, he handed his plane over to a reserve crew. We took off after midnight. The first to get into the air at 0030 hours was Nestor Kroutogouz, of course. He tended to just grit his teeth if someone went ahead of him, but this time the leading position was his by right because he was carrying photographic bombs and would have to capture images of the port area from two approaches, one at the beginning and the other at the end of the raid.

The fires in Helsinki were visible all the way from Lake Choudskoye, over which we flew, holding course for the city. This time the raid was somewhat drawn out and therefore seemed less intense, but in terms of the total force used it yielded nothing to the first. The ground defences fired as tirelessly and ferociously as before, and not in vain – Doubitskiy's and Paukov's crews were shot down. Other regiments incurred losses too.

Kirill laid out his bombs and put us on the return course, but we were not destined to reach home: we received an order to land at Edrovo. Lots of aircraft and people ended up there because many of the other aerodromes were fogbound that morning. Few had managed to return home by midday. Bataly was still closed, but the meteorologists were promising better visibility followed by clear weather in half an hour, so what was the point was of sitting and rubbing elbows in the Edrovo bazaar? By the time we got to Bataly it would be open. We took off from Edrovo in a small group (five or six crews) and pulled for Bataly. Kroutogouz followed on our tail. This bloke spent too much time trying to show his strength, not only demanding recognition for being as accomplished as the most experienced men, but trying to outdo them in everything, almost making a spectacle of himself with his fearlessness. He hadn't yet realised that the most outwardly courageous and bold flyers were also the most careful and prudent. I had had to put him in his place a few times, marking him down for deliberate demonstration of his 'capabilities' during piloting tests.

Having arrived in the regiment as a senior sergeant, Nestor was already an officer with battle decorations. He was always looking to make an impression. A serious accident occurred during a take-off at Serpukhov when engine failure made Simkin's plane slide off the airstrip and blow up on the spot. Kroutogouz, seeing the other crews were frozen by the spectacle, taxied around them and without waiting for signals from a scared starter, took off past Simkin's burning plane and flew off on the mission. This time, after the Helsinki raid, that devil wanted to be the first to land, even though fields of foggy rags were still hanging over the aerodrome and all the other crews, believing the mists were just about to disappear, were in a holding circle. Kroutogouz wasn't happy about the delay. He slowed down and went to break through the milk, but he missed the landing strip, hit the pine tree tops, got stuck and crashed. It was an ending typical of so many attempts to find a fogbound aerodrome.

We buried them next to each other, like brothers, in a village cemetery in a pine forest on a hillock in Bataly, unknown to the rest of the world. Nestor was at the edge of the plot, Misha Isachenko – the navigator – next to him, then gunner/radio-operators Barinov and Mandrikov. There was a fifth man among them – photo technician Lieutenant Evgeniy Chernyshev. They were superb men and all of them just twenty-two or twenty-three years old.

Back then we all tried to guess whether the weather frustrated the commanders' plans or whether it had been necessary to wait for the Finns' reaction before deciding what to do next. A second raid on the same targets didn't happen until 17 February (eleven days after the first) and was carried out by only a limited force; the third one, at full strength again, was launched on the 26th. Strikes were made not only at targets in Helsinki but also on the seaports of Turku and Kotka.

After Finland's withdrawal from the war the brass from Soviet military command visited its capital. They expected to see ruins, but it turned out that most of the buildings were still standing. Someone suggested that the Finns, foreseeing the bombardment, had built a dummy city next to Helsinki and the ADD had unloaded on the decoy. But that wasn't the case. We hadn't touched the city because we hadn't been tasked to do so: our targets were military, political and administrative installations – the port, wharf, railway junctions, industrial works on Helsinki's outskirts. Golovanov's order had been 'to refrain from a massive strike upon the city itself'. Destruction had been achieved by choosing the right mass and class of bombs to match the nature of each individual target. As for the stray bombs that landed in no small number in the city proper, the 100kg devices that made up the bulk of our arsenal couldn't do much damage to the large, solid buildings there.

After the third strike we didn't leave our dispersal points immediately because the Stavka was engaged in determining whether a fourth was needed. Our push played a not inconsiderable part in influencing the situation. The Finnish public began to speak out against the war and there was confusion in government circles about what to do next. After the first strike Paasikivi, a representative of the Finnish government, visited the Soviet ambassador in Sweden to negotiate conditions for withdrawal from the war. The Soviet Union demanded an unconditional ceasefire and a break with Germany. It seemed that Finland was just about to hoist the white flag but then Helsinki fell silent. The Stavka did not expect this turn of events, and Golovanov wasn't happy about it either. As spring approached Moscow was advised that Finland was now ready to consider withdrawing from the war, but at approximately the same time the German Minister of Foreign Affairs, von Ribbentrop, arrived in Helsinki, and after formidable negotiations he prompted President Ryti to declare that Finland would not quit the war except by agreement with Germany. 'Extra measures' would have to be applied to resolve the situation. A Karelian Front operation completed the task: at the beginning of September 1944 Finland ceased to resist and quit the war.

Of course, as we waited for a decision back in those March days we didn't sit idle: we smashed German installations in Narva, Tallinn and other locations on the south coast of the Gulf of Finland. When the weather was good we made three sorties a night, at the same time letting the Finns know we were still around. The ground defences at Narva, and especially Tallinn, were well organised and looked very powerful, but during those moonlit nights the main danger came from fighter planes. Here and there the air on the target approaches was criss-crossed by luminous, dotted machine-gun traces, flying from the most unexpected directions so that it was hard to tell whether the bullets were coming from friend or foe. The side of the aircraft illuminated by the moon was the most vulnerable. Visibility was so good from that direction that it was as though the planes were projected on a giant cinema screen, and this exposed us to rapid and sudden attacks. Our division was spared by Fortune but others were less lucky.

Spring came to Bataly. We had to leave while the snow still lay on the ground, and we flew across to Prilouki in the Ukraine. It was already warm there. The footpaths were dry, but the aerodrome was covered by *chernozem* [black earth, the most agriculturally fertile kind of soil – translator's note], sticky as congealed fuel-oil: it could pull the jackboots off your feet. However, in the middle of the field there was a kilometre-long, rock-paved airstrip with a chipped concrete surface. A narrow taxi path – only a little wider than a plane's undercarriage – led to the parking area. The planes lined up in single file before taking off for a combat mission, drawing up to the edge of the airstrip in turn, then immediately beginning their run, barely taking off before they ran out of runway. Landing was a lot more hassle. Everybody returned from a mission at the same time, gathering in a crowd and stepping on each other's toes before forcing their way to the landing strip. It was necessary to get clear of the strip as quickly as possible after touchdown to avoid the plane's tail being chopped off, and the flyers had no time to hesitate. Having slowed down a bit, they turned right at the end of the strip and, heading for a free space, rushed onto the mud at full speed, trying to get as far away from the strip as possible before the plane got bogged in the viscous soil. At dawn we were greeted by the bizarre spectacle of several dozen scattered planes bogged up to their wheel-hubs; it looked like an abandoned battlefield or a ploughed meadow where gigantic birds had been forced to land. Tractors, straining with all their might, dragged the aircraft out onto the concrete and towed them to their stations. There the sleepless technicians washed them, inspected them and got them ready for the next night's flight.

Spring quickly turns into summer in the Ukraine and soon the new green grass could easily bear the weight of our heavy planes. Thank God the Germans hadn't managed to knock us out when the aircraft stood wing to wing in a cramped parking area. Now we dispersed them in zigzags along the edges of the aerodrome and a sudden, belated German raid which caught us sitting on the ground at night looked dashing but didn't do much damage: the flak guns had obviously cut the attackers down to size.

By that time the front line had rolled noticeably westwards. Soviet planes had mastery of the air, and south and south-west were our new target directions. The regiment was still fighting below strength, but quite a few young crews had arrived from the schools. At Bataly we hadn't managed to train even one crew to the skill level required for combat operations; Prilouki was a different story. The summer weather was stable there, the aerodrome was dry and planes were available for training flights. After Pavel Radchuk's death I'd been appointed to his position as deputy regiment commander and had to organise all the regiment's flying. This sometimes meant I had to refuse to make combat flights. When the regiment was out on a mission I buzzed over the aerodrome. Then one of the young pilots who was ahead of the rest would be ready to make his first combat sortie. Gradually the others would catch up, and finally we would all fly out together on an operational bombing raid. Then new crews would arrive, eager for their turn to head out on a sortie.

Foreign towns and cities began to crop up among the names of the targets we were assigned relatively nearby – Galati, Constanta, Bucharest, Ploesti ... Oil fields, fuel dumps and tankers blazed. And how they burned, whole fields of them! We observed this astounding spectacle from a distance of 200, sometimes 300 kilometres. The ground defences here always had large-calibre guns, with searchlights as dense as a pine forest. Two other targets, Kerch and Sevastopol, fired at us especially fiercely too, throwing up what looked like completely impermeable walls of solid fire. During the fourth raid on ships in Sevastopol harbour on 8 May 1944 they managed to hit our left engine and broke our oil feed system. I failed to notice the damage and kept flying along the attack heading until Arkhipov had dropped our bombs upon the burning seaport. As we passed over the Crimea on our way back the oil began to heat up dangerously, the pressure fell towards zero and I had to turn off the engine. Unfortunately the propeller kept spinning like a windmill, creating unwelcome and considerable resistance. The plane gradually began to lose altitude. If the weather had been good we would have made it home, but fog was descending at Prilouki and planes were being directed to land anywhere they could. Under the circumstances we turned towards the nearest aerodrome, Noviy Boug. I knew it well for I'd landed on it very recently when bad weather covered the east of the Ukraine. There were facilities for night take-offs, searchlights, a homing station. In the past front-line aircraft had been based there: now it was home to defence fighter planes which protected the city of Krivoy Rog. We made one circle after another over Noviy Boug, sending signals identifying ourselves as friend and one red flare after another asking for an emergency landing, but not a single light shone from below. Everything was dead quiet. Our altitude was falling, but I hadn't yet lost hope of raising at least one man who would rush to help a heavy plane in trouble and turn on a couple of lights, at least the landing floodlights. My efforts were in vain. Reaching another aerodrome was out of the question, and where would we go anyway? Was anyone on duty elsewhere? Maybe other bases would be closed like this one? Our altitude dropped to 1,000 metres. A little bit more and it would be too late to bail out. But the plane was brand new and still in one piece! Was there any way out? I felt desperate.

It was a moonless southern night, black and impenetrable. I headed about 30 kilometres south-east by guesswork and, reckoning that there should be flat steppe below, I decided to land. It would be too dangerous to come down on the undercarriage: any kind of obstacle would mean certain death. What if I got everyone to bail out and tried it on my own? 'Petya,' I said, 'stuff as many white flares as you can and a few red ones into your pockets and bail out. If you land on flat ground send me a signal with the white ones and give me some light for landing. If it's bumpy send up the red ones.' The radio-operators were in no great danger and I decided to keep them on board – they would have time to bail out anyway.

I circled and waited for signals. Arkhipov did his job absolutely precisely. At last there was a white flare and then another: he was surveying the ground. Then another white one and a few more ... I slowed down, closed in, turned on the landing lights and aimed at Petya without putting the undercarriage down. The lights slid over young, green crops. I levelled out a bit lower and the plane headed towards Petya and his flares. We were about to touch down when I saw a small gully overgrown to the same level as the crops (Petya couldn't see it!) and it was exactly where I planned to land. Fortunately I hadn't yet turned off the right engine. Giving it full throttle and making it let out a roar as if in pain, I skip over the damned gully. Now I couldn't see the flares any more and had lost nearly all speed. I turned off the engine and ploughed our belly into the soft field. The screeching and sharp braking suddenly gave way to complete silence. We flew out of the cockpits and turned on our pocket torches: the propellers were bent, the lower engine cowlings and undercarriage nacelles were crumpled, but it would fly again. We were lucky not to have landed on the undercarriage – had it gone into the gully we would all have been burning down there by now.

With the first rays of the sun I had a look at the surroundings: there was a flat field in front of us and a black forest in the distance. In this terrain we would be able to take off again. Petya and I walked towards

Noviy Boug, came out onto a road and reached a garrison by hitching a lift on the first passing vehicle (who would refuse to do airmen a favour?). We reported the accident to our commander and talked to the local brass.

The Germans had bombed Noviy Boug the previous night and, having no flak guns for defence, the aerodrome had survived only because of the darkness – the fighter pilots based there couldn't fly at night. We, in spite of our 'friend' signals, red flares and behaviour absolutely typical of a plane in trouble, had been identified as a 'fascist carrion crow'. It had been easier for them to come to this conclusion: less hassle, no worries. Fortunately they had no flak guns, otherwise they would have shot us down. And none of the local commanders got it in the neck for our belly-landing. They pretended to be ignorant of the circumstances, and what was it to them if I cursed?

By evening a C-47 transport plane had arrived to pick us up, delivering technicians, tools and equipment to lift our aircraft. They had to replace the engines too. A month later, taking off from the same spot, I flew to Prilouki – and that aircraft would go on a lot more missions.

*   *   *

Dnepropetrovsk had been liberated from the fascists back in October 1943 but I hadn't heard from my mother or father for a long time. They had no news of me either until my father's long time friend brought him a magazine with a photo of me wearing a Gold Star. This prompted my father to write to his brother Fedor in Moscow to see if he knew anything about what had happened to me. Fedya replied and also passed on my family's new address to me. We immediately began to exchange letters. I helped them with money but what I wanted most of all was to see them – after all, Dnepropetrovsk was so close. At the end of May the division commander sent his C-47 on a mission to the south and he said to me, 'Get on board. It'll drop you in Dnepropetrovsk, and in a day or so I'll send an Il-4 to pick you up.'

My joy was unbounded. My mother, father and I spent two days together. They'd seen a lot of trouble but were safe and sound, though still concerned for the fate of my younger brother Zheka. Before fleeing from Dnepropetrovsk the fascists had deported him to Germany [as a slave labourer – translator's note]. He hadn't been heard from since. Then in 1944 he managed to escape. He made his way to the front line and fought there till the end of the war as a machine-gunner, was wounded twice and got a medal 'For Valour'. In 1946 he was still doing army service in Belorussia. Not counting on a successful outcome, I wrote a letter to the military district commander with a request that he send my brother to the regiment I was in charge of now. To my surprise a week later Zhenya himself arrived wearing red infantry shoulder badges. It didn't take long to decide which duties should be assigned to him. He was already an infantry machine-gunner and he asked to become an aerial gunner. He did some training, acquired the necessary skills and took up his position. Initially he flew in my crew. Then – to keep him out of trouble – I transferred him to another one. But that was much later. In late May 1944 I was at home in Dnepropetrovsk: my two days flew by in an instant.

Early the next morning, before sunrise, I headed for the aerodrome. The plane had been flown in by Zhenya Yakovlev. He moved to the front cockpit, I got into the pilot's seat and we took off. After making a couple of circles above my parents' house I flew low over the tree tops along the boulevard, switched to climb and turned towards Prilouki. I would not see my parents again until after the war.

* * *

At that time my schedule was approximately as follows: three or four nights with the juniors around the aerodrome, then a couple of combat missions. The Yassy–Kishinev operation was still ahead of us, but we were already bombing the German troops around the two towns. During preparations for a raid on Yassy the regiment commander told me, 'Colonel Tikhonov will go with you in the front cockpit to monitor the results of the raid.'

This was no joke. The navigator and I prepared even more meticulously than usual, calculating which place to take in the formation and how we should pass around the target in order to give the division commander a full picture of the raid and assess its final result. Tikhonov's presence meant Petya and I wouldn't be able to smoke that day. Usually Petya rolled a little cigar out of newspaper and stuffed it with tobacco or *makhorka* [low-quality, poorly processed tobacco – translator's note] somewhere in the middle of the flight. He would light it up and, tapping my leg, would hand it to me before making another for himself. I would shut the right window and open the left one so that the tobacco smoke was sucked out together with the sparks. The butt went the same way. Of course it was stupidity, especially since the engine start control panel and its usually leaky petrol taps were on the right-hand side of the pilot cockpit. We acquired the habit of smoking in flight not because of an insurmountable desire to inhale tobacco smoke but from plain foppishness. This time, however, we would have to refrain: Tikhonov would be monitoring not only the raid on Yassy but also the operational readiness of the crew.

All the division heads stood by to see our plane leave. Before take-off I agreed with the flight leader the special light signals by which our plane could be distinguished from the whole mass of others when everyone crammed over the aerodrome before landing. We took off in the middle of the trailing regiment, climbed to the right altitude and flew by the horizon reading. The night was clear and starry. There was silence, if you discounted the buzz of the engines. The only words came from Arkhipov who gave adjustments to the course now and then and counted off the time. The commander was silent too. But then the divine aroma of expensive cigarettes reached me from the front cockpit. I inhaled avidly. 'The commanders live a good life,' I thought with unintentional envy, but at the same moment someone nudged my leg and a lit cigarette was handed to me. I took it carefully in my fingers, said thanks to the colonel and, slowly, deeply inhaling its aroma, smoked it to the very end. The commander fed me some chocolate too. What a treat!

The guns on the front line shot up into the sky at full tilt but we could see gaps which were free of fire and crossed without problems. Yassy lay ahead. While we were still some way off we began to see the burning outlines of the railway station and the area where troops were concentrated. Then, coming closer, we could make out the beams of dozens of searchlights and intense flak fire. I calculated how to reach the target and, after discussing it with Petr, closed in. The nearer we got to the target, the denser the shell bursts became, but our bombs were laid densely too. The division commander had no reason to be frustrated by the results of his men's work that night. All hell raged on the ground and in the air. The earth must have been shaken by flak fire and exploding bombs, but for us the spectacle was soundless. The searchlights had not touched us yet; they had been carried off by someone else and the main bulk of fire was concentrated there. If they had known who was on board our plane they would have thrown the whole lot at us: division commanders didn't fly over to the Germans every day.

Petya didn't simply bomb that day – he showed real class. He dropped the bombs successfully and, avoiding searchlights and shells, we sneaked past on the sly. We were on the periphery of the flak area (which, of course, was weaker than the centre) and I reduced altitude so as not to collide with those coming in to attack. Then, as planned, I put the plane into a left turn for a look over the target. The commander didn't understand why I had made this manoeuvre. 'Where are you going?' he asked, perplexed.

'Around the target, Comrade Colonel, to make it handier for you.'

Tikhonov seemed to gasp for breath for a second, but the next moment he uttered a roar: 'What the hell? Get out of here immediately!'

I shot sideways like a cork, stayed on the traverse for a while (as far as possible from the bursting shells) and then headed home. I felt terrible, only now comprehending the stupidity of the escapade. Essentially I had repeated Mikhail Uroutin's mistake when he nearly handed the Germans General Loginov over Korotoyak. I was worried that the commander had lost faith in me: I valued his opinion enormously. But on the way home Tikhonov gave me cigarettes as if nothing had happened and was really animated. I landed as soon as we reached Prilouki – the flight operations officer saw my signals, sent the other crews off in all directions and cleared the way for us. The division commander shook my hand cordially and didn't reproach me for my stupid decision. The next time he needed to fly he went with me again.

Targets in Belorussia followed. These sorties turned out to be anything but simple: a grand Belorussian offensive operation was being prepared. First we targeted aerodromes: Baranovichi, Minsk, Borisov. Then on 22 and 23 June we raided the enemy's fortified districts on the front line near Mogilev and Zhlobin with 1-tonne bombs. The night-time weather, especially on the eve of the breakthrough, was terrifying for this kind of work – low clouds, rain, pitch darkness. We flew with terrible strain on our strength and nerves. To drop a tonne of bomb you need an altitude of no less than 1,000 metres – any lower and you get wiped out by the blast wave. But in the prevailing conditions where were we going to find that kind of height? We flew at a bit below 1,000 metres and sometimes touched the rain clouds or even saw low-level clouds rushing beneath us. Don't let them get any thicker! The conditions were extreme, on a razor's edge. We couldn't postpone or redirect the raid: the machinery of the operation had been launched and nobody but long-range bombers could crack those fortifications. Blazing buildings, artillery fire, searchlights and flares revealed the target location. If we made what in school we had called a 'C-grade' bombing run we could quite easily have harmed our own troops. A 1-tonne bomb is no joke and calculations for placing it have to be exact. The bombing was dense, the darkness cut by bright flashes. Arkhipov brought us to the target and bombed it from minimum height. After the weapon was dropped the plane lurched upwards and Petr found time to warn me, 'Hold on there, commander!' Our tonne lit up the whole world and shook it so violently that the control wheel jerked out of my hands. We were on our way home. The enemy put up no defence – he had been completely neutralised. But the crew of Vasya Galochkin – a very experienced and able flyer, seasoned even before the war – met its death after turning on to the homeward course. The search for him continued for some time, but without success. That night several crews from other regiments died too.

CHAPTER TWELVE

A Jubilee and an Excommunication

A considerable force of long-range bombers had been concentrated at our operations directorate. General Loginov's corps hadn't been diverted to other tasks and the corps commander himself ran operations not from a stationary command post but from an aerial one (ACP). He had created it himself and it was the only one in the ADD. He either patrolled with his group in the operations zone, advancing to the front line, or landed on one of the combat aerodromes. Ours in Prilouki was no exception. His C-47 would take root in a free bay, and hard-wired and radio communications would be set up to link it with the regimental and divisional CPs, with Moscow (the ADD and Stavka), and, when regiments were in the air, with the combat formations. All information about the aerial and combat situation, intelligence data, reports from below and orders from above were drawn together at the ACP. Of course the main CP run by the chief-of-staff didn't stop working, but the aerial CP significantly increased the degree of efficiency with which the whole corps' combat activity could be controlled.

On 26 June 1944 we bombed Borisov aerodrome. It would have been a mission like any other but instead of Arkhipov I was assigned Colonel Zuev, head of the ADD's ground test service. He had arrived from Moscow not really as a monitor but rather with the intention of getting the hang of combat work. I'd been ordered to fly with him. His position in the ADD suggested he must be a good bomb-aimer. That was what mattered and if needs be, the rest of us would find the way to the target. But that sortie was more special for the fact that it was my jubilee 300th. As would become clear later, this fact was known not only to the commanders and headquarters but also to my friends. They never said a word about it before take-off. We were all superstitious (some more than others) and rather afraid of exchanging unnecessary farewells or any kind of meaningful words before sorties. Who knew what might happen?

We took off at the end of the group, calmly and silently approached Borisov aerodrome and managed to be there while the illuminating bombs were still in the air. We found the target and the navigator dropped our bombs. It looked as though everything had gone well: he hit the target and something caught fire below. The searchlights didn't find us and the flak guns hadn't hit us. We returned to Prilouki where I landed, taxied to the parking area and began to cool the engines, not hurrying to get out of the cockpit. The bright lights of the cockpit stopped me noticing that I was being approached along the wing. It was Gleb Bazhenov, of course, and someone else was with him. Gleb hugged my head, pressed me against him, shouted out congratulations and, not giving the engines a chance to cool down, shoved his hand inside the cockpit and turned them off. 'They'll be all right,' he said. Someone else's hands stretched towards me. 'Stop dawdling and get out!' Gleb ordered, hurrying me along.

When I got down off the wing I was mobbed by the other guys but Gleb dragged me to the stabiliser. There in the darkness I discerned a white newspaper scattered with plates and mugs. When did they manage it? I detected a strong smell of *samogon* from afar. I was offered a tin mug and someone held a gherkin out to me. But before I had time to grab it or breathe in [people usually breathe out before gulping a shot of vodka – translator's note] I heard a shrill voice from the darkness: 'Major Reshetnikov – to the corps commander!' Hell! Everything snapped inside me. What would the general think when he detected the smell of *samogon* on me, straight after I'd taxied to the parking area? Would he conclude I'd been drinking while flying?

There was nothing for it. Running, as was proper according to army regulations of the time, I rushed to the corps commander's plane. I climbed the ladder and saw him at the desk near the pilot's cockpit. Rather than take even a step towards him I shouted loudly down the length of the fuselage, 'Reporting as ordered.' To my horror Loginov, spreading his arms wide and smiling cheerfully, headed towards me, saying over and over: 'My dear fellow, you're the first in the corps to make 300 sorties! Well, thank you, my congratulations!' He hugged and kissed me as I stood like a statue with my lips tightly closed, not daring to say a word. Then the whole operational staff of the CP congratulated me in turn, shaking my hand. Loginov concluded the ceremony: 'Well, off you go to the canteen – they're waiting for you.' Trying not to breathe I thanked the general, said the words appropriate to the moment and rushed outside. I don't know if he noticed the murderous smell.

In the airmen's canteen long tables had been pushed together for a celebration and a multi-coloured placard was stretched along the wall. There were ceremonial toasts and jokes drowned by laughter. Somebody banged out pre-war jazz rhythms on an old piano. We left in the quiet, sunlit dawn and by nightfall I was on the aerodrome again, ready to fly a new mission.

The regiment commander, Alexander Ivanovich Shaposhnikov, reclined in his Willis [American-made light vehicle – translator's note] next to the CP, having a snooze in the setting sun. With one eye half-open and some irony (which put me on my guard), laziness and deliberate foolishness, he asked me, 'You're not off to fight, are you?' There was some kind of dirty trick implicit in his intonation. Unable to figure out what it was, I tried to fall in with his tone and answered that I was.

'But you're not allowed to!'

'What do you mean, "not allowed"?' I was confused.

'Just that. So grab your machine and fly with the youngsters.'

'Is it just for today?'

'No, brother, it's for good.'

'That can't be.' I felt the anger starting to rise and couldn't understand what was going on. 'What made you decide to do this?'

'No, my dear fellow, it wasn't me. Tikhonov called and said it was an order from above.'

The division commander was still in his headquarters. Alexander Ivanovich gave me his Willis and I headed to the city. 'The order came from the ADD commander,' the division commander said. 'He said, "He's done enough flying on combat missions: let him train the young ones." So do it.'

Whether this was true or whether he had initiated the excommunication himself was anyone's guess. Thirty years later I asked Alexander Evgenievich Golovanov about it directly. The Chief Marshal of the Air Force answered in the following way: 'It was not just about you. The war was approaching its end: it was time to think about the post-war development of the ADD and to begin to conserve the seasoned commanding personnel. Yes, that year many seasoned young commanders had their combat sortie accounts closed: we were not short of flying crews anymore.' Thus, a year before the end of the war Golovanov had not only begun to think about the post-war fate of the ADD but had also started to lay its groundwork.

Between the day of my excommunication and the end of the war I managed to beg only six operational sorties from the regiment commander and 'insolently' stole one more, flying off on a mission against his will. Instructing young pilots became my main duty but sometimes as a warm-up I would make other flights, often on the slightest pretext: to pick someone up after a forced landing, to reconnoitre sudden bad weather, to test-fly a dodgy plane. I spent much more time hanging around near the landing T during take-off, watching training flights by lieutenants who were already flying on their own, giving the regiment's crews permission to go out on a combat mission and then awaiting their return. Gradually regular checks of flying techniques were reintroduced according to the rules and regulations of the pre-war period. It was my duty to oversee them too.

* * *

The front was moving further and further west. We were not supposed to fall behind. Our targets were only 10 minutes from the line of engagement but the flight up to it over Russian territory took hours. We didn't have to go far to relocate to another aerodrome – only about 200 kilometres to Bushev, west of Kiev. It was an ordinary open field on *chernozem*. The ground was soft and peppered with sparse grass. It got soggy when it rained but while the weather stayed dry and hot nothing interfered with flying from it.

One after another the youngest crews opened their flying accounts. They were eager to get into combat and were terribly proud of belonging to the front-line brotherhood. For every crew their first operational sortie generates a wave of emotions and impressions. Everything is new and everything comes at once. Even a take-off with a full load of operational bombs wasn't exactly the same as one made with the same weight of dummy ones. And not everyone could do it at the first attempt. It was vital for every crewman to be in complete control of himself on his first flight. The second time out he would feel like a seasoned falcon who had seen something of life.

Alexander Ivanovich was still uncompromising in his determination that I should not take part in combat sorties and only once did he allow me to go on a mission: to take part in a raid on a fortified district near Kovel. He wouldn't listen to me any more. Having been cut out of operational flying himself, he would while away the nights at the CP and he kept his navigator – Maxim Alexeev, the regiment's senior navigator – back with him. But once (it was at the end of August), without any hope that the commander would show clemency when he found out, I persuaded Maxim, who was my friend, to make a sneak attack on a good target so we could 'get some fresh air'. Tilsit turned up and among the targets there was a bridge across the Neman. Take-off was to be in the dark. We couldn't have had better luck.

We did our calculations, prepared maps and put on our leather jackets. We had chosen our victims, an ordinary crew, ahead of time. Their plane had been kitted out with the kind of bomb load appropriate for destroying bridges. We drove up to their machine, deplaned the flyer and the navigator from their cockpits, took their places, turned on the engines and took off in the queue under another's call sign. It was hooliganism of the first order, but we badly wanted to break through the defensive flak above a strong enemy target and drop bombs on it. What made us do it? Zeal for revenge? A feeling that we were shirking our battle duties? Neither can be ruled out, for the war was still raging. But there was something else. I'm afraid it's impossible to understand fully the logic of what we did. When the regiment took off on a combat mission and I stood with a starting pistol on the quiet and deserted aerodrome my soul was flooded with a stinging feeling of awkwardness, vexation, almost shame. It was as if I had refused battle having found some easier job to do and sent young men into danger in my place. And who is going to argue with the fact that danger itself is charged with an attractive and magnetic force?

The flight with Maxim went easily, even cheerfully. The time passed quickly in lively conversation. As we approached the shores of the Baltic we began to search the blackness of the starry sky carefully. The reason for the extra vigilance was that during the work-up of the task the chief of reconnaissance had set a flea among the crews, warning them that the Germans had jet fighters over this part of East Prussia. What a thing to contemplate: apparently these aircraft had no propeller but flew at nearly 1,000 kilometres an hour! Did they really? Nobody had seen them but people said they existed. Imagination drew a long fiery tail across the skies in search of prey. We didn't see jets: they hadn't yet begun to fly at night.

Tilsit didn't surprise us with anything new. It shot at us desperately and reached out with searchlights but it continued to burn and explode: a lot of matériel had accumulated in depots and trains there. Maxim took us towards the bridge: bombs exploded and there was a good deal of shooting going on. Tilsit was defended particularly well. I had to descend a bit to let Maxim fix the bombsight on the thin thread that cut the Neman river. Every metre counted here. No manoeuvring – just follow a straight line. It was no accident that the bridges had cost us many planes and airmen, more than any other targets.

We failed to break through unnoticed: they caught us in their searchlights and began to pour well-aimed fire in our direction but failed to make a hit. It seemed the illuminating bombs hanging over the bridge had become a considerable nuisance for the flak gunners. After the bomb drop Maxim and the radio-operators began to assure me noisily that the batch had crossed at a narrow angle and knocked out the centre of the bridge, having exploded in several places in its girders. Let's hope so. I hadn't witnessed it myself.

After landing we called in to the CP, as we were required to do, to report the completion of the mission. All hell broke loose. The 'escape' had been discovered very quickly because there had been witnesses on the ground. The commander wanted to call us back immediately but the chief-of-staff talked him out of it. You might think that Shaposhnikov would have cooled down while we were in the air, accepted the incident and tempered his anger. No. When he saw us he roared like a wild boar, rushed towards us and, not mincing his words, fell upon us with such fury that all the witnesses to the scene flinched. We took the hits steadfastly, not suspecting that the worst was still to come. I knew Alexander's anger must peak somehow, but I didn't expect perfidy. However, he was looking for the most fiendish possible punishment for us. Banging his fist on the table, he pronounced sentence: 'No vodka for them!' We nearly burst out laughing at his pronouncement. Choking with laughter and hiding their faces, all the other guys turned to the walls.

At last we had a chance to give our account of the mission. Maxim's report about the explosions in the bridge girders and the damage done to the structure elicited a spiteful snigger from the commander: 'He broke the bridge! The whole division wasn't enough to knock it down. And, you weren't the only ones who bombed it.'

Yes, a bridge is a tricky target. You can pepper it with bombs but if they pass through its network of girders it will shake from the explosions but still remain in one piece. The Neman bridge was bombed by the whole group and probably significantly weakened, but out of Maxim's precision batch only one or two, at most three, bombs fortunate enough to blow up in the structure's wobbly joints might have completed the job. However, no reports were taken on trust – there had to be evidence and Lounev saved us. That night he brought excellent photos on which the destruction of the bridge was obvious. It softened the commander's attitude. He didn't remit our sentence, but he did stop being angry, and the previously cordial relationship between us was restored.

* * *

There were intense summer raids on German positions between the strips of the advancing fronts and we didn't notice the arrival of the Ukrainian autumn. Then the ground at Bushev began to grow soft under lengthy rainfall, but the western aerodromes still occupied by front-line aircraft were not yet ready to receive our planes. We had to make a temporary move to a firmer, though cramped, airstrip nearby. Loginov's whole corps based around Kiev was living out of suitcases but its operations weren't being wound up yet and regiments would rush off on combat missions at the smallest break in the weather. When showers and thick, persistent fog pinned the whole district down, everyone was idle.

One day, in anticipation of a night grounded, a group of officers was invited to the Kiev circus. Emil Kio – a famous illusionist – was to perform. Tickets were given to Heroes of the Soviet Union and the most heavily decorated men. The corps commander ordered us to 'Come to the circus in your decorations!' Towards evening, having overtaken each other on the roads leading to Kiev using whatever transport we could get our hands on – overloaded *polutorkas*, Willises, motorcycles – the 'Loginov Guards' gathered under the tarpaulin dome of the circus in an 'invasion of stars'. Only when we had taken our seats did we understand the secret reason for the order to turn up in our decorations: all of us had seats in the front row encircling the arena and the solid line of decorations on our chests was an absolutely incredible sight. The spectators were enraptured. Flowers apparently initially destined for the performers flew down to our feet from the upper rows. We felt quite embarrassed, but happy too.

Just before the beginning of the show Evgeniy Fedorovich Loginov came through the central entrance accompanied by two very tall, handsome men – the division commanders, Vasiliy Gavrilovich Tikhonov and Alexey Petrovich Sherbakov. Although Evgeniy Fedorovich was quite short he wasn't lost in his general's uniform against the background of these giant colonels. We automatically stood up to greet our commanders and that stirred the spectators to even greater excitement.

During the second part of the show the arena was occupied by Emil Kio and his colourful array of pretty female assistants. The maestro was exasperated and clearly angry – and rightly so: his girls' minds were elsewhere. Instead of watching their boss they spent most of the time glancing at our row (and, of course, finding reciprocal attention there). It was not by chance that our boldest ladykillers didn't come back to their regiments till morning.

Of course, only the corps commander could have organised such a thing. What an extraordinary man he was – unpredictable and out of the ordinary in everything: views, deeds and decisions. He had a lively and active mind and an undying thirst for action. He had more initiative and was more sagacious than many others charged with organising and leading combat operations. Blocking planes combined into regiments was his idea: only he had an aerial CP and he was the first to introduce countermeasures to the German radar. His debriefings and airmen's conferences attracted not only those for whom they were intended but also many other commanders.

The day after the circus trip our regiment flew over to Gritsev near Shepetovka. An advance operative group, armed with its estimation and intelligence data set up, was already waiting for us there. We had to transfer the data onto our flight maps and enter it into logbooks. The first night the crews went out on a combat flight.

Russian target names had completely disappeared from our schedules and the toponomy now had a consistently foreign accent. I must admit this made us all feel easier in our hearts. October whistled with winds, dragged in low clouds and poured fine rain on us, but our regiment was robust and still managed to carry out two sorties each night. The next group of young lieutenants was now breathing down my neck. The most impatient hurried me, prodded me, tried with all their might to secure a combat mission as soon as possible. However, I have to admit that more even-tempered ones arrived too.

Gritsev was a big village – a district centre. Several stone houses towered above the main square, and around them were huts, vegetable and fruit gardens, fences and unpaved streets. A river flowed through the village and nearby ran a good-quality highway, all the way to Kiev. Counter-intelligence had warned us that this was Bandera territory [Stepan Bandera was a well-known leader of Ukrainian nationalist forces which fought against the Germans and to a larger extent against the Soviet Army till the late 1940s – translator's note]. We had to set up stronger guards around the soldiers' quarters, but the commanders still preferred to lodge in private households. Billeting officers offered me a room in a solid stone house on the outskirts of the village, thinking I would turn it down because of its location. There was a narrow field behind the house and a dark pine forest in the distance. In fact I agreed without hesitation, but General Tikhonov, who paid us a visit after finding out about my lodging's position, isolated as it was from head-quarters and the billets, demanded I be resettled immediately closer to the centre. To appease him I stayed overnight in quarters two or three times, but I didn't abandon that house. I had been allocated a spacious, light and warm room with white walls and curtains, a wide bed with a deep feather mattress and a pile of pillows. My young and attentive hostess was Stepanida and she had a small family. What reason was there to leave that blessed nook? And I would have felt awkward having to tell my hostess that I was moving to a safer place; it would have sounded like cowardice. To be suspected of timidity, and by a woman: there could be no worse disgrace!

When the 1st Ukrainian Front advanced through this area the com-mander, Army General Vatutin, had been billeted in this very room. The lively spirit of this kind-hearted and friendly man was still in the air and he lived on in the vivid memories and joyful stories told by Stepanida and her family. During that time the house had been well guarded and Bandera's men hadn't shown themselves at all in the neighbourhood. Now there was only talk of them, nothing more. To all appearances this village wasn't a particularly tempting target for them: the fact that a regiment was based there meant they were sure to meet with armed resistance. They preferred to pillage elsewhere, in areas more remote than ours. So it was that on 29 February 1944 Vatutin was ambushed by Bandera's men on a road near the front line. He was heavily wounded in the attack and died of his wounds on 15 April the same year.

I carried not only a pistol but also a light submachine gun with a magazine full of ammo. I had to sleep mostly during the daytime, but if I had to take my rest at night I walked to the house along the most out-of-the-way footpath across the cemetery. Quite a few gangs of various kinds flourished during the war. Some of them, those closer to the west of the Ukraine, belonged to Bandera's forces; others waged wars of their own. In Prilouki Tikhonov had been visited by people from nearby villages who complained of marauding raids by a gang with a hideout in the thickets of a narrow island formed between the meandering channels and marshes of a small creek, the Uday. Small militia [police force – translator's note] detachments had slipped in there. They had apparently managed to track down the gang's lairs and to engage the bandits, but they failed to capture them or wipe them out. The gang was getting more and more brutal, and their bloody tracks were becoming thicker and spreading ever further.

Vasiliy, as senior commandant for many dozens of kilometres of the neighbourhood, had to take action, but how could you send in airmen for a swoop with bayonets fixed? He decided to resolve the problem the Air Force way: he ordered reconnaissance conducted by U-2, pinpointed landmarks and possible hiding places on plans, and then prepared a flight of bombers and sent them on a raid. He didn't forget to involve me.

On a clear summer morning, steadily circling in at low altitude, we smashed all the marked locations, dropping high-explosive splinter bombs on several approaches, treating the island as if it were a training ground. And although no trace of the gang could be seen from the air, it had been quiet in the neighbourhood since then. I guess the men had managed to leave the area in time but hadn't taken the risk of returning.

The situation was worse around Granovka, our new aerodrome south of Doubno. This time it wasn't just local rumours: regular operational dispatches told of bloody massacres of local people and attacks on Soviet institutions and even military installations. They hadn't threatened the Air Force units yet, probably fearing retaliation. Later on, however, a major – an officer from the operations department of our division – was abducted at night and never heard of again. That was the handiwork of a Polish nationalist gang.

CHAPTER THIRTEEN

The ADD Loses its Status

In early December 1944 a strange, but initially barely noticeable, event occurred. It hardly affected us at the time (our job was to fight the war!) but it was more than significant on a Long-Range Bomber Air Force scale. The ADD was reorganised into the 18th Air Army and made subordinate to the Chief Marshal of the Air Force, Novikov. The number of regiments remained the same, but the number of divisions, which now comprised three or even four regiments each, had been reduced, and the number of corps was halved. Although our combat strength underwent little change in the new organisational structure, the status of the 18th Air Army looked much lower than that of the old ADD.

This kind of reorganisation was not hard to justify at this stage of the war: the most remote targets were now in operational range of front-line aircraft, strategic advances on the fronts were proceeding according to plan and there was no longer any need for the maximum centralised application of ADD forces, as had been the case when it was directly subordinate to the Supreme Commander. However, there was a feeling that the reorganisation had been prompted by circumstances as yet unknown to the majority of us.

Back then I had no way of knowing about the collisions that were taking place between the two highest commanders of our country's Air Force – Chief Marshals Alexander Novikov and Alexander Golovanov. Only many years later would I find out the truth and understand much more about what actually happened in 1944. For a long time Air Force Commander Novikov had been attracted by the idea of placing the ADD – that powerful striking force – under his command and of engaging it in daytime operations. The aerial armies at the fronts were not particularly strong strike forces but they did possess innumerable fighter aircraft capable of reliably covering the operations of long-range bombers to prevent combat losses from attacks by enemy fighters. The Air Force commander understood that daylight strikes would be noticeably more effective than night-time ones: the change would provide better aiming conditions and allow a denser concentration of forces over a target because the raids would be carried out in daylight; in addition it would mean that a significant part of the night-time bombers' support staff could be transferred to the assault echelon. To tell the truth, the operational range of fighter escorts was no greater than the depth of the enemy's tactical defence, but by that time the distance to our targets was almost no further.

Golovanov had been well aware of Novikov's pretensions and was on the alert, obstructing in any way he could the implementation of this idea that threatened the ADD not only with another reorganisation but with more unpredictable consequences, up to and including the loss of its integrity and independence. A secret struggle was on. Novikov knew how much the Supreme Commander trusted Golovanov. Almost no suggestion or request Golovanov referred to him had met with refusal. To Novikov's considerable irritation sixteen aircraft repair plants, several flying and technical schools, maintenance workshops and depots, and technical bases had all been transferred to the ADD from the Air Force by Golovanov's use of this channel. Even the civil air fleet, which was previously part of the Air Force, had been transferred to Golovanov's control as ADD commander at his request, as were the air-borne and parachute troops somewhat later. Golovanov was sure of his strength; he behaved confidently and independently with the highest approval. 'There was more than one occasion,' the ADD Chief-of-Staff Mark Shevelev later told me, 'when Golovanov pulled me up for my phone calls and visits to Air Force headquarters to resolve operational issues: "What do you visit them for? We're not subordinate to them."'

How could Novikov raise the thorny question of the transfer of long-range bombers to the Air Force? One day at the end of autumn, when another group of Soviet leaders was visiting Helsinki, Novikov found himself next to a Politburo member, Zhdanov, and drew his attention to the fact that despite the series of mass ADD raids, the centre of the city was pretty much intact. Was Novikov aware that the residential areas of the city were never on the target list? Most likely he was, but Zhdanov might not have known and he didn't turn a deaf ear to Novikov's words. He reported all he'd seen to Comrade Stalin. Maybe in those undamaged walls the Supreme Commander found a reason for the strange non-compliance of the Finnish leaders, who, contrary to expectations, had not been in a hurry to pull out of the war immediately after three heavy ADD raids? It seems Zhdanov's report significantly altered Stalin's attitude towards Golovanov, and Novikov didn't miss this rare chance to best his rival. Stalin readily agreed to his proposals and the issue was resolved instantly: the ADD was transferred to the Air Force.

Everything was done without Golovanov's knowledge because he was sick at the time. Foreseeing a long period of treatment, he sent Stalin a report and a request to be relieved of his duties as ADD commander. Contrary to expectations another order followed, even before his discharge from hospital: Golovanov was to become head of the 18th Aerial Army and simultaneously Deputy Air Force Commander. Novikov had already radically reorganised the whole structure of the former ADD and sent home the Civil Air Fleet and Airborne Troops, which were previously subordinate to Golovanov. Now he vindictively excluded from the names of regiments, divisions and corps the very notion of 'long-range', turning them into ordinary bomber units. The very concept of a 'long-range bomber air force', which had existed since the First World War in various forms, disappeared in one stroke. Even those of us at the front felt this vicious blow to professional pride. Golovanov saw the collapse of his favourite child as a disaster.

* * *

Granovka was our last operational aerodrome on Soviet territory. The spring of 1945 came too early and brought a good deal of unforeseen trouble. The aerodrome got soggy and under the weight of our heavy wheels the metal strip we inherited from the departed fighter planes quickly drowned in red mud. Adjacent aerodromes also went out of service one after another. It became hard to operate. Large numbers of heavy planes were now gathered on small airfields and we needed to leave for new locations, to look for strips with hard surfaces. One overcast, sleety day the regiment dragged itself over the Western Boug, stretched out so as not to attract anyone's attention or jostle each other during landing, and turned towards a Polish aerodrome, Zamosc.

From low altitude a pattern of fields, roads, farms and villages completely different from the Russian landscape suddenly came into view. The unfamiliar features of the nearest suburb of Western Europe opened out before me. The town near our new base also turned out to be unusual in terms of the style of building and the architecture of squares and streets. It retained features of antiquity, of the Middle Ages, and was surprisingly unharmed by years of war. The mysterious lives of unfamiliar and foreign people were going on there. The large and motley selection of small shops, beer houses and restaurants was striking.

Spring was already in full swing here: puddles twinkled on the roads and sparrows brawled in the sun. People walked about in light coats with their heads uncovered and looked very well dressed, even smart by our standards. But by evening a cold wind had begun to blow, a dense snowfall started and a blizzard howled. Winter had returned from nowhere and swaggered around for a couple of days before retreating. The spring had to start all over again.

In March and April 1945 the strongholds of East Prussia were stormed day and night. Large numbers of long-range bombers alternating night and day raids opened the way to the walls of Königsberg's citadel. The land troops expected us to launch powerful strikes with the highest, even mathematical, level of accuracy. Our targets were incredibly solid, more solid than any others in the whole war, and they were small, almost point-sized from the air, but the attacking files of troops were quite nearby. The job could be done only in mass daytime raids, and by this stage of the war daylight sorties had been all but eliminated from the front-line activities of our long-range bombers. For most of the crews this was a new kind of mission, but our general level of flying skills and strong combat spirit gave us no cause to doubt we would succeed in what we had been asked to do. Our ability to carry out these raids was not obvious to everyone at supreme headquarters, however.

Without hesitation Air Force Commander Novikov decided to deliver a powerful and concentrated strike on Königsberg's strongholds with the full weight of the main forces of the 18th Aerial Army covered by fighter planes. On a clear day, 7 April, more than 500 long-range bombers escorted by 150 fighter planes (there would be 100 more over the target) broke up the last centres of German resistance with large-calibre bombs, opening the way to the citadel for our troops. The attackers poured into the breaches and the citadel fell. Our ground-attack planes had managed to neutralise the main bulk of the ack-ack batteries and pinned most of the German fighter planes to the airstrips – those that had managed to take off failed even to get near the bombers.

Seeing my 'humility', Shaposhnikov sometimes gave in to my requests to fly and during recent months he had stretched his generosity to four more operational sorties. On 16 April, the day the decisive Berlin operation was unleashed by Stalin, the commander didn't dare deny me: he allowed me to join a combat flight by the whole regiment. That night just before dawn, at the moment when the operation began, the 18th Aerial Army's 750 aircraft came together in the area of Seelow Heights, heading in from the east to strike at the centres of the German second line of defence.

While we were on our way the night was clear but dark and moonless, densely sprinkled with stars. We flew strictly by the horizon, observing the preselected altitude. No manoeuvring was allowed in the dense flow of planes streaming westwards: altitude, bearing, estimated speed – we had to stick to each of these like an instrument following a part in a huge orchestra. We couldn't see even our nearest neighbours. There was only silent blackness and gleaming stars.

When Poznan was under our right wing a large-calibre flak shell suddenly burst above us – just one. Apparently some cranky gunner had sent a single shot into the night sky for no particular reason, at random. All hell broke loose. The sky around us, which had previously looked so empty, instantly glittered with signals: 'I'm a friend'. Flares poured out on all sides at many different altitudes – we saw them above and below, to the sides and behind. I flinched at the spectacle, understanding only now how tightly packed we were in our rush towards the target.

The sky began to grow pink at our backs and ahead of us the whole of space became lighter, although it was still night-time on the ground. Artillery barrage and bomb strikes seethed below. We approached the fortified area assigned to us and launched our own bombs into the mass of explosions already peppering the ground. As we turned we noticed a chain of light beams drifting over the ground and shining towards enemy lines. Those were the famous 140 searchlights that were turned on instantly in order to dazzle the enemy at the moment when the offensive was launched.

I didn't yet know that this was my last operational sortie, my 307th. But that was how my combat career ended. The regiment flew to bomb the German troops and their fortifications more than once before the end of the war, but the strain was gradually easing, and sometimes it seemed that we were being held back by our superiors. In fact this conclusion was not just gossip. At the end of the war our relationship with the Allies, outwardly quite cordial, suffered from serious and sometimes dangerous internal tension. The Allies were not happy at the prospects for the post-war situation in the East European states and Germany itself. And although the supreme commanders continued to decorate each other with their countries' highest honours, considerable forces were kept battle ready, 'just in case'. Any conflict of words could ultimately turn into the use of force by nations which had recently been our allies. We kept our eyes on them but everything turned out well, thank God.

On the night before 9 May we couldn't sleep at all. The light was on in the room with curtained windows where between six and eight regiment commanders and navigators lived. We, flopped down on our beds, talked endlessly. Then we jumped up, paced from one side of the room to the other or went out for another smoke, even though we were already up to our eyeballs in nicotine. Somebody fruitlessly turned the tuning knob on an old radio set, procured heaven knew where and how, catching snatches of phrases in Slavic languages that seemed to be asserting the war was over. But we'd caught such combinations of words before, ever since the beginning of May, and the war was still dragging on.

Then there were deafening shots outside the house. I turned off the lights and threw the window open. Who was firing and where from? It was impossible to tell. We reached for our pistols. Maybe, a gang had broken through into the town? It wasn't impossible – there were several gangs around the place and even more rumours about them. Then someone ran past, frantically yelling 'Victory! Victory!' A minute later, having leaped out of the building, we too were firing our pistols into the night sky. We were gripped by overwhelming excitement and an inexplicable feeling that we had been thrust into the middle of an incredible dream.

The corps commander, Loginov, appeared near regimental head-quarters. Fearing dangerous consequences from the chaotic shooting – and not without reason – he finally managed to make himself heard: 'Line up the regiment!' The shooting gradually died away. Shaposhnikov calmed us down, put everyone up into rows and reported to the corps commander. 'Load arms!' he ordered. When we were still and quiet, Loginov congratulated us on the victory, thanked us for our valour and remembered those who had fallen in combat with eternal glory. The regiment saluted three times, honouring the victory, and then went back to quarters for a rest, as ordered. But rest wasn't really an option. Excited and agitated, we returned to our room, turned on all the lights, swung open the windows and, not knowing how to give vent to our emotions, we sang, laughed, clowned around. Then we all looked at each other with an air of gloom: the joyful celebration wasn't heading for its logical climax. There was no getting away from it – lesser occasions than this one demanded wine and we should definitely have some now. But it was dark outside; where were we going to get it?

I stepped up to the challenge. Once, our arms technician, Arzali Alkhazov, during a casual chat under the wing of my plane, had begun to talk about his home and kinfolk, who lived somewhere in the mountains of the Caucasus. He said he'd had hardly any letters from home and had lived at the aerodrome throughout the war (I don't know where he slept – or even whether he slept at all). Day and night, like clockwork, how-ever exhausted he was, he rolled and hung the bombs: it seemed he had been born to the work. But somewhere he had a home, a family and a not very young mother. Well, we could get by without him, couldn't we? I arranged a holiday for him. At the end of April, having returned to the regiment, Alkhazov brought me a 1-litre bottle of superb, rather strong, home-made wine. 'This is for you, Comrade Lieutenant-Colonel (in March I'd been promoted a rank). My Mum sent it to me.' How could I reject his mother's present? And now, preening myself, I put it on the table, without hurrying. Everyone got only a little bit. Despite its Caucasian strength the wine couldn't make us tipsy in those small quantities, but the appropriate ritual had been observed and we were happy.

The shooting outside the house stopped; the night seemed to have settled down, but we didn't get away without misfortune. A young navigator called Ogourtsov, having had one too many, had gone some distance away from quarters and in his lonely joy he let off a pistol volley. The armed Poles he came across were tipsy as well. A skirmish occurred and Ogourtsov was killed. A letter from his mother was found in his map-case: in it she begged her son to pity her, to be careful, not to go on combat missions, for the war was about to end and others could handle it without him. Ogourtsov was an obedient son (he had been openly keeping away from combat missions) but he had still met an unfortunate death. We felt sorry for him.

A very joyful and ceremonial victory lunch was held by the regiment the next day. And at dawn the following day Shaposhnikov ordered us to get our regimental Douglas ready for a flight, drove his commander's Willis into it and, inviting along Chief-of-Staff Rytko, the new senior navigator Ivan Kindyushov and me, he flew the plane to Berlin.

We landed at Werneuchen aerodrome. We barely managed to find a parking spot among the mass of aircraft that had inundated Berlin, the city which had attracted the attention of the whole world. We put the Willis on the ground, got into it and headed to the prostrate capital of the Reich as part of a dense crowd of vehicles. Files of scared Berliners with eyes full of suffering dragged themselves along the roadsides back to their city, pushing and dragging handcarts and bicycles loaded with household goods and chattels. Berlin was still smoking in places and was in terrible ruins. As if begging for mercy, white bed sheets of surrender hung down from windows and balconies that had escaped destruction. Queues of prim German women and bewildered children stood near the Soviet soldiers' field kitchens with saucepans. Without asking the way we set out for the Reichstag, following a huge stream of vehicles moving in the same direction. The building was full of holes, marked by burns and dense pockmarks and covered with the names of Soviet soldiers: it was dead and human figures were running over its huge body like ants. This stern and imposing structure had probably never been photographed so much in all its life as it was at that time.

We stood for some time near the Brandenburg Gate and then walked down the Unter den Linden. It was hard to imagine this city in its splendour and pomposity, crowded with smug soldiers and respectable citizens. Everything had gone, turned to dust – both the city's spirit and the flesh of its bygone grandeur. Houses raked with fire, blackened by gunpowder and soot, towered like old teeth stained by tobacco smoke; the broken roads lay contorted and the perforated statues of Prussian conquerors strutted pitifully on their pedestals. Apparently the whole of Germany looked like that. When would this nation, which had gone astray by following deluded pretensions, rise from the ashes? In half a century? A century? Would she ever rise again? It was no less strange and amazing to see in the alleys, squares and avenues known to the whole world, amidst shadows and the skeletons of great pieces of architecture, Soviet soldiers and officers smoking cigarettes, not yet cooled down from the recent fighting and still armed. Our gallant old fellows with big moustaches climbed into squeaky carriages which had horses or sometimes bullocks harnessed to them. Allied soldiers of all ranks sauntered here too, cheerful and unconstrained. The scenes we saw that day astounded at every step in their contrasts, paradoxes and improbability.

Day gave way to night. We knew that we couldn't get by in Berlin without a commandant's patronage – there was nowhere to eat or to stay overnight. In the Wilhelmstraße we found the commandant of one of Berlin's districts, a young, handsome, battle-seasoned lieutenant-colonel. He received us warmly, fed us and organised somewhere for us to rest. He showed us other corners of Berlin and, in deep twilight, drove us to the underground bunker of Hitler's Reich Chancellery. Many of the rooms were still intact and everything inside them evoked acute interest and curiosity in us. We stayed there quite a while and lost our way when heading back to the commandant's office through the unlit ruins of Berlin. The streets were dead, not a single light in the windows; the doorways were empty and echoing, although in the distance (sometimes closer) we heard submachine gun bursts, solitary shots and even the bass voice of cannon. We were still trying to find our way, blindly darting round corners as we came to them. None of us could speak German and for this reason our attempts to elicit information from random (and apparently terrified) passers-by were unsuccessful. As a result we slept in our vehicle in the middle of a large square. In the morning we found out that the square was called Alexanderplatz and Wilhelmstraße was very close. The commandant entertained us with a splendid breakfast, presented us with elegant pocket pistols and accompanied us to the aerodrome before bidding us farewell.

CHAPTER FOURTEEN

What Price Peace?

The front-liners hadn't thought about their post-war fate up until the last moment of the conflict. But now the war had gone away and the first days of celebrations were over. What next? Post-war life couldn't be simply a continuation of our interrupted pre-war routine. Too much had changed since then, in society and inside all of us. We would have to start from scratch.

The time had come for every officer's record and competence to be examined. Some would leave the service, having used up their age and health; others would be expelled for professional inadequacy and moral unsuitability. But there was a third category: those who had decided to exchange their flying trade for a ground-based occupation. The fittest and most robust flying personnel stayed in the ranks.

All sorts of strict and uncompromising commissions and inspection teams from Moscow crawled all over the garrisons which were still dispersed along the fronts. While the war was on we hadn't really believed that people of very high rank even existed, but it seemed they had been working away somewhere and hadn't forgotten us. They had been waiting for the end of the war with even greater impatience than we had. They were stylish, smart, decorated – and we were miles behind them. We began to work out our tactics for dealing with them: how to answer their questions, what to bring to their attention and what to hide. We had no experience in this field. Their task was (we understood it straight away) to demonstrate that we couldn't do a bloody thing, were good for nothing – in fact that we were nothing. During harsh disputes the words yes and no would roll off their tongues but then the phrase 'Your time's up!' would be thrown at us. As for the business of flying, they began to drum into our heads the fundamentals of pre-war organisation and flying methods.

My salvation arrived unexpectedly. One day my surname echoed down the corridors of our hostel: I'd been urgently called up to head-quarters. 'Get ready,' the regiment commander said, 'a passing Douglas is waiting for you on the aerodrome. You are going to Moscow, to Monino Academy for a training course.' My documents were ready, I packed my trunk in an instant, threw it in a captured vehicle and having ridden up to the plane, I leapt into the fuselage. We taxied off within a minute. Fare thee well, my regiment. But for how long?

I studied with no particular zeal – Moscow was close to the academy and it was a source of temptation. The city was certainly poorly fed and not yet restored to order, but it was also joyful and resilient. The bohemian community was thriving and I was attracted by its libertine ways and carefree attitude. I made new acquaintances among front-line poets and the young literary fraternity – and even had some affairs of the heart. This world was attractive but I couldn't find a foothold in it and soon felt that it was the time to get a grip. Alexey Fatyanov – the most popular poet of that time – said to me, 'Haven't you had enough of flying? Come on, join the Institute of Literature. They'd accept you!' But I had no intention of leaving flying. It was the first and most important thing in my life. It was to become the main reason why, after graduating, I resolutely refused to switch to the full-time academic studies that General Vorobiev – the course chief – tried to talk me into.

Dragging myself through to the end of the course, I graduated with no worse marks than the rest (although my graduation reference noted: 'Could have studied better') and by the summer I was back in my regi-ment. It was based 70 kilometres from Kiev in Uzin, a dirt aerodrome with three hangars and a big village nearby. There was a serious lack of roads in the area, no electric lights, no sewerage.

Shaposhnikov had been accused of some kind of failures of command. He was frequently called to answer to those in authority. Finally demoted from his position, he was appointed a squadron commander and sent to the Far East of Russia. He was not the only victim of the raging orgy of retribution that befell the command staff of the Air Force (and other services too). Nearly the whole Military Counsel of the Air Force followed Commander Alexander Novikov to jail. Later ADD Commander Alexander Golovanov was stitched up and left without a job. Evgeniy Fedorovich Loginov was demoted too and was appointed a deputy corps commander. They tried to roll Tikhonov but he moved to the Academy in time.

All of those who'd been in German captivity for any period of time were removed. Some were let go 'with blessings' and felt quite happy about the situation, but others were put in jail. Gavriil Lepekhin was among the latter. General Verov, a new member of the Military Counsel of the 18th Aerial Army – and an insolent and morally unscrupulous man – visited our regiment; after he left, two squadron commanders – Smirnov and Tonkikh, slandered as 'contemptible POWs' – were expelled and the chief-of-staff of the regiment, the battle-seasoned navigator Ivan Vas'kin, followed them. At various times all of them had been shot down over enemy territory but their reputations had remained spotless: there was nothing the Soviet people or those in authority could reproach them for. Had there been any legitimate reason for their demise they wouldn't have been allowed to leave so easily.

We could only gasp as time after time we received the terrible news that combat officers had been dismissed or arrested. Serious changes were taking place in the organisational structure of the Air Force and absolutely radical ones were under way in the long-range bomber group. In April 1946 the 18th Aerial Army was reformed into the Long-Range Air Force of the Soviet Military Forces, which consisted of three major aerial groups. The corps, divisions and regiments acquired heavy-bomber status. It's very likely that the extremely serious nature of the new post-war order had forced the powers that be into the changes. In a hurry to reveal its previously secret might to the whole world (and particularly to the Soviet Union), the United States hadn't held back from using an atomic bomb. It was quite understandable that the leaders of our country simply had to have a strategic means of attack in their hands, and this role was entrusted to the long-range air force in its new form.

In March Stalin had suddenly dismissed Air Force Commander Novikov. He was convicted on the most absurd charges: deliberate acceptance of low-quality aircraft for service. The *narkom* for the aviation industry, Shakhurin, was removed from duty and later arrested on the same charges. A high commission was appointed to investigate the sins of the Air Force commander and at its head was the Deputy Minister of Military Forces, Boulganin (Stalin himself was the Minister). Novikov was arrested on 23 April and sentenced to five years in jail.

Golovanov was quick to appraise the situation and didn't hesitate to call for the removal of the 18th Aerial Army from the Air Force and its subsequent transformation into an independent unit. The procedure didn't take long and on 6 April the decision was made. Golovanov was appointed the commander of the Long-Range Air Force. Long-range bombers began energetically to spread their wings, which as yet were not very powerful. Back then what could we put up against the atomic bomb and its bearer, the B-29? The longed-for bomb and our Tu-64 were still on the design table. The Il-4s that had survived the war and a few four-engine Pe-8s were good enough to reach only European targets at best.

I was now the regiment commander and these questions were beyond my direct concern. The regiment was supposed to be able to fly confidently in any weather conditions and at any time of the day, to bomb accurately, to overcome enemy resistance and to be battle ready with the minimum of delay: it was my duty to take care of these issues. But many other undertakings, mostly unrelated to the job, fell to me too.

We were expecting a new plane but we had no idea that it would be a clone of an American one. In spring 1945, before the atomic strikes on Hiroshima and Nagasaki, a couple of B-29 strategic bombers made forced landings in the Far East of Russia after a massive raid on Japanese targets. This unexpected gift from God resulted in prompt action: Stalin ordered the trophies flown to Moscow and charged Tupolev with the task of copying them in every detail. Of course the task stung the eminent aircraft designer. At that time he was working as hard as he could on a new four-engine Tu-64 bomber with performance characteristics higher than those of the B-29. But Stalin rejected his objections and demanded he build an exact copy of the Superfortress.

Strange as it might seem, the task turned out to be incredibly complicated but highly fruitful. The fact was that Tupolev's project relied on Soviet aircraft production technology as it existed at the time, and it hadn't developed significantly during the war. The Americans, who had shot ahead in this field, already had a different, more promising technology. During construction of the clone, which took place under Stalin's supervision, a technological revolution occurred in our aviation industry and in a whole group of related engineering sectors. There were real breakthroughs in materials science, electronics, instrument-making and the development of machinery. It was this that enabled us to create radically new flying machines, including jets, in an incredibly short period of time.

The Soviet atomic bomb was about to be built and the Tu-4, production of which commenced simultaneously at two powerful plants in the Volga Region, was assigned to carry it. Although these carriers of atomic cargo still had only enough range to fly one way from their Arctic bases to reach the likely enemy number one, who sat beyond the ocean, the most important goal had been achieved: the United States had lost its monopoly on nuclear strikes. It had become dangerous to blackmail the world without risking a blow in return.

My regiment was robust, flew confidently, bombed well and struck aerial targets accurately. While the accident rate was quite high in the air force generally, that kind of misfortune passed us by. But how difficult our life had become. The aerodrome came to a standstill during bad weather. Our *chernozem* got waterlogged, the roads became slushy, the town was completely cut off from the outside world. There was an

8-kilometre-long sugar mill branch line on which it was possible to reach the nearest railway station by walking on the sleepers. In bad weather, when it was impossible to fly or drive, I used to walk that route, rushing to regular meetings in the division's headquarters and then returning home the same way. Our houses and barracks were lit by candles and kerosene lamps. A pathetic diesel engine gave light in the offices only occasionally in the evenings. I couldn't find a reasonable generator or enough fuel. And I couldn't get hold of building materials to improve the life of the garrison in any way.

To be honest I was a hopeless economic manager and the professionals were as lazy and dull as if they had been picked with those qualities in mind. Having failed to distinguish themselves in anything, they were eager to flee the garrison to better positions as office managers in higher departments in the rear. My reports and requests for some sort of help drowned at the senior levels of headquarters. During reports I made personally at district offices the generals would graciously pat me on the back and lie shamelessly, making empty promises and almost pushing me out the door to get rid of me as quickly as possible. The brass avoided coming to our garrison because it made them acutely aware of their own helplessness when confronted by a pile of everyday problems. And they feared the roads: no one heading towards our base could count on a quick return home. A straightforward case of appendicitis could have been quite enough to kill you; it nearly was for our radio-operator. Hospital-class surgeons were available only in Kiev and Vinnitsa, and during landing at our aerodrome it was easy to nose over, even in a Po-2, so they were very reluctant to come. At last we managed to make arrangements with a pilot that when he brought the surgeons to our base he would land between lines of soldiers and officers who would stand on both sides to catch the aircraft by hand and prevent it from lifting its tail during braking. That's exactly what happened whenever it was necessary to fly doctors in. One Po-2 was about to lift its tail, digging mud with its undercarriage, but the hefty blokes hung onto the stabiliser and pressed it down to the ground. The radio-operator was saved but the surgeons were not able to fly back any time soon, not until a small patch of ground got dry.

Families suffered terribly, especially those who rented corners and rooms in village huts. The shops were empty and the high cost of post-war life threatened to ruin anyone. But we lived somehow. We even arranged our own club in a large apartment and it was never empty. There was one more source of 'cultural' life – the sugar mill club – but drunken hordes gathered there from across the whole neighbourhood and it was no place for a sober soul. However, people were aware that the first year after the end of the war couldn't offer them any other way of life and they seemed to bear their cross without complaint and without losing heart, with a bright faith that there would be change for the better. After all, we'd won; how could it be otherwise? In the summer life was easier and livelier. Soccer games started up; new movies were shown in the open air at night. But flying seemed to be the only genuine consolation in the cheerless gloom. When the aerodrome dried out or was hardened by frost, it was good to fly and everyday hardships receded for a time. For a while we would feel we were not redundant.

* * *

By now Tikhonov had begun to grumble at me more and more often: 'The regiment commander and still single? It's not right!' I maintained silence, not thinking too much about the issue and even somewhat fearing the loss of my freedom if I married. Back then I was cautiously paying court to Natasha, a girl from Kiev and a student at a teacher training college. She lived in great poverty with her mother – a maths teacher. Her father, a prominent agronomist, had been shot by the Germans during the occupation of Kiev. I saw Natasha rarely but on summer Sundays I took off for Kiev in a Po-2 and, having flown past her balcony (she would rush out), I landed at Zhulyany aerodrome and headed to the city. There was no greater joy for us than going to the theatre. We rushed to a performance in the evening and then I stayed overnight in a hotel before starting up my Po-2 at dawn on Monday and flying back to the regiment.

In 1947 we married and it turned out to be no mistake; it was for good.

* * *

There was a lot of trouble in the regiment. Discipline grew slack in the terrible living conditions and, taking into account the fact that soldiers and sergeants were supposed to serve a fixed period of eight years with no holidays, arguments were hardly to be wondered at. The soldiers were also unhappy with the fact that, having left school somewhere between the ages of sixteen and eighteen, they now faced the gloomy prospect of never getting a school-leaver's certificate. I decided it would be good to open a night-school for them and give them a chance to complete their education during their military service. Although the move contradicted army regulations, I went ahead anyway. The local teachers supported me and the school began to operate. How happy the soldiers were at graduation ceremonies when their certificates were presented. Many of them went to university after being demobbed.

In my third year as regiment commander I was called up to a sitting of the Military Counsel of the Aerial Army. Nothing had indicated there was a storm ahead, but during a review of the discipline situation they came down hard on my regiment. And rightly so. The soldiers', and sometimes the officers', tricks were inspired by village moonshine. The counsel threw accusations at me like a hail of stones. The situation which had developed in the regiment was more than I could deal with and it meant that there was no way to avoid punishment. Army Regulations said: 'One must not complain of the strictness of a penalty'. Well, I wasn't all that keen on my position; I prized flying work a lot more highly and only hoped that I wouldn't be stripped of that part of my career. They finally decided to dismiss me from my position as the regiment commander and gave me a new assignment which meant a demotion. I was sorry to leave my home combat unit as an outcast and give my position up to a man from outside who had 'missed' the war, but I left my Guards Red Banner regiment well organised and ready for operations by day or night. Nobody complained about that.

Two days later Chief Marshal of the Air Force Nikolay Semenovich Skripko, who had replaced Golovanov, called me at my apartment. He very sympathetically asked me about my intentions and offered me a place on a course at the Academy. I refused and requested he assign me to flying work, in up-to-date equipment if possible. He promised to accommodate me.

CHAPTER FIFTEEN

The Superfortress Russian Style

I was filled with unimaginable joy when I found out about my appointment as a deputy regiment commander to Vasiliy Ivanovich Morozov, whose regiment was due to be one of the first to switch to the brand new Tu-4s. He had been an excellent commissar of a brother regiment in our division, deeply respected by all, and he was a reliable and resolute combat airman. He had been a division commissar too, but a new regiment was formed in the middle of the war and he became its commander. We'd known each other really well, and after the war we frequently encountered each other as regiment commanders at conferences and other gatherings, sometimes for the Corps, sometimes for the Aerial Army. He had a good, strong regiment.

Before getting into a Tu-4 I managed, to my joy, to fly in some two-engine American Mitchells (B-25s) and four-engine Liberators (B-24s). Both machines had three-wheel undercarriages, which made them similar to Tu-4s in terms of the way they landed. Regardless of my long-term aims, it was very good to fly the 'Americans'. Apart from the pleasant flying conditions they offered, when I piloted the aircraft I experienced a previously unknown feeling of comfort.

Familiarity with the Tu-4 came later, in Volga Province, where I was retrained in a practice regiment. When the training was complete I was allowed to make independent flights. Reaching that level of skill was not, God knows, such a big achievement. All we did was daytime flying in simple weather conditions round the circle above the aerodrome. We more or less had to teach ourselves the complicated stuff.

When they departed the practice regiment left us several machines, although they were not exactly in the first flush of youth. Then two brand-new ones were flown in from a plant. Some pilots didn't master the Tu-4 straight away, especially the way it had to be landed. It didn't have the kind of cockpit I had been used to and I had to probe for the ground through the spherical glass of the bomber-navigator's cockpit, which sat ahead of the pilot's, in the forward part of the aircraft. That took special skill. The Cobalt radar bombsight was a hard nut for our navigators to crack. Its main feature was an exceptional ability to fail for one of countless different reasons at the most important point in a flight. The navigators never flew without their pockets full of screwdrivers, spanners, fuses and spare parts, and sometimes they would invite ground-based engineers onboard. It was hard to get the Russian-made, American-style electronic devices to work well. Nevertheless, we managed to tame those bloody boxes and panels, and they played no more tricks.

The aerodrome hummed non-stop. I'd never been involved in such gripping work in my life. In good spirits, I and two or three other instructors changed planes endlessly, working through regular flying tasks with the crews. We had come a long way by the summer – we bombed properly, flew long and complicated routes, shot at aerial and ground targets (there was something to shoot with – 10 cannon). We set about night-time operations too. Other army regiments were involved in the same activities as us but so far they had been unable to catch up. And every day one plane after another rolled out of the plant workshops, sometimes outrunning the rate of crew training. The new aircraft couldn't be put into service immediately and filled the plant parking areas to the limit, the planes awaiting their new owners.

Then, with a group of the most skilful crews, I was charged with the task of flying aircraft from the plants not only to our regiment but to other units too. Sometimes the transfer group was led by Vasiliy Ivanovich Morozov (if we flew the planes to our location) but more often the role of leader fell to me. It happened that the aircraft, which had left the workshops a while ago, were not ready for handover by the time of our arrival, for the test-pilots, working literally to the point of exhaustion, hadn't had time to check them. To make things happen faster Alexander Alexandrovich Belyanskiy – the director of Kuibyshev aviation plant – got our pilots to work with his aircrews and tried to talk me into working for him full time: 'What's so good about service in the ranks for you? Just say yes. I guarantee you the rest.' I knew that Belyanskiy had been plant director since the war – a prominent industrialist, a general – and had tremendous authority with the country's leaders. My transfer to another diocese would be just a matter of a phone call for him. This proposal sounded very attractive but, having hesitated a bit, I decided not to leave my familiar role of operational flyer and instructor, particularly now when I was completely absorbed by the work of flying and the regiment's affairs were going quite well.

It was still winter when the Long-Range Air Force Commander, now Marshal Zhigarev, arrived unexpectedly at the division. Accompanied by a large retinue, not so much Moscow higher-ups as army, corps and divisional top brass, the marshal dropped into the aerodrome, drove around the garrison and called a meeting of commanding officers, telling them they should be ready to give a status report. Responsibility for giving our regiment's report fell to Vasiliy Morozov, but then, out of the blue, I was called to the meeting too. The marshal listened to the regiment commander's report in silence. We had major trump cards: the regiment was not only battle ready for any weather or time of the day, but had a higher level of training than the others and flew without accidents, which was valued very highly at that time. Fortunately, despite his background as a political commissar Morozov was incapable of verbosity, and his simple, laconic and absolutely understandable report aroused no desire in the marshal to look for any faults. But then Zhigarev got me to stand up. He came up to me and asked two or three questions, including one about my previous service, and as a result it became clear that he knew something about me. When I finished my report, having answered all his questions, he suddenly turned to the Aerial Army Commander, Aladinskiy, and asked him sharply, 'What did you demote him for?' Aladinskiy was perplexed; he took a while to collect his thoughts but still failed to answer. The atmosphere was oppressive.

A month later Nikolay Ivanovich Sazhin, Vasiliy Ivanovich Morozov and I were called up to Moscow one after another. Sazhin was appointed corps commander, Morozov was given control of his division and I was put in charge of the regiment. Later a change occurred in the Aerial Army – a new commander took over.

It became harder to work. I didn't give up flying duties, and, having burdened myself with the rest of the work that fell to a regiment commander, I began to feel that every day was too short. In addition, changes had occurred in the management of the regiment. For a start, the unit had failed to perform at major ministerial exercises a couple of times – it missed a radio-located target on a training ground during bombing. And although we were not the only ones to make the mistake, that was no consolation. The navigators believed that they had mastered the bloody Cobalt, but they hadn't: they approached the unfamiliar ground and all its suspicious flashes with too much confidence.

We had to shake up the groups of navigators in each crew, to unearth even the most minor mistakes during debriefings. Significant system errors, which we hadn't suspected, began to be exposed during public examinations of our mistakes. Of course we began to visit other unit's training fields more often in order to practise aiming and drop bombs. Soon we began to improve again. The average quality mark for operations climbed and a competition for the best batch of bombs set in. The regiment had been bringing back quite a few excellent marks by ordinary

standards but among them there was always one for a batch that had hit
the very centre of the target or the closest point to it. A champion would
be announced during debriefing and presented with a crystal cup or bowl
– quite widely available items back then, for which there was always an
awards budget in the regimental treasury. The whole issue was about
generating a healthy competitive spirit: anyone, even the youngest navigator, had a chance to come in ahead of all the renowned commanders
and in public. The regiment's marks for operations climbed quite high
and then held steady. Other units acquired a reasonable safety margin
too.

It was about this time that we managed to get the division commander
to set aside the ground floor of a new barracks as an officers' club. After
all, a regiment without a club is no regiment at all.

The training period was set for the end of the year as usual. We took
off with the whole regiment. After reaching the end of the flying range
we closed in for a raid on a radio-located target at a training field we
hadn't been to before. We lay in the attack heading with the usual
trepidation but also with a feeling of confidence – all we needed was a
target. My navigators didn't grumble: the target shone brightly; there
was no windshear; and communications were good, with no interrup-
tions. Bombs from my plane opened the parade. Everything went
according to schedule. I listened attentively to the reports: my boys
bombed with no gaps, one after another, and none of them had stuffed
up yet. At last they came in closer. The regiment stretched along the final
straight line and set off home.

By the time we returned the result was already known – one got a
4, the rest 5 [a typical Russian assessment system allocating a mark
between 1 and 5 – translator's note]. Nobody had ever done that well in
bombing using angles (that is, angle reflectors visible in radar sights in
any weather, day or night). The division's navigation department almost
suspected us of cheating, assuming that someone had set up fires near the
radio-located target and by using them we had adjusted our aim via
optical bombsights. Otherwise how could such results be achieved? Our
honour was seriously dented. We would have to repeat the strike. The
division's navigators headed to the training field to monitor everything
personally. They wouldn't have to put out fires: the training field was
covered by a solid layer of cloud, which meant there was no possibility
of peeping, but for us the target shone as before.

This time the route had been simplified and we returned home in the
middle of the night. No bombing results had been reported from the
training field and I sent everyone home to sleep. But sleep wouldn't come
for me: I was eager to see the results reports which were to be dispatched
by a plane by morning. Having tossed and turned for two or three hours

I got dressed and headed to headquarters. I was surprised to see nearly all the commanders and navigators on the doorstep, awaiting the same report. Perhaps it was on that morning that I felt acutely how firmly cemented our brotherhood of officers was, how dear to us the regiment was, its honour and its dignity. This time the minutes of the training field inspection contained only 5s. The argument was over.

As time went on I felt that although I was still full of youthful strength and health, my destiny as a flyer was becoming hazy. The young cockerels – recent graduates from training centres who didn't yet have significant achievements as pilots under their belts but were armed with the latest knowledge after their years at high school – followed the wave of front-liners from all units who had already gone to the academies. And regiment commanders, not foreseeing their quick return, parted with those men quite willingly, holding back only those who were irreplaceable, the strongest and most experienced flyers and especially the instructors. But three or four years later the same cockerels, now with academy diplomas, began to reappear in the regiments (sometimes in the ones they had previously served) and they confidently forced out the mature squadron commanders, already eyeing up regiment commander positions. The men who had been to an academy had accumulated a fair bit of knowledge but they couldn't organise flights, debrief them or even check piloting technique. However, they were protected by their diplomas, the more so as the service duties incumbent on them were still carried out by the same 'uneducated' flying commanders. In all conscience it was the latter who should have been sent to academies in order of merit. But we don't know how to see the future, and when we encounter it we reproach ourselves all too late for the mistakes of the past.

We had to take some kind of action. I remembered General Vorobiev, but he'd died in an accident by then. Then I wrote a letter to Evgeniy Fedorovich Loginov, at the time chief of the faculty of commanders of the Air Force Academy, and submitted a report to the new division commander, General Dryanin. Loginov replied immediately: 'Come over. We'll teach you.' The division commander was silent. I once reminded him of my report during a meeting: 'And who's going to do your job?' he asked. That was the end of the matter. And my age was building the final wall in front of me. But then yet another long-range air force commander (after Golovanov they changed with incredible frequency), Alexander Alexandrovich Novikov, appeared in the regiment. Only recently, in February 1952, having done nearly a year on top of his sentence, he had been released from jail. But freedom had met him coldly. The Army was closed to him because he had been discharged, stripped of his rank and decorations. The former chief marshal asked for employment in Aeroflot and was appointed head of the department of geological exploration. Only after Stalin's death were his chief marshal's rank and two Gold Stars returned to him, and at the same time Novikov was appointed to the Air Force.

The regiment was flying on the day of the commander's visit. I don't remember why but I was running the flights from the starting CP and not from the flight control point as usual. The commander asked for a stool, put it on the fresh grass and fell silent. This was apparently his first visit to a working aerodrome after his many bitter years of imprisonment and he was obviously enjoying himself, squinting under the bright sun, breathing deeply in the steppe air, looking intently at the blue line of the horizon, silently observing the sequence of take-offs and landings and the flights of aircraft over the airstrip. He didn't invite either the army commander or the division commander to talk, never interrupting the silence of the men sitting next to him.

When the planes had taxied in for refuelling the commander ordered us to report to him on the regiment's state of affairs. In the evening at divisional headquarters he briefly set out the commanding officers' new tasks and at the end asked those present if there were any questions. The atmosphere was easy, relaxed – I sensed accessibility and humane cordiality behind the stern, starred chief marshal's uniform, and said that I intended to ask him to allow me to take study leave. 'I will definitely support you,' the commander replied.

In accordance with Novikov's recommendation I joined the General Staff Academy. In the autumn of 1954 I bid farewell to my regiment, kissed my wife and son, for whom it would be much more comfortable to remain there than stay in temporary digs in Moscow, and off I went. My situation was unusual not so much because I was the only regiment commander in the Aviation Faculty (I was among men who had already surpassed that level and stood above me by two or three ranks), but rather because of my poor education. Unlike all the others I had no academy diploma, and without one it was difficult to join the General Staff Academy.

On this visit Moscow hardly existed for me, except when I found food for the soul at art exhibitions or theatres on the odd Sunday when the academy was closed. With the last bell announcing the end of classes my new friends from the study group, having impatiently flicked through their notes and abstracts in preparation for the next day, sealed up their personal safes and headed off to their families. In the deafening silence that ensued I stayed at the academy till nightfall; never leaving my textbooks, plans and maps, I worked to learn the stuff with which the rest were already familiar. My efforts paid off: I didn't fall behind or spoil the average score of the class, and I managed to defend my diploma thesis with an 'excellent'.

CHAPTER SIXTEEN

Cold War Skies

My studies were coming to an end. The clerks from personnel departments who appeared before graduation generated a quiet tumult in our ranks. Muscovites who had worked in central departments before enrolling at the academy were alarmed: what if they were sent to remote areas? The process aroused only curiosity in me: I was ready to go anywhere. But when the garrison from which I had recently been dismissed as regiment commander was named, something shook inside me, a hot wave swept over my head and, so as not to give away my true state of mind, I hastily and abruptly said, 'Agreed.' I don't know if any other options had been set aside for me but I grasped this first one as a challenge from fate.

My old front-line regiment had disappeared from Uzin, having been disbanded, and the base had changed. A paved road now led out to the highway but the whole neighbourhood was still drowning in mud and by night the streets and houses were plunged into darkness from which the same diesel generator on its last legs was unable to drag them. But the change in the aerodrome was like a miracle: 3.5 kilometres of thick concrete 100 metres wide, taxi paths, parking areas, facilities, a three-storey flight control point.

Alexander Molodchiy was in charge of the long-range intercontinental jet bomber division. I'd known him for a long time, since flying school where we'd graduated together. We saw each other after that, serving in neighbouring regiments of the same brigade, but he couldn't remember me. I wouldn't have remembered him either if the rapid rise to glory of this gallant, superb airman – twice Hero of the Soviet Union – had not resounded through the whole country. He was going to join the General Staff Academy but thankfully he was still at the base when I arrived. Without wasting any time he set about helping me to handle planes which were unfamiliar to me. He worked to get me up to the mark in all weather conditions, day and night, not only from the commander's seat but from the instructor's too.

During those crucial years I'd spent at the school desk devoting myself to science, a lot of things had changed, not only in the armament of long-range bombers but also in the way battle readiness was maintained, in the specifics of armament application, in the principles of pilot training. Molodchiy had begun to fly a Tu-95 to the north, to the high latitudes of the Arctic, even the Pole, and to the most remote eastern meridians. Such flights were the best test of the stability and reliability of the aircraft's whole body. And it wasn't the exotic nature of the Polar expanses that drove him to fly there: the division was taking up a military mission and its main operational direction was north, across the Pole. Molodchiy handed the division over to me before his departure for the Academy, as prescribed by the order. I would have to run the show from now on. It was the only division flying this type of aircraft and we were building up experience from scratch.

The core of the flying personnel had been put together well. We would have to pull the rest up to the mark and be able to enter the operational arena not with single crews but in formations of regiments. The goal was the same – to the Pole, beyond the Pole, along the shores of the continents of both hemispheres, working through manoeuvres, interaction with ground defence and the Navy, combat missions in remote areas. All this was included in the combat and operation curriculum but it was a thrill in itself.

I would have flown these superb machines that knew no limits to their range with a light heart if I had not been cursed by the drudgery of routine matters, the very thought of which plunged my soul into gloom as soon as the undercarriage touched concrete. Molodchiy had shouldered a lot of the work of forming the division during construction of the aerodrome, but I got my share of hard times too. Routine tasks always had to take last place behind the directives and plans that came from above. The stages of aerodrome construction were based on principles established long ago: first, an airstrip with minimum facilities; then a regiment or even a division landed and reported to the top on its readiness for combat missions. Houses, roads, shops, schools, clubs – all these came later, their construction stretching over many exhausting years. The pile of garrison problems that landed on my shoulders seemed insurmountable, but now I had people who were reliable and experienced in dealing with everyday challenges and we managed to push some things ahead. And although there was still a shortage of accommodation, nobody had to leave the division now.

The regiments maintained a good level of activity, and more and more often the inversion trails of our aircraft cut the skies near the Pole, above Choukotka, the neutral waters of the Norwegian Sea and the North Atlantic. Sometimes NATO fighters would hitch up to the sides of our aircraft. They would fly past, take a few photos, glance under our belly, hang alongside while there was enough fuel, and then cast off. Some of their airmen would wave and smile. Our crews brought back more than a few photos and films too.

The Arctic wasn't barren and soundless. There was a network of radio stations on the coast and the islands, new aerodromes were going up – some with thick concrete topping, some on rolled ground in the tundra. There were ice-covered ones too. Once the Air Force Commander in the Arctic, Leonid Reino, invited me to have a look at an ice field near the shores of the Laptev Sea. We got into a transport aircraft and were soon on the spot. A homing radio station, starting CP, airstrip marked with black groundsheets – everything was like any other aerodrome. But beyond were endless icy wastes. I took a walk along the airstrip markers, scrutinising the ice and tapping it with my feet as if this armour many metres thick would move under my fur-lined jackboots. Silently I imagined a picture of an impending landing and then a take-off. The recent unfortunate take-off of a Tu-16 from the ice airstrip of one of the North Pole scientific stations flashed through my memory. The machine had swerved and met its end amidst the ice floes. What if mine slid off too?

'What d'you reckon?' the commander asked me.

'It doesn't sag underfoot. I guess it'll not crack under a plane, although it's going to have to take more than 100 tonnes on landing.'

'Do you really have doubts? This ice is unbreakable. But you're worried about cohesion, aren't you? Don't be afraid – it's not going to disappear.'

I had a feeling that General Reino really wanted to use my visit as an opportunity to test his facility under the weight of the heaviest combat aircraft. And I needed to check how the four-engine machine with reverse thrust deceleration would behave on an ice airstrip. Nobody had ever landed on ice in such a machine, and in combat conditions the experience of having done it before would not go amiss. There was no point in thinking about it for too long: the visibility was excellent, a light breeze was blowing over the airstrip. If you don't use the gift of good weather in the Arctic you may lose it for many days, even weeks.

I returned to the base aerodrome and left it first for another on tundra on an island in the Kara Sea (this was the main task assigned to me). Having taken off from there I headed straight to the ice airstrip. I landed carefully and touched the ice softly – if the plane jolted once or twice during an unsuccessful landing you might not be able to keep it under control and it would slide sideways. But the bomber went smooth and straight, still on the two main undercarriage wheels. I lowered the front wheel very slowly. Then I touched the brakes lightly and felt as though the plane had shrugged its shoulders, striving to throw itself sideways. I took the inner engines' airscrews off block and when the powerful back-draft deceleration engaged, the bomber abruptly shed speed, wobbled for an instant, but steadied straight away. I could now release the outer screws. The machine sat firmly on its feet and was completely obedient.

Now I would have to take off. The wind was weak, certainly not blowing hard enough to influence the length of the run-up or the machine's stability, so what was the point of returning to the beginning of the airstrip, taxiing fruitlessly for about 3 or 4 kilometres? I turned around to a course opposite to the landing bearing, pulled up the flaps, made the engine work, took off on my run (the brakes wouldn't hold me anyway) and headed towards the base aerodrome. Later a regiment commander, Leonid Agourin, landed on this ice, and other crews followed him, but this skill wasn't widely used.

The Tu-95 was a very young machine which hadn't yet been through every conceivable set of flying conditions and we had to make adaptations to it. But sometimes the conditions themselves put thorny problems in our way. This was certainly the case during the first landing on a tundra aerodrome. One night we received an urgent mission from above and it fell to regiment commander Yuriy Pavlov: a long night flight in a north-easterly direction with a landing on the Arctic shore. There was only a tundra aerodrome in the destination village and nothing else. Our aircraft hadn't yet made a landing on an airstrip like that. How would it go? The propeller might be damaged under the impact of lumps of frozen snow – and the compressor blades for good measure. If he made it down without damage he would then have to take off again and that was an even more dangerous exercise: you couldn't examine the propellers and blades after take-off. Everything turned out well and Pavlov's success at that one tundra aerodrome allowed us to draw some general conclusions.

By that time several landings by Tu-16 bombers had taken place and there was considerable foreign interest in the machine. We were not blessed with a network of aerodromes that could take heavy aircraft and it was impossible to hide them in protective shelters, so scattering the regiments on out-of-the-way bases was the only option. In this way we hoped to avoid potentially large losses in the event of a sudden strike by the enemy.

The aircraft designer, Andrey Nikolaevich Tupolev, swore furiously and warned Long-Range Air Force Commander Soudets that the machine was not meant to land on dirt strips or tundra, and that he would take no responsibility for the consequences of this barbarism. Neither could we imagine how the plane's construction would behave during protracted jolting on a steppe airstrip or on rolled snow; wouldn't the propellers suck up heavy ground particles which would grind their vanes and compressor blades, putting screws and engines out of operation? We had to investigate all these possibilities and set about testing the machine on special flights.

One summer day I flew in an experimental plane to an aerodrome in Volga Province where a whole investigation brigade – operators, monitors, aerodynamic specialists and even Tupolev's own test-pilot – had arrived. The field that was to be the site of our experiment, a rolled area of steppe, was near a concrete strip. The machine behaved superbly during testing but of course we were most interested in how it would react to take-off when fully loaded. The dirt aerodromes were needed not only to evade immediate danger but also to act as bases from which fully equipped operational missions could be launched and to allow scattered planes to take-off in the shortest possible time. The place chosen for the new test was a vast expanse situated far away from aerodromes and centres of population. The steppe spread from horizon to horizon. The grass had already shrivelled under the hot sun and the ground had hardened quite well. Two planes – a Tu-16 and a Tu-95 – were prepared for take-off. It was noticeable how the Tu-95's wings sagged and its consoles drooped; the pneumatic gear had gone flat. The flight weight approached 160 tonnes but the refuelling crew kept pumping kerosene into the bottomless tanks: the machine could take more weight in fuel than its own total tonnage when empty.

Marshal Soudets, Aerial Army Commander Toupikov and their numerous entourage were loafing about under a tent near a staff vehicle, waiting for the take-off. Mikhail Arkatov – commander of a neighbouring division – was the first to get the Tu-16 into the air. His take-off was discussed for some time; the tracks of his run were measured and weights recalculated. Then came my turn. The machine barely moved, even with the engines at full power. It crept to the start point, apparently straining to the limit. The run didn't begin much better. During the first few hundred metres the flyer on my right-hand side, cracking under the psychological strain, anxiously babbled, 'Commander, it's not speeding up! It's not going to take off!'

Yes, it felt as though the machine, having picked up a bit of speed, couldn't find any more, but I could see that the airspeed indicator was still moving slowly upwards without pausing – in fact it was even showing some acceleration. The mighty 50,000 horses roared, dragging the heavily loaded bomber along. Now it had gathered a bit of momentum and, increasingly feeling the lift of the wings, it began to move as if it was travelling on good concrete. The run had taken the whole 4 kilometres (if not more than that), but it was important to check that dry, well-rolled steppe could be called into service as a reserve aerodrome when necessary. In the end we built quite a few on open ground, with barracks, canteens, control facilities. Of course fuel and ammo were despatched to these outposts as well. Just in case ...

As a pilot it gave me quite a bit of satisfaction to carry out that fully loaded take-off but as a commander the dirt aerodromes on which our operational plans relied so heavily always made me worried and depressed. The winters were rarely frosty. After spring the soil dried out till the middle of summer but then autumn would roll in. And how long were those aerodromes, on which such significant funds and resources were spent, in operational condition? Perhaps just two to three months a year, and then only if the summer was dry. But war doesn't take account of the weather. What if a summer rainstorm broke out at a crucial time, just after planes had landed on a dirt strip and refuelled to the limit? After all, this had happened many times during practice. The only way out would be to leave before conditions got wet and then hang around in the air for several hours to use up or even jettison several dozen tonnes of fuel until the weight of the plane was low enough to allow a landing. Then it would be necessary to head for a concrete strip. We got away with it during practice, but it was hard to imagine the consequences of such a manoeuvre in wartime. We certainly didn't place our faith and hope in those aerodromes. In fact commanders organised their manoeuvres to avoid landing on the dirt strips as far as possible.

Andrey Tupolev came down hard on our creative thinking about the way we could use the Tu-16: one landing on an earth strip equated to three on concrete, he said. It meant extra wear and tear, and the Air Force wouldn't get away with it. It certainly didn't happen immediately but the idea of landing on dirt strips gradually evaporated, giving way to more rational solutions to the problem.

We were very restricted with regard to flying at low altitudes. Our on-board electronic countermeasures equipment was weak, to put it mildly, against the enemy's ground defence radar detectors and aiming stations. Low-altitude flying would have been much more effective at protecting us from being prematurely detected during the most exposed parts of the flight, for the radar's radio waves hardly touched topography or the surface of the sea. During practice with our own ground defence, if the flight plan had been kept secret, our aircraft would fly undetected and untouched at low altitude through a huge area. The radiolocation fields of our probable adversary, whose general pattern we knew pretty well, weren't much different from the Soviet ones and that gave us a considerable chance.

We began to make flights at an altitude of between 100 and 300 metres without permission, not seeing any rebellion in what we were doing, but as it turned out, the plane's structure was exposed to increased strain at that kind of height, especially in summer when the air was made turbulent by evaporation from the land. Tupolev's verdict: one hour at low altitude was equal to two hours of a plane's ordinary service life. Of course it was costly and it was not good to waste service life, but back then we couldn't reject this one reliable means of sneaking up on targets more or less unnoticed. And later, when new and more powerful electronic countermeasures and even long-range anti-radar missiles came into service, we still couldn't abandon low-altitude flying.

*   *   *

A mission unlike anything we could ever have predicted was assigned to the crew of deputy squadron commander Andrey Durnovtsev – on 30 October 1961 he had to release a 50-megatonne nuclear bomb over a training field. The power of the Hiroshima device has been estimated at between 0.12 and 0.16 megatonnes, so you can imagine what kind of monster sat inside what was hanging under Durnovtsev's plane. 'Kouz'kina mat' ['Kuz'ma's Mother': part of a Russian saying, 'to show someone Kuz'ma's Mother', that is, to give them a thrashing – translator's note], as it had been nicknamed by nuclear professionals using Krushchev's phrase, wouldn't even pass through the chutes of our giant and a customised plane had to be prepared. The bomb hid inside the fuselage with only its withers and massive hips sticking out. Durnovtsev had managed to get about 100 kilometres from the training field after dropping his load (rushing away at full speed while the bomb descended on a parachute) before his plane was overtaken by eight waves of air, which were visible and coloured blue. Under their powerful blows the supports of the aircraft's onboard lights were torn off, some chutes were crushed and panelling was deformed in places, but the plane's superstructure held up and Durnovtsev returned safely to his aerodrome.

Krushchev declared to the world the advent of a new Soviet bomb of unprecedented destructive power: his message underplayed the bomb's real capacity by nearly a third (as it turned out, according to the final calculations the device's explosive power had significantly exceeded the predicted level). This one-off could not be mass produced, but could any nation refrain from flexing its muscles and denying itself the pleasure of generating dismay in the camp of the likely enemy?

* * *

Towards New Year 1961 an order was issued to appoint me deputy corps commander. The corps was huge – several divisions with three regiments in each, plus individual scattered regiments. The corps commander, Major-General Chousarov, wasn't happy about my appointment. Apparently his nose had been put out of joint by the more than ten years' age difference between us, which he saw as a threat to his position. By nature he was a somewhat dry and laconic man with no sense of humour. He displayed some notorious oddities, which had become the subject of confidential jokes: he couldn't stand smokers and was fond of exercising with 32kg dumb-bells, forcing his entourage to do the same. All things considered, these were not the worst habits he could have indulged in. I had given up smoking back in the academy and my abstinence was enough to exempt me from the weightlifting. But the commander himself was exceptionally strong. They said that once during the war as he closed in for landing in bad weather conditions he touched a hillock overgrown with bushes with his fuselage. His plane was smashed and he was thrown a long way out of it, but he was alive and in one piece. When they found him lying in the bushes his huge fists were still squeezing the control wheel, which he had pulled out by the roots.

The professional skills I had acquired as a regiment and division commander turned out to be of little use in my new position. I had to fly out to the units a lot, but when I was working in one place it was hard to keep track of what was happening in others, unless there were telephone dispatches from the corps CP. Flying went on twenty-four hours a day. Of course all locations had regiment and division commanders – officers experienced in flying, who were responsible and, generally speaking, reliable men – but I had no way of knowing who they were sending into the air, other than by looking at the official data.

That winter two regiments each experienced a disaster – young, poorly trained flyers found themselves in the air at night, flying in conditions they didn't have the skills to deal with. The investigation into the accidents was harsh. It was headed by Marshal Soudets who rushed in from Moscow. He made short work of those who had thoughtlessly allowed those pilots to fly, but we couldn't bring the twelve young, fit men back to life. Let there be no more. It wasn't the result of the marshal's punishments, of course, but there were no more flying accidents for a long time. It fell to me to sort out many issues and implement some reorganisation to get things back on track.

The corps commander worked away quietly but he'd been right to worry about his future. It was summer when he called me to his office. He was alone, and the marks of worry showed all over his face. It seemed he had just put down the phone after a rather unpleasant conversation. He began with the news that he'd been offered the new role of Arctic Air Force Commander, and that I was supposed to be appointed to his position. Although it sounded important, the job offered to him wasn't higher than the one he occupied at that moment, to put it mildly. In addition, he was no longer very young: he didn't want to disrupt his well-ordered family life. 'You only came here recently,' he went on. 'You don't have much experience of work in the corps. There's no rush, and this position will not get away from you. You should decline the offer.'

The situation was extremely awkward. Nobody had talked to me about the new position but the commander was already demanding that I decline it. If I had been offered the chance to leave for any other place immediately to get out of the commander's way I would have disappeared without hesitation, but the situation was developing along other lines. The commander waited for my response. 'I've got nothing to put up against your arguments relating to your appraisal of my service – you are here to take decisions as the commander. I do not expect any new appointment and am not fishing for a new position – such claims are humiliating and unworthy of an officer. But if I am asked about it directly, I, as a military man, will not be able to decline a new appointment and for that reason I won't do it.' I made my pronouncement calmly and firmly.

The next day, having left me in charge of the corps, the commander followed orders and flew to Moscow. Late that night the Deputy Long-Range Air Force Commander, Chouchev, landed at our aerodrome, calling me to him. Colonel-General Grigoriy Alexeevich Chouchev was strict in the military way. He was markedly punctual, adhered firmly to logic and common sense, and would always find simple and clear solutions to seemingly impossible problems. Seven years earlier, when he was the commander of our Aerial Army, he had persuaded Chief Marshal Novikov to commandeer me to the General Staff Academy. He was notorious for being tough and sometimes excessively harsh in his relationships with his entourage, but he'd always been very calm and cordial towards me. This time, however, his bearing was gloomy and reticent. As we met at headquarters he demanded sharply that I make a report on the state of affairs in the corps. He listened intently, in silence, and then asked several apparently irrelevant questions. After a long silence during the walk to the hotel he suddenly said, with a note of reproach in his voice, 'Why did you waver, Comrade Reshetnikov? We've trained you, relied on you and when you were offered a more difficult and responsible position you declined it.'

I nearly choked. 'How's that – declined? Who told you that?'

'Well, the corps commander reported to the chief commander that you consider yourself unprepared, inexperienced for the job, and moreover you have health problems and for these reasons you declined it.'

I was stunned and perplexed. I had to tell him about the unpleasant conversation I had had with the corps commander the day before. Chouchev was outraged, turned round there and then, headed back to corps headquarters and, despite the midnight hour, called the chief commander using a special phone line. He described the essence of the situation. In the morning, without setting about any other business, he flew to Moscow. Apparently the only aim of his visit had been to talk to me. As a result the order was issued to appoint me.

It was a complicated time: our confrontation with the West was becoming more and more acute. The world was increasingly violent. Missile forces were growing stronger. 'Our dear Nikita Sergeevich' [the way the Soviet media commonly referred to Krushchev during his time in office, 1954–64 – translator's note], having recklessly come to believe that the new weapons [of mass destruction – translator's note] would meet any threat without resistance, announced that the Air Force would be slimmed down and went through it like a destructive whirlwind, subjugating the top brass to his blind faith. The new military plans were founded on the use of ground-based missiles and had no use for the Air Force. Our supreme commanders had no choice but to believe that the winds of change were truly blowing when the commander of Odessa Military District, Hero of the Soviet Union Colonel-General Boris Sidnev, who had raised his voice to defend the Air Force, was instantly dismissed and transferred to the reserve. Regiments and divisions were slashed to the roots, driving flying and technical personnel in all directions; aviation schools closed, repair works were handed over to missile units, construction of aerodromes ceased. Aircraft were scrapped in their hundreds at dismantling bases, including brand new ones that had just arrived from the plants. We would come to regret this time deeply.

The Long-Range Air Force was under threat of destruction. But Vladimir Alexandrovich Soudets (no one else could have done it) managed to preserve its assault force with hardly any losses, resorting to major organisational restructuring and slashing managerial staff. A considerable part of the senior and even supreme commanding personnel was transferred to the work of manning missile units and formations. They were initially created within the Long-Range Air Force, and once each unit was ready it would go on watch. They would have continued to develop under the remit of the Long-Range Air Force, but when the time came to build new and larger formations the Supreme Air Force Commander wavered for a moment. He faced the prospect of having to run both aviation and missile units, and he considered the latter artillery rather than Air Force resources. The Ministry of Defence immediately took advantage of the opportunity: the missile units were removed from the Long-Range Air Force and used as the basis to create a new type of armed wing – the Strategic Missile Force.

But the Air Force survived, bearing its pain and healing its wounds bit by bit. Having made a mess of things and realised their errors, the service's supreme leaders began to return it to its proper role. The Long-Range Air Force was also saved – and I should point out that this happened in an environment where heavy, air-borne missiles with conventional and nuclear charges and an operational range on land and sea of several hundred kilometres appeared to be waiting in the wings. New means of navigation, electronic countermeasures and reconnaissance had matured as well. The Long-Range Air Force now looked qualitatively different, ready to meet the challenges of a new kind of warfare.

Missiles suspended under an aircraft's wings didn't bring anything especially new to the art of piloting, but when we launched them it was a different matter, especially those of the first generation. In some cases a missile would leave the pylon and either lose the target once it was flying on its own or its engines would stall. It would then begin to shy from side to side and after losing power it would tumble out of control. There was always a chance that people might be on the ground below, although uninhabited places were usually chosen for trials. Before it was too late a signal would be sent to the self-destruct charge; the missile would be blown up and settle down on the ground in ashes. Then investigating engineers would rush to the location in helicopters, collect the debris and try to understand the reason for the failure. Minute examinations and control checks would begin on the weapons. After several successful launches everyone would assume that we had the Devil by his beard, but then another failure would follow. Design faults turned up in these missiles right until they were written off.

There was no operational charge in a training missile but it still weighed several tonnes and had volatile fuel components too, which tended to explode when mixed. We never got into big trouble with these devices but there was an occasion when one missile hit a derrick and smashed it. Geologists had set the derrick too close to our training field boundaries, in spite of the ban on doing so, and its metal 'shone' brighter than our targets nearby. Fortunately there were no geologists on the spot when the accident happened, and they didn't come back. Elsewhere, in the Far East of Russia, a launch route passed over Soviet territorial waters and shipping was banned from the area. But once a Japanese fishing boat sneaked into the prohibited waters and it became the target for a wayward missile, which smashed into its deck superstructure. A major scandal was only avoided when the boat's captain, apologising profusely, begged our authorities to forgive his transgression into foreign territory and let him head home, for his vessel was still afloat. They had to agree.

No launch was guaranteed a happy outcome: every single one raised anxiety levels, among not only the crews but also the commanding staff involved. Of two or three missiles selected for training, one would be certain to fail. But it was impossible to predict which one – and how painful it was to be the regiment which had been allocated the dud as its single practice device (a launch did not come cheap and we were only sent one missile at a time). Such a regiment, no matter how skilled, was doomed to have an unsatisfactory practice score for a long time until it was offered a chance to redeem itself. The scoring criteria were extremely simple: if you hit the target – excellent; if you didn't – D grade. In a combat situation the technical faults wouldn't have frustrated us: we planned to use several missiles for each target to compensate for their low reliability. Even if a single one reached its destination its power-ful charge would guarantee destruction. Having worked with these weapons even the weakest imagination could foresee the earth burning and life on it becoming extinct under the impact of nuclear detonations. Hundreds of nuclear power stations and chemical plants, dozens of dams and levees protecting cities and whole states from the sea would be open to strikes, either aimed or accidental. Were we far away from the apocalypse of the nuclear war? No, it would come close, and more than once.

When, on Khruschev's watch, the Soviet Union contrived to transport strategic missiles to Cuba under the nose of the United States the tension in the military stand-off rose to boiling point. We stood shoulder to shoulder as armies do on the eve of a battle, waiting for the enemy's first careless move, ready to unleash the most disastrous, in fact the last, mass slaughter in world history. Nuclear devices were dispatched to our strategic bombers. Although they were never handed over to the crews or hung on the locks that was still a terrifying moment. Several hours later the weapons were returned to their underground dumps by order of Moscow. It was their first and only stage appearance. But if just one of them went off, no other would be needed.

The airspace over Cuba was not the only area of tension. Day and night NATO aerial scouts dashed along Soviet sea coasts, sometimes crossing them. Our ground defences drove them away but they kept coming back. Nuclear-armed groups of American submarines and sea-borne aircraft targeted at the most important parts of Soviet infrastructure were on combat duty in all the oceans. Our Navy and Naval Air Force watched them, but we were also charged with the task of monitoring the potential enemy in the Atlantic and keeping an eye on the forces he was transferring to the Mediterranean. Our first pair's reconnaissance flight was unsuccessful. They had already passed Ireland when a technical failure occurred on board the leading machine. Under other circumstances the crew would have continued with their task without batting an eyelid, but this time the situation was special and they returned to the aerodrome. The second pair also failed to reach the target, having encountered difficult stormy weather. Behind the practical reasons for the decision to abort these flights were some hidden psychological ones. In an attempt to preserve the prestige of the division the commander himself – General Ivan Shikhanov – led the third sortie. He got his share of extremely difficult weather conditions, which it would have been better to avoid altogether, but he made it through. The radar detected an American sea-borne group somewhere between the Azores and Gibraltar. Shikhanov ran through the clouds, came out under their lower edge and at a height of 200 or 300 metres flew over an aircraft carrier several times, photographing its upper deck and escort. Then he did a swift turn, entered the clouds and set off home. His wingman – a missile-carrier – had stayed at high altitude, flown traverses and photographed the situation at sea on the radiolocation sight screen. His sights could take in an area about four times larger than the space available to the radar of the leading machine. The wingman was the first to detect targets from huge distances, directed his commander to them and, staying at high altitude, waited for his return. Sea-borne fighter planes chased him and got Shikhanov in their pincers, not allowing him to turn. They raced in front of his nose then came up next to the pilot's cockpit waving their fists but they were unable to interfere with his flight. The pictures were superb. The battle order of the sea-borne group looked classic: the aircraft carrier *Enterprise*, a colossus, her deck covered with planes, was surrounded by a circle of escort vessels.

After that we established silent, and not very friendly, but regular contacts with the sea-borne groups. The contacts seriously alarmed America, but those were neutral waters and to open fire would have been equivalent to starting a war. The world didn't become more peaceful because of our vigilance but it seemed to us that it was we who guarded it from trouble. No matter how stealthily and silently the sea-borne groups headed off into the ocean, nobody managed to cross the Atlantic unnoticed. However, the searches were certainly not what you would call easy. On one sortie an experienced pair, having reached a group of ships, couldn't find the main target – an aircraft-carrier among the escort vessels. It seemed that, foreseeing an encounter with her pursuers, she had leaped out of the ring. But fighters hovered, which meant she was somewhere in the vicinity. It turned out she was getting away to the south and our planes had to chase her. On another occasion an aircraft carrier's radio operations were detected on a very unusual bearing. The radar marking left no doubt that they belonged to a large vessel, but it turned out to be a decoy – a medium-sized ship which had been densely equipped with reflectors. The object of our search was moving with her retinue in full radio silence, hoping to avoid another encounter with Soviet bombers.

All this provided great practice for our crews in searching for and approaching mobile targets in remote areas. There was a great deal to intrigue in the manoeuvres of ships and the tactics of American sea-borne aircraft. The anti-aircraft defences of sea-borne formations were an almost insuperable obstacle. In combat conditions our contact with these vessels could only have occurred from long range, at rocket-launching distance. But aircraft carriers were far from invulnerable. The performance of our missiles was such that they would find a naval target better than any other. However, there was no harm in taking a look at them directly, in peaceful neutral waters.

I believe that for the Americans our uninvited visits were not only a nuisance but also a useful means of conducting their own training. The sea-borne fighters certainly fell upon our aircraft in droves – numbers much higher than would have been sensible in a combat situation. None of them seemed to suspect that the arrival of fighters to intercept Soviet bombers far from the target only confirmed the accuracy of our approach. Well before visual contact, it guaranteed the presence of her majesty the aircraft carrier in a naval group. They led us to her themselves.

The waters around the Azores were the most suitable area for these dates with US fighters. Naval routes from Norfolk to Gibraltar lay there. But it wasn't easy for our bombers to fly to the Azores through bad oceanic weather and there were no reserve aerodromes beyond the last patch of Soviet territory – the Kola Peninsula. It must be said that the aerial route was secured in places by Soviet Navy salvage ships, but thank God we never had to resort to their services.

The situation in the Atlantic was becoming more and more tense. Our planes began to be regularly intercepted on the beam of England and Iceland and accompanied by NATO fighter planes. This wasn't a big worry, but in order to shake off the attention our crews would sometimes cross this zone at low altitude, under the coastal radar's visibility floor. The aircraft carriers tried to get rid of us (and maybe to probe our capabilities) by manoeuvring south of the Azores and began to press closer to Madeira. All this led us to consume more fuel and although it would have been a sin to complain about the capacity of our fuel tanks, we had to resort to in-flight refuelling.

Reconnaissance operations in the Pacific were even more complicated. Hawaii, sometimes Wake Atoll or even areas much further south, was the main base via which sea-borne aviation groups went to their patrol zones. Alexander Molodchiy – a corps commander in the Far East of Russia back then – didn't restrict planes to only one top-up refuelling on the way out but sometimes sent out another for the return journey. After a prolonged reconnaissance in order to make their way to coastal aerodromes, bombers would deploy refuelling hoses and top-up their depleted tanks while still over the ocean.

Contacts with the aircraft carriers continued for many years. Observing no hostile intentions in our activity, the Americans gradually began to get used to us and stopped getting angry, judging from the change in the gestures mimed at us by the fighter pilots. Only a few remained openly aggressive and strangely they were mostly black. It seemed they were more patriotic than their white brothers. But what was the point of getting angry? We didn't carry missiles or bombs and our cannon were in the stowed position. There were incidents, however. Once, having got behind our plane, a fighter pilot started quite a cordial miming chat with our rear gunner. The guy, perhaps misunderstanding the American but more likely in foolishness, turned the cannon towards him. The fighter pilot got angry, moved forward abeam of the pilots' cockpit, tapped himself on the head and pointed his finger towards the tail, complaining to the commander. In conclusion he lowered his own gun carriage as if to say that he had something to hit back with if needs be. The commander immediately grasped what was the matter and without hesitation despatched a popular colloquial combination of words to the rear to restore order. After that he damped down the conflict with the fighter pilot with an apologetic gesture.

Our headquarters had long ago compiled detailed photographic files for each aircraft carrier. (No doubt our bombers had also been photo-graphed from all angles, although we changed our hull numbers after each flight.) But flying continued at the same intensity, for the job consisted not so much of collecting new information (we were not short of intelligence data) but rather in showing our opposition, or to use the modern term, making a 'demonstration of presence'.

By now these sorties seemed quite routine and ordinary for a strategic bomber, but in-flight refuelling, many hours of isolation from any kind of aerodrome, encounters with potential enemy fighters in the muddle of clouds over the ocean with no witnesses, flying at low altitude over swarms of ships armed with guns and missile-launchers which were watching and shadowing us through their gunsights – all this sharply, even lethally, raised the cost of any human error or unforeseen complication caused by matériel, weather or aerial conditions. But there was a real buzz about those often audacious flights, which pushed risk to the limit. Those who had carried out such a task once or twice acquired good standing with our superiors and at headquarters; they got the best marks for flying and operational skills. And the aircraft commanders and crews who had lived through the experience would find in themselves new depths of character and willpower. There are no stronger ways of building a man's character than those that draw a military airman into real danger, a risky situation where all hope rests on his resolve, composure and skilled professionalism.

Then we were tasked with another duty – to reconnoitre the area of the Norwegian Sea patrolled by American submarines. The boats would sit under the water, not giving themselves away at all, and would creep out to breathe only at night – quietly and with no lights. In the daytime they would detect a plane earlier than we could detect them and then they had enough time to hide unnoticed. For this reason none of us ever saw a nuclear submarine with a ballistic missile. But there was one occasion ...

That day our flying altitude was largely determined by the weather. The lower edge of dense clouds, which were depositing rain in places, varied between 200 and 300 metres and only beyond the beam of the Faroe Islands did it rise to about 800 metres. Steep, gloomy waves with white crests heaved beneath us, but when we approached the Faroes we gasped in astonishment at the sudden change in scenery: the sea was scattered with many hundreds of fishing boats among which towered a giant vessel – an ocean-going fish-processing plant. We passed towards Jan Mayen Island, looking over the fishing boats, but there were no traces of submarines. However, on the way back, when the sea was again deserted, an excited shout rang out from the rear gunner: 'A submarine! Behind us! It's dived!'

With the maximum possible roll I turned around 180° and when the estimated time had elapsed I returned to the previous bearing. The sea was desolate but the rear gunner's cry resounded again and I repeated the manoeuvre. My navigator recorded the coordinates, although there were no traces on the waves. I was already on a third approach when a large, rounded body came out of the depths of the sea, shimmering with a metallic lustre. It rolled over and disappeared into the waves again. 'It's a whale!' all of us shouted at once. No other important 'discoveries' were made by our reconnaissance. There would be no more submarine searches.

Basically, our duty was not really reconnaissance but rather combat operations against naval groups of the potential enemy, and we were not an independent force but a means of reinforcement for the strike efforts of the Navy. But the Navy's Supreme Commander, who made us conduct searches, wanted to attach us to his operations and even insisted on kitting out the strategic planes with reconnaissance devices. We managed to ward off this plan and although we carried out naval tasks conscientiously, our main targets were always land based.

The most important part of combat practice was, of course, 'special training'. This vague term concealed from the inquisitive everything related to polishing the skills needed to deploy nuclear weapons. Dropping a device fitted with a 'special charge' is very different from bombing with conventional explosives. The measures you need to take to protect yourself from damage caused by your own megatonner are out of the ordinary, let alone the series of absolutely precise and strictly sequenced operations that have to be carried out en route to get the charge ready for explosion and make the bomb leave the lock at the right moment.

All the bomb-carrier crews and their planes were listed on a daily basis, not only at our headquarters but also with the highest authorities in Moscow. The nuclear charges were stored under the supervision of specially trained engineering units in warm, roomy, well-lit premises and were never taken out to the surface, except at the time of the Cuban crisis. Lessons and training flights were conducted with blank 'special bombs'. Only once were we allowed to have a real one. A test in the atmosphere was prepared by the state leadership. And once we'd been entrusted with the device we couldn't miss the rare opportunity to get as many flying crews as possible involved. Let them see it, feel it, understand what they were dealing with!

Judging from the suggested conditions for the explosion, this quite small, smoothly shaped, elegant bomb contained no less than 2.5 megatonnes. There were quite a few candidates for the drop but the task fell to Iona Bazhenov – a superb and well-trained pilot. It was decided that the whole regiment would escort Bazhenov. Planes would be placed in battle order to investigate the effect of the blast wave on aircraft construction and to determine a crew's minimum safe distance on different bearings. Altitudes were varied as well: the aircraft closer to the explosion were positioned higher than the ones further away. I sat in the right-hand seat next to a young flyer, choosing a place for myself on the right flank of the formation, further away from the bomb but at a relatively low altitude. I could see Bazhenov and the whole formation from there.

The whitest possible inversion clouds, sterile in their cleanliness, lay above Novaya Zemlya [an archipelago to the west of the Soviet Arctic domain – translator's note]. Their upper edge was at between 4,000 and 5,000 metres and we flew in 'steps', at altitudes between 9,000 and 12,000 metres. It was quiet in the air. Everyone listened only to Bazhenov. I craned my neck to examine the rows of aircraft once more. Everyone was in the right place – no need to make corrections. Of course, Bazhenov aimed using radar. He saw the target clearly and the training field gave approval for the drop. Communications with the training field CP were calm and precise. The final order was imminent. Then the signal was given – 'Drop'. I lowered goggles fitted with dense, black light filters, pressed the red button of the automatic pilot to switch it off and took the control wheel with both hands. My young fellow flyer had lowered his goggles too. He mechanically took hold of the automatic pilot handle with his right hand, not yet realising that it had been switched off. 'Grab the control wheel,' I prompted him. He quickly moved his hands to the handles of the wheel and we both froze, leading the plane strictly along the course and glancing at the spot where 'it' was about to occur.

The light filters were so dense that the cockpit gadgets were almost invisible and the sky was drowned in thick twilight, as if night were about to descend. But suddenly the brightest fluorescence lit up the space beyond the clouds, gilding them. It illuminated the whole surroundings with an even light, penetrated the cockpit and lit up the instrument panel. It lasted for seconds. The light faded as quietly as it had come, but seconds later we were shaken several times, as strongly as if we had raced over a worn-out multi-track railway-crossing at high speed. Heavy thuds shuddered through the whole fuselage and jarred our backbones. The wings swayed a little, the nose swerved, the pointers began to swing across the plates of the aneroid devices. We shifted the rudders, steadying the plane, and it flew quite obediently again.

Now the spectacle began. From the smooth surface of the clouds a huge white dome began to rise and grow rapidly on the left-hand side. Having barely become a hemisphere it burst through the clouds, dragging behind it a wide, smoky pillar that quickly climbed to an altitude already higher than ours. A colossal turban, hanging at about 20 or 30 kilometres up, puffed out of the top of the pillar, highlighted with the most delicate tints of all the colours of the rainbow. The whole regiment flew around that turban as if making a lap of honour, cautiously glancing at it from underneath. Then we set a southerly course towards the aerodrome.

How far would this colourful monster float, disintegrating en route and dispersing radioactive dust? I have to admit that back then I didn't think about it. I was happy that the drop had been successful, the explosion had gone to plan and the whole regiment had returned without losses. But the image of the turban was still before my eyes, captivating in its stern grandeur. The dosimeters sticking out of our chest pockets like ballpoint pens didn't show anything serious. The aircraft were in one piece and the technicians could find no visible sign of damage. Bazhenov's plane was the exception. No matter how fast it had retreated from the blast point it had still been closer to the explosion than the rest. Darkened blotches of metal were now visible under the white enamel; brown burn marks were present. They were also visible on unpainted areas underneath the plane. The glass of the cockpit had clouded too. Here and there cracks had occurred in the weakest portions of the duraluminium cover. The effects of the megatonner were no joke, even at points the calculations said were a safe distance from its detonation. Bazhenov's plane was exhibited to the flying personnel of many regiments, but it was then quietly written off to get it out of harm's way and flown to the training ground of the Kiev Engineering Aviation School.

It seems that was the last atmospheric nuclear blast. Testing moved underground. And although mankind is still hostage to nuclear death, all wars continue to be waged by conventional means.

*   *   *

The next crisis ripened in 1967 when Israel invaded the Sinai peninsula and Egypt failed to defend it. Having exhausted its resource of verbal arguments our government resolved to use the coercive approach. I was ordered to prepare a regiment of strike planes to bomb Israeli military installations (a list of them was attached).

A battle alarm signal was despatched to one of the garrisons. Bombs were hung, tanks filled with fuel. Flyers and navigators peered at maps, plotted routes to targets, studied the enemy's ground defences. However, they did not research the effectiveness of the American-made Hawk surface-to-air missile complexes as thoroughly as pilots examine that kind of thing today. The complexes had our intended targets within their field of fire!

My special telephone lines wouldn't shut up. Directives followed one after another, each contradicting a previous one. The voices were anxious, nervy, impatient. No wonder: the Long-Range Air Force Commander, Agaltsov, and his headquarters barely had enough capacity to relay the massive flow of orders and directives from several channels at General Headquarters which finally flooded into my tormented garrison.

I was struck most of all by a strict warning about the necessity of avoiding combat losses under any circumstances. I understood quite clearly that this was a matter not of sparing crews' lives but of protecting the prestige of our state, which would be badly compromised in the eyes of the world if red stars were found on a downed plane. Having grasped very quickly that this could not be guaranteed, someone in Moscow was inspired by an idea, which was embodied in another order: we were to take all documents away from the flying personnel, and to remove the stars from the planes and replace them with Egyptian markings instead. Without delay.

Bloody hell! The documents were no problem – that wouldn't take a minute. But how was I to find enough chemicals to get rid of the star markings and enough paint to replace them? Plane markings look tiny only from afar, but it could take several days to draw them accurately. By the way, exactly what did the Egyptian circles and squares look like? We made haste to find out and when we did, we were stupefied – they were in four colours: red, white, black and green. We needed special paint – not the kind for painting fences, although it would probably have done the job. We painted our poor keels, fuselages and wings carelessly and quickly. The paint was supposed to be left to dry for at least a day, but forget about that – it was time to take off.

We sent the first pair to the start aerodrome where they were supposed to be refuelled and then head out on a combat sortie. But just at that moment foreign radio stations all over the world announced that the Soviet Air Force intended to strike at Israeli military installations. How had they managed to find out? Either because of these broadcasts, or because the powers that be had simply cooled down, Moscow took the pressure off. First there was a phone call: 'fly only by special order', which never came. Then the all-clear signal arrived. Everybody sighed with relief – commanders, flying personnel, families frightened to death. The men returning from the aerodrome were welcomed as though they had survived a war. I felt happy about the 'retreat' but deep down I was also ashamed. I had been embarrassed by a humiliating attempt to interfere on the quiet in someone else's war. And had any of our men happened to get left in the sands of Arabia, all obligations to them would have been renounced without batting an eyelid.

In 1968 we reached out a 'brotherly hand' to Socialist Czechoslovakia. The Soviet Air Force, mostly transport aircraft, played a significant role. A regiment from our corps had a role in the operation. Its task was to deploy radio interference to neutralise the radar of all other (not only Czechoslovakian) aerodromes from which it was possible to launch planes to observe our air force.

Colonel Krivonos's crews were superbly trained, self-disciplined to the maximum and understood immediately the finer points of any task, no matter how complicated. The invasion began on schedule. Krivonos's guys had already been in their planes for about an hour waiting for the signal to take off, but Moscow was silent. The August night was stuffy and the air had not yet cooled down after the heat of the day. You can wear out the flying personnel that way, even before take-off. I requested an approximate start time from the Long-Range Air Force CP. To my surprise it had been delayed almost till morning. I estimated that the crews could probably catch about three hours' sleep. Some of the leading crews were lodged in the aerodrome barracks, not far from the planes; the others were a bit further away. Suddenly, in the middle of the night, well before the stipulated hour of reveille, the order to take off arrived. I called Krivonos (like me he was dozing right by the telephone): 'Get going! Immediately!' I could imagine how he felt, but he didn't even have time to swear.

I waited for the report of the first take-off – they wanted the news in Moscow too. For me the most important thing now was that the first plane got on its way. It didn't matter which one. The regiment's departure time would be recorded as that moment. As I expected it was not the leader but the smartest guy in the regiment who was the first to leave. Good man! He was the one who would get a watch as a reward. The take-off order was mixed up for some time, but that was no big deal – Krivonos's guys were so experienced and skilled that they would all find their places in the ring around Prague. It was hard to say who they jammed with radio interference, but whatever the case, the Soviet Air Force encountered no opposition in the air. Having been on duty for the allocated two hours the regiment returned safely to the aerodrome.

*   *   *

In autumn 1968 the position of first deputy commander of the Long-Range Air Force became available and it was offered to me. Ten days later I became Marshal Fillip Agaltsov's deputy.

Agaltsov was no ordinary man. During the Spanish Civil War he was commissar of the group of Soviet airmen who fought on the republican side and when he returned home he was promoted to the rank of Division Commissar before becoming Commissar of the Air Force. He visited Stalin more than once, in both his office and his apartment at the Kremlin. During their conversations Agaltsov told the leader with the utmost openness about how seriously backward the Soviet Air Force was compared with German planes our flyers had encountered in aerial combat. He also outlined the dangerous consequences this state of affairs might have if it was allowed to persist. There was quite a bit of risk involved in this kind of straightforwardness: impressed by a whole series of outstanding aerial expeditions and records, the whole country was in euphoria, considering itself the mightiest air power in the world. And its creator, of course, was Stalin himself. Now he was hearing a difficult message. Foreseeing the forthcoming storm, in January 1941 Agaltsov departed from the path of commissar, exchanged the two rhombuses on his collar for two major's bars [officers' insignia used in the USSR before 1943 – translator's note] and, having asked Stalin to appoint him as a regiment commander, left Moscow for the Baltic shores, where he received the rank of colonel just two months later, in March. He was at the front for nearly the whole of the war, and by 1945 he had become a lieutenant-general – an air corps commander. After the war he was in charge of an aerial army for some time. Having gone through quite a few high positions, he'd been far away from long-range bombers, but suddenly in 1962 he was appointed commander of the Long-Range Air Force. With his strong military and political background he could lead a structure of any size with great success. But in January 1969 the time came for him – born with the century – to go and I was appointed to his position.

Having become commander I had to take control of a whole group of state committees appointed to oversee the design of new aircraft, missiles and electronic equipment. It became clear to me during my first days in the new job that there was no more insidious field than armaments supply. It was easy to lose your bearings in the complicated connections between egotistical corporations. Illusions of successful solutions came and went, mean-spirited ambitions and pretensions flaring up all the time. The most run-down industrial producer, still working with ante-diluvian technology but maintaining a monopoly in the field, was in a position to openly ignore for many years the timeframes set out for fulfilling orders, letting them overrun several times before finally offering up some awkward and heavy item with a pathetically poor level of use-fulness. State committee meetings sometimes turned into battles where the highest priorities in the search for truth were department and personal interests – certainly not the interests of defence.

Testing of the Tu-22M long-range bomber was already in progress when I assumed my new post but the machine wouldn't perform at all. Initially planned as a modification of the supersonic Tu-22, which had already been in service, it had picked up more and more engineering developments. Now – having received variable-wing geometry, more powerful engines, a radically new cockpit and engine layout, not to mention serious modifications to the armaments system – to all intents and purposes it was a completely new type of aircraft. It was quite natural that with these additions the machine had become noticeably heavier than the initially prescribed weight, and even the new, more powerful engines couldn't drag it up to double supersonic speed. The standard 2,500 metres of airstrip stipulated by performance requirements – let alone 1,800 metres – were insufficient to allow her to take off. Then, to get over that problem, even more powerful engines with 20 tonnes of traction were installed. But in the meantime the plane's weight had grown again. It would take much longer to refine the aircraft and only its fourth modification – the Tu-22M3 with 25-tonne traction – went into mass production to arm the regiments.

It was over this particular machine that major military–diplomatic debates broke out with the Americans. They included it in the category of strategic bombers, but in reality it didn't meet the criteria. It looked very formidable when heavy missiles were loaded onto its pylons, but it was still only a bomber with a European operating range. The Americans (who sat on their bases next to the walls of the Warsaw Pact countries) were most annoyed by the rod sticking out of the fuselage for in-flight refuelling. As a result of a political agreement it was dismantled and taken away to storage.

In those same years (the early 1970s) the problem of creating a strategic supersonic bomber became most acute. The need to build one essentially stemmed from the Americans' decision to add the B-1 to their arsenal. We needed something similar: a couple of Machs, a mass of about 200 tonnes and an operating range of about 10,000 kilometres. On top of that we needed in-flight refuelling capability, long-range missiles, good defence, modern electronic equipment and electronic countermeasure systems. Creating it was a super-complicated task. In the course of implementing it I had to work with the designs of Pavel Sukhoi, Alexey Tupolev (Andrey Tupolev's heir) and Vladimir Myasishchev. An attempt by Tupolev to create a military version of the Tu-144 passenger aircraft didn't work out, but his Tu-160 overtook the most interesting projects that Sukhoi and Myasishchev came up with – and for which no production base was found. By the early 1990s the Tu-160 had become one of the most powerful bombers in the world.

*   *   *

At the end of the last week of 1979, when our troops hadn't yet entered Afghanistan, I was charged with the task of carrying out a bombing raid on the north-west outskirts of Herat. 'The rebels are dug in there,' I was told. Were there just ten of them or a whole division? Were they inside a house or rallying in a town square? No one knew anything. Headquarters was galvanised into action – paperwork was brought out, calculations were made, intelligence officers began to exchange phone calls. I examined large-scale maps. It was a large compact city, pressed against the mountains, with a river and roads. In the reference books its population was given as only 160,000. What should we drop bombs on? Where was the aiming point? We were going to slaughter a lot of people, that much was certain, but would we destroy the rebels? Maybe the local people were the rebels?

To be honest I knew about the opposing forces in Afghanistan only in the vaguest of terms, not being too dissimilar to my superiors in this regard. The rapid and bloody change of leaders was making us cautious. Loyal friends were instantly becoming deadly foes and being replaced by unfamiliar new figures. The game was played at the highest party leadership level in both countries. The people – that eternal and defenceless victim of politicians – took no part in this marathon, as usual.

But an order is an order. There was no time to lose. The designated regiment was put on alert and got its mission. Although a long-range regiment was involved, it was based far away from the target and with a full bomb load on the way out it wouldn't have enough fuel to make it home. A large intermediate aerodrome had been chosen in the Transcaspian area, but it had no suitable bombs, just small fry. And there was not enough space to park the whole regiment. We had to limit ourselves to a squadron. The squadron transferred some of the weapons that would be needed but the rest were delivered by a group of strategic aircraft. On an unfamiliar aerodrome where no one knew what we had flown in for, each crew took upon its own shoulders the job of hanging the bombs on the locks, using any means available. Fuel tanks were topped up. It was best to take off under cover of darkness – it's difficult to make a raid in the daytime: after all these were heavy bombers, heading out to target a city. What would people think of us?

I asked to clarify the situation before take-off, but there was still no detailed information available, not even confirmation of the previous data. We switched to waiting mode, but there was still no news about exactly how many rebels there were in Herat or their location. Were they really there at all? The Supreme Commander accused us of letting the moment pass because of our sluggishness. He said we had not taken the rarest of opportunities to strike at the 'enemies of the revolution'. So I had no occasion to 'distinguish' myself in the fight against the 'rebels' in Afghanistan.

Four years later the long-range bombers did once help our 'limited contingent' of troops there, striking at a formidable *mojahed* garrison [a common name for the anti-Soviet Afghan rebels during the war in Afghanistan between 1979 and 1989 – translator's note] that firmly held quite a high mountain with a small plateau, keeping important communication junctions under fire and even effectively resisting our aircraft and helicopters. A regiment had been prepared for this task. It was shifted closer to the spot and armed with heavy bombs. Then one dark, cloudy night it struck. The planes worked faultlessly. The strike density on the relatively small area gave the garrison no chance of survival: it fell silent and would never show itself again.

*   *   *

In the 1980s I was the Deputy Supreme Commander of the Air Force and had to take decisions on a huge variety of tasks. I considered my most important duty was to help the Supreme Commander as much as I could in his duties. The Air Force Supreme Commander, Pavel Stepanovich Koutakhov, was a harsh, domineering man who demanded absolute subordination from those below him. But it is no exaggeration to say he worked exceedingly hard, often forgetting the time of the day and the burden of his years. It was impossible to work more slowly next to him. Our windows were lit right into the night. We knew our job and never let our Supreme Commander down. There didn't seem to be a single day when, escorted by his armaments experts, he wouldn't rush to see people in industry, the ministries, scientific and research institutes, design bureaux or plants. He managed not only to put right the consequences of Krushchev's destruction, but also to clear the way for resurrection of the combat air force in its new capacity.

It was then that the Soviet Air Force reached the pinnacle of its might. The fighter complement comprised the main part. Even the number of long-range bombers was slashed to make way for its endless growth. Still considering the threat of war to be very real, we spent a fair bit of time working with operational maps. We knew our 'enemies' almost by sight, including their first and surnames. There is good reason to suppose they weren't in the dark about us either.

During practice manoeuvres Koutakhov would always begin hostilities with a short period spent repulsing enemy aircraft raids. Then almost without a pause he would switch to an operation to seize mastery of the air. The games were conducted not only from the maps. Weapons rumbled on both sides of our borders with other socialist countries. Concentration of troops sometimes reached critical mass. On more than one occasion I thought, 'Maybe it's not a drill after all.' Our commanders would describe any attempt to ward off our aggression with the following words: 'The enemy, under the pretence of manoeuvres, ...' Which one of these endless 'pretences' would be fateful?

The air forces of the Warsaw Pact countries were drawn into these war games, but they took part very reluctantly. They were too scared out of their wits to use electronic countermeasures, avoided any complex manoeuvring above their cities and refused to restrict the flight of civil aircraft even a little bit or to cede more of their airspace. Bulgaria was perhaps a bit more courageous, as was the German Democratic Republic, but it was best not to have anything at all to do with Romania. However, our 'brothers in arms' would readily agree to play a role over Soviet territory, sparing their own countries unnecessary trouble and strife.

After the deaths of Brezhnev [Soviet leader, 1964–82 – translator's note] and two of his followers, Andropov (who held office from 1982 to 1984) and Chernenko (who was in power from 1984 to1985), an unusually fresh wind suddenly began to blow through the political skies. A new word, *Perestroika*, resounded. If only we had known where the process would end, but no one knew, not even the new general secretary [Mikhail Gorbachev – translator's note]. A river of progress was breaking down the old floodgates with a growing roar and no one would be able to return it to the old channels.

The year 1986 was approaching its end. That summer I clocked up my fifty years in the military air service. It had been a difficult and troubled but marvellous and unique world all my life. It was time to leave. I don't remember a more bitter minute in my whole career.

A new era was beginning and other people will tell its story.

Glossary

ADD – Long-Range Bomber Air Force
bayan – a variety of accordion
chastooshka – joyful comic singing
chernozem – black earth, the most agriculturally fertile kind of soil
Comsomol – Young Communist League
narcom – *Narodnyi Kommissar Oborony* (People's Commissar of Defence)
NKVD – People's Commissariat for Internal Affairs
Osobyi Otdel – 'Special Department' of the counterespionage service
polizei – police force made up of collaborators
polutorka – 1½-tonne truck
samogon – moonshine
Sovinformburo – Soviet Information Bureau, the Soviet news agency during the Second World War
starshiy politruk – senior political commissar
Stavka – general headquarters of the armed forces

Index